SEX, MONEY, HAPPINESS, AND DEATH

SEX, MONEY, HAPPINESS, AND DEATH

The Quest for Authenticity

MANFRED KETS DE VRIES

Raoul de Vitry d'Avaucourt Chaired Clinical Professor of Leadership Development, Director, INSEAD Global Leadership Centre, France, Singapore, and Abu Dhabi

First published 2009 by
PALGRAVE MACMILLAN

Palgrave Macmillan in the UK is an imprint of Macmillan Publishers Limited, registered in England, company number 785998, of Houndmills, Basingstoke, Hampshire RG21 6XS.

Palgrave Macmillan in the US is a division of St Martin's Press LLC, 175 Fifth Avenue, New York, NY 10010.

Palgrave Macmillan is the global academic imprint of the above companies and has companies and representatives throughout the world.

Palgrave® and Macmillan® are registered trademarks in the United States, the United Kingdom, Europe and other countries.

ISBN-13: 978–0–230–57792–3
ISBN-10: 0–230–57792–X

This book is printed on paper suitable for recycling and made from fully managed and sustained forest sources. Logging, pulping and manufacturing processes are expected to conform to the environmental regulations of the country of origin.

A catalogue record for this book is available from the British Library.

A catalog record for this book is available from the Library of Congress.

10 9 8 7 6 5 4 3
18 17 16 15 14 13 12 11 10

Printed and bound in Great Britain by
CPI Antony Rowe, Chippenham and Eastbourne

To my children, who helped me to understand that no one grows old by living, only by losing interest in living; and to my mother, who built the foundation.

CONTENTS

CONTENTS

PREFACE

The tragedy of life is not that it ends so soon, but that we wait so long to begin it.

W. M. Lewis

Three things in human life are important: The first is to be kind. The second is to be kind. And the third is to be kind.

Henry James

The true measure of a man is how he treats someone who can do him absolutely no good.

Samuel Johnson

Sometimes if you want to see a change for the better, you have to take things into your own hands.

Clint Eastwood

As a professor of management and leadership, it was some time before I acknowledged that much of the management research published in academic business journals is overwritten, convoluted, and often extremely boring. Worse, when I ask business practitioners how helpful these research findings are to them in their work, the response I receive is not encouraging. They view most of the studies as quite irrelevant. Learning from experience—making sense of what really happens in the business world (or in the world in general for that matter)—doesn't seem to be a priority for many management scholars. Although (in theory) there should be continuity between theory and practice, in practice that doesn't seem to be the case. Many management research contributions are merely fodder for management mandarins. The Zen master Ts'ai Ken T'an once noted, "Water which is too pure has no fish." And that's exactly the case with many research publications in business: far too often, pure management theory doesn't address the complexity of knotty, real-life business problems. Whatever ingenuity these researchers demonstrate in their experiments—whatever the potential usefulness to the business practitioner—seems to be taken out of the equation. Many of these research publications provide as much practical help for executives running their businesses as reading their daily horoscope. We could even argue that the horoscopes are more useful as they often contain a modicum of practical advice.

MAROONED IN AN IVORY TOWER

To management mandarins, publishing in one of the "A" journals has become a rite of passage, a significant marker on the royal road to promotion and tenure. While it might be an accurate assessment of a management scholar's talent for data manipulation, in this ritual very little thought is spared for long-suffering business practitioners. Although business schools, like medical or engineering schools, should do research at the forefront of knowledge, and help to create better organizations, they often fall short of that noble purpose. They are more concerned about how to impress their colleagues. Business school research, and the practical knowledge that helps practitioners to create more effective organizations, should be cross-fertilizing. Instead, too often, they're ships that pass in the night.

What should have been the pursuit of common sense in an applied school has been lost in the search for academic recognition. Common sense is conspicuously absent from the stream of research publications coming from most business schools. This adds to the isolation of executives. Instead of having access to a group of people who could be really helpful to them by working on their problems, they're confronted by a group with an agenda quite different from theirs.

What adds to this sad story is the gullibility of many executives. Because they're desperate to solve the problems of an increasingly complex, global business world, and are alienated from the scholarship that might have supported them, executives are suckers for management witchdoctors. They are far too eager to take the bait of quick-fix answers to the problems they encounter and as a result have to deal not only with their disillusionment with management research, but also the dangerous company of the witchdoctors themselves.

Of course, the interesting question is why these people fall for witchdoctors so easily. It may have something to do with high levels of executive *angst*: What else explains why so many of these management fads are given a serious hearing? Why else would otherwise sensible executives be so eager to consult the witchdoctors? "Miracle" cures, like one-minute management, management by objectives, six sigma, business process re-engineering, total quality management, and benchmarking—notwithstanding their pseudointellectual base—have been (and are) very attractive to executives. They offer seemingly simple answers to extremely complex problems. Unfortunately, despite their much heralded promises of salvation, the usual scenario is quite different. Most of these great business solutions fall short of what they promise. Eventually, the scales drop from the executives' eyes and they're like the little child in the fable who points out that "The emperor has nothing on at all!" But before they discover that the emperor has no clothes, they will make decisions that affect the lives of thousands of people.

As a management professor, I'm very familiar with management mandarins who sit in ivory towers, and with the snake-oil salesmen, business gurus who peddle faulty wares. I have been asking myself what needs to be done for their work to be more relevant. Does it have to be this way? Is there a way to create greater rapprochement with business practitioners? Or is it hopeless to expect anything to change? I must confess that it also crosses my mind to wonder whether I'm the right person to criticize the current situation. After all, am I not said to be one of these so-called gurus myself?

I come from a family of very pragmatic entrepreneurs, and the search for relevance has always been driven home to me. When I played with conceptual ideas during my studies, some of my family members would always ask me how my ideas were going to help them run their businesses better. To hold their attention, I had to come up with an acceptable answer. This is a partial explanation (or rationalization) of my concern for relevance. I've always wanted to be in a position that would enable me to give executives sensible advice.

This personal search for relevance hasn't always been straight-forward. Having been introduced in my studies of economics to *homo economicus*—that remarkable, imaginary, instant calculator of pleasures and pains—I began to search for a more realistic way of understanding how people really behave. My dissatisfaction with *homo economicus* led me to the study of management and organizational behavior. But even here, the constructs of human beings seemed oversimplified. Traditional studies in organizational behavior were directed more toward structures and systems than people. Disappointed once again, I decided to enter the world of psycho-analysis, psychiatry, and psychotherapy. Becoming a member of a helping profession—the word says it all—appealed to me as a way to make better sense of people's behavior. It was a very good choice: I quickly discovered that it was hard to escape practical issues on this route, which turned out to be a fantastic way to combine theory and practice. I was brought face-to-face with serious people issues. I learned an enormous amount about what makes people tick.

MORE THAN MEETS THE EYE

With hindsight, I have found it a great advantage to operate in the two worlds of management and psychotherapy. My familiarity with both has made me a sort of bridge between the two domains. I have not only obtained insight into more traditional organizational problems, but I have also learned how to use a different lens to decipher those problems. It has been a great way to understand better people in all their complexity; it has provided me with a three-dimensional view of the human being.

From the world of psychotherapy, psychiatry, and psychoanalysis I've learned that often there is more to a problem than meets the eye. Frequently, the real crux of a problem turns out to be invisible. Learning from my clients made me attentive to out-of-awareness behavior. I learned that much seemingly rational behavior is actually quite irrational. The clinical orientation to problem solving that I acquired—having learned to listen with the third ear—gave me an additional tool to make sense of what would otherwise have been incomprehensible actions. I realized that organizations cannot perform successfully if the quirks and irrational processes that are part and parcel of the organizational participants' inner world are not taken into consideration. My clinical background helped me to spot the 600-pound gorillas that were running amok—the deep-seated underlying psychological conflicts that really caused organizational problems. It gave me a lot of insight into people's foibles. Most importantly, it taught me to take espoused rationality with a grain of salt. As the anthropologist Ashley Montagu once said, "Human beings are the only creatures who are able to behave irrationally in the name of reason."

In my search for relevance—realizing that unconscious dynamics can have a significant impact on life in organizations—my desire was to help organizational leaders (and followers) recognize and plan for those dynamics. I wanted to provide them with greater insight into both manifest and latent behavior, contributing to greater realism in problem solving. I also wanted business practitioners to see through the false promises of snake-oil salesmen, and prevent them from being seduced by their siren's call. Many of the books and articles I have written over the years are attempts to spread this particular point of view.

My other agenda, as far as my contributions to management are concerned, has been to advocate less mandarin-like behavior among my colleagues, and make management professors more attuned to the issues that preoccupy executives. It disturbs me when I discover that many of them have very little of relevance to say when placed in front of a management audience. I find it embarrassing, given that this is the constituency to which they should be attuned. From what I've learned from my own experience, however, dealing with the real problems of real people is a great way to focus our minds. This approach makes us realize what life in organizations is all about. And stepping down from the ivory tower and really listening to what executives have to say is a good start to becoming more relevant to the business community.

At the business school where I teach, my goal is to span the Ivory Tower and the Main Street of business, to bring the rigors of academia to the practice of management. In whatever I teach, I try to help *real* executives to solve the *real* problems they're struggling with. I act in this way because I want to make a difference. And as I have suggested before, I am not only referring to more immediate, surface problems. I want the people with whom I work to explore not only their external reality but also their internal reality. And it is my impression that many management mandarins would like to do the same, if they could only break free from their self-imposed constraints. When it really comes down to it, all of us like to create meaning for others.

My role as director of INSEAD's Global Leadership Centre has provided me with a fantastic base to help executives deal with their most pressing and relevant issues. Supported by a cadre of well-trained coaches, leadership coaching has become part of the makeup of most programs at our school. Each year, many thousands of executives are exposed to leadership coaching in one way or another. Learning from each other—the leadership coach-client interchange—is a very fruitful process. From the consistently positive feedback that we have received, it's clear that giving executives the chance to discuss what is really troubling them has been extremely helpful. Important as deeper knowledge about finance, marketing, technology management, and other business matters may be, for many of them, these interchanges are a great opportunity to deal with their most pressing organizational conflicts. And it's not only the participating executives who are touched by these interventions; they have a contagious effect on other faculty members who are becoming aware of the kind of issues they need to address.

ANOTHER 600-POUND GORILLA

Having a more realistic outlook on organizational matters is one thing, but, as we all know, there is also life outside organizations. In my role as a psychoanalyst, psychotherapist, and leadership coach, I'm frequently privy to the kind of information I would never have received as a management professor. Many executives talk to me not only about the more typical organizational problems but also about other more general, existential issues. And—as I've also learned from my leadership coaches—it may be the latter that preoccupy them most. Executives explain to me why they are doing what they are doing. They talk to me about their fears, desires, concerns about money, search for happiness, disappointments, and even their fear of death. Often, they ask me if I can help them with their existential problems. And although these issues may seem far removed from what is considered part of the management domain—making me vulnerable to the accusation of being yet another mandarin—they are very much part of the executives' reality. Given their persistent and repetitive nature, they warrant further exploration. They are definitely not ivory-tower topics.

When I'm presented with these problems, my real challenge is to help people to help themselves. There have been many occasions when I've been asked for advice because the people who asked me didn't like the answers they had given themselves. I try to point out to them—not always successfully—that all the answers they need are to be found inside them; they only have to be quiet enough to hear them. But, as many of us have discovered the hard way, deep listening does not always come naturally. Before we can change our routines, or change direction, we've to stand still and pay close attention to what is really going on. This means asking ourselves difficult questions such as why we are running, where we are running to, and, most importantly, what has made us run in the first place. What we may discover—if we're courageous enough to take this less traveled road—can be quite depressing, especially as the fear of becoming depressed might be a major reason why we're running so fast in the first place. It takes courage to stand still and to find out who we really are.

I point out to the executives I deal with that there are times—if we want to see a change for the better—that we have to take things into our own hands. We cannot always use others as a crutch. But this advice isn't always welcome. If they had the option, quite a few of my clients would prefer to remain in some kind of dependency situation. What they have to learn is that although everyone's future depends on many things, it depends mostly on ourselves, what we make of it. They need to accept that they're responsible for the world they live in. They need to own their own lives. There are no miracle cures that will provide the solutions.

An additional challenge for me is to make these executives realize that life is not all about the symbols of power and position; it's not all about money. How can I make them discover that how they spend their time is more important than how they spend their money? They've to realize that status is an elusive entity, popularity an accident, wealth very fickle, and that only character endures. I try to point out to them that material things are not the most important things in life. What is truly important has to do with meaningful relationships, making a difference, and creating meaning. The great use of life is to spend it on something that will outlast us. What example do they want to set for others? Mahatma Gandhi once said, "My life is my message." In that respect, going through life is like looking in a mirror. What you see on the outside has to resonate with what you see inside. Harmony between your inner world and external reality is essential.

INSIDE THE MINDS OF EXECUTIVES

Apart from my work as director at INSEAD's Global Leadership Centre, I am personally involved in two workshops, "The Challenge of Leadership," and "Consulting and Coaching for Change." One of my ex-doctoral students has described these workshops as "identity laboratories." They are of a more transformational nature, with many participants making major life decisions during and after them. In these workshops I help participants work through the particular issues they are struggling with in a journey of self-exploration.

Although it is the nature of truth to struggle toward the light, engaging in such a journey is not always an easy process. There will be many roadblocks on the way. Usually, I have to deal with many defensive maneuvers as executives can be reluctant to see what is really going on. People do not always like what they see, either. The psychologist Carl Jung was very aware of the significance of this reluctance. In his autobiography, *Memories, Dreams, Reflections*, he wrote: "Whenever there is a reaching down into innermost experience, into the nucleus of personality, most people are overcome by fear and many run away ... The risk of inner experience, the adventure of the spirit, is in any case alien to most human beings. The possibility that such experience might have psychic reality is anathema to them." But I can be stubborn. I do not give up easily, notwith-standing the many defensive reactions that crop up. To quote the playwright Henrik Ibsen, "It is no use lying to one's self."

As we take this journey together, I try to make executives under-stand that the real voyage of discovery consists not in seeing new landscapes, but in having new eyes. Not only do they need to be brave enough to undertake this journey, it is also important that they start using themselves as an instrument of discovery. They have to be sensitive about the bipersonal field they are living in—they need to be observant about the way others influence them. I explain to them that the future is not out there some place waiting for them. We help create our futures through the power of imagination and the act of discovery. Each of us is gifted in a unique and important way. It's our privilege and adventure to discover our own special light.

When thinking about life's challenges—the journey all of us are taking—it's interesting to reflect on the life of the painter Paul Gauguin, which was characterized by many transitions. After an adventurous early life, including a four-year stay in Peru, he settled into a comfortable bourgeois existence, obtaining a position with a firm of stockbrokers and marrying a Danish woman with whom he had five children. During this period, Gauguin discovered that he had a talent for painting, but essentially remained a Sunday painter. However, his disillusionment with material wealth and the business world led him to a search for a society more unspoiled than his native France. He left his wife and children and went to the island of Tahiti where he began his second career as a painter.

Gauguin's early years in Tahiti were happy, but by 1897 he was syphilitic, suicidal, and severely depressed because of the death of his daughter. He was struggling with the meaning of existence. He spent his last years meditating on the human condition, as depicted in his most famous canvas, *Where do we come from? Who are we? Where are we going?* Gauguin viewed this painting as his testament. It was his attempt to sum up his feelings and philosophy and to think about what was to come next. He wrote, "I shall never do anything better, or even like it." The canvas depicts a variety of figures, all of them Tahitian, sprawled across its wide frame, each engaged in a particular and significant act, raising symbolic questions about the human condition.

Gauguin evoked awareness of the journey of life. Not only did he question how to do it, he lived it. However, when I listen to execu-tives, in my roles as a teacher, consultant, therapist, or leadership coach, I have noticed that people frequently try to live their lives backwards. They try to have more things, or more money, in order to do more of what they want to be happier. Although I realize that it's good to have an end to journey toward, it is important to remember that "the journey is all, the end nothing." As most of us have discovered, arriving at one goal is the point of departure toward another. It's our day-to-day experiences that count. The purpose of life is to live it, not to plan to live it later. We need to love the moment.

This reminds me of a Zen parable about a man who met a tiger—and fled. The tiger chased him to the edge of a cliff, where he caught hold of a wild vine and swung himself over. The tiger sniffed at him from above. Terrified, the man looked down to see that, far below, another tiger had appeared, waiting to eat him. Meanwhile, two mice, one white, one black, began to gnaw away at the vine he was hanging on. Out of the corner of his eye, the man saw a luscious strawberry near him. Grasping the vine with one hand, he plucked the strawberry with the other. How sweet it tasted!

The apostle Matthew tells us, "Do not worry about tomorrow, for tomorrow will worry about itself. Each day has enough trouble of its own." Life exists only in the present moment. The past is gone, the future is not yet here, and if we are not in touch with ourselves in the present moment, we cannot be in touch with life. Life must be lived as it comes along. By living our lives one day at a time, we live all of the days of our lives. Life is not a race, but a journey to be savored each step of the way. We cannot go back and start a new beginning, but on any day we can make a fresh start toward a new ending. The doors we open and close each day will decide the kind of lives we will lead. To quote the writer George Orwell: "To see what's in front of one's nose requires a constant struggle." Heaven or hell is not determined by the direction in which we travel, but by the person we have become when we arrive.

TAKING THE EXISTENTIAL ROUTE: THE ROAD MAP

In this book I try to do something different from the many books I have written on organizations and leadership. While I have always been driven by the notion of being relevant in whatever I am doing, in these chapters I aim for relevance of a more existential kind, going beyond the more humdrum issues that trouble executives. I address the kinds of questions executives put to me as a clinician. Although the people I meet are usually wary of people in the helping professions, because I speak their language—and have a good understanding of the organizational issues they struggle with—it is easier for them to open up and tell me about some of the other issues they are struggling with.

I do realize that to give advice on organizational matters is one thing, to give advice on "living" another matter altogether. Some people may even view it as presumptuous on my part. Is it really possible to give advice on these matters, or can we only learn by doing? Is dealing with life's major challenges purely an experiential thing? True enough, in taking this road, you need to live. You need to be there. You need to learn from your experiences.

I feel, however, that the time is right to deal with these issues, as I am no longer young enough to know everything. I've reached the age where I realize that the only true wisdom is the realization that you know very little. And although age doesn't necessarily bring wisdom, I hope that I have been lucky enough to learn a few lessons on the way. Writing this book has been a great way to understand better the depth of my own ignorance. It is a real challenge to try to make sense of issues that resonate very much in yourself.

It is a truism to say that we learn much more from our failures than from our successes. It has often been said that wisdom cannot be taught. I've learned from the school of hard knocks that our character is formed more by our failures than our successes. Adversity has the effect of eliciting talents that, in more advantageous circumstances, would have remained dormant. In that respect, life is a succession of lessons that must be lived to be understood. To me the only thing worse than making a mistake, is making a mistake and not learning from it. If we look at it closely, wisdom might turn out to be nothing more than healed pain.

I've learned that it takes courage to face one's own shortcomings, and wisdom to do something about them. There is a Spanish saying that tells us, "It is not the same to talk of bulls as to be in the bullring." In some ways, life is like an onion: we peel it off layer by layer, and we may weep at times while we do. We all seem to be seeking the meaning of life, whatever that may be for each of us. But perhaps more pragmatic is to have our external experiences resonate with our inner reality. The major task that each of us faces is to give birth to ourselves.

The origins of the chapters in this book are stories told to me by executives that touched a chord with me. I'm not referring to stories about business problems. Such problems will be resolved, one way or another. I'm referring to the stories behind the stories—the themes contained in these stories. I want to tackle some of the metaissues many executives—or for that matter most people—struggle with. And, predictably, the stories behind the stories have to do with issues concerning the human condition. These are my musings from the underground, chapters based on the questions my executives were trying to find solutions for.

The first part of the book, on sexual desire, is the longest. It's a very complex topic and even necessitated an excursion into evolutionary psychology. But it's a topic that has always fascinated me as I have struggled myself with the demands of biology and society. Over the years, I have realized that there isn't much of a safety net against attraction. Like it or not, sexual desire will always be with us. Listening to the stories my executives told me, made me realize how difficult coping with desire can be. Desire is so often the catalyst that makes us do the kinds of things we would never otherwise have done.

The second part deals with money. In my roles as management professor and consultant, psychoanalyst, psychotherapist, and leadership coach, money pops up all the time. Having met a number of exceedingly rich people, I've been fascinated by what money did to them and how deeply it affected their lives. An encounter with one of my students, an investment banker, inspired this part. He followed me down a corridor, asking, "How much money will be enough?" I was struck by the irony of his question, knowing that he was by far the best-paid person in his organization. Clearly, for him, there was never going to be enough money. Some people confuse self-worth with net worth.

The third part of the book is about happiness. It's the oldest in this collection and based on one I wrote several years ago called *The Happiness Equation*. This essay grew out of the responses I received to a question I asked CEOs at the end of my leadership workshop: "Imagine you are asked to make a graduation speech at your school. What would you tell the students? What themes would you touch upon? What have been some of the more important issues in your life?"

The theme that recurred constantly was how to be happy. Reflecting on their ideas about happiness led me to write a short article that I eventually turned into a longer essay. At the time, I was in a rather depressive state of mind, but perhaps that's the state to be in when writing about happiness. I was in good company. The philosopher Bertrand Russell was also in pretty bad shape when he wrote his essay on happiness. In fact, much of his best work was done when he was trying to escape the world around him.

The last part is on death. I started this part anticipating the death of my mother. At one point, I considered the process to be finished— but then my mother died. Although I had been preparing myself for my mother's death for many years, when it actually happened it hit me much harder than I ever expected. Her death led me to rewrite the part. It made me realize the absoluteness of the fact that you've only one mother; it underlined the power and intensity of the mother-child relationship. Now that this part is complete, I realize that writing it has been my personal way of helping me work through my grief.

Although death is the end, and logically should end the book, I felt that this was a rather dismal way of finishing this collection. The Afterword deals with authenticity, altruism, wisdom, and humankind's search for meaning, and is informed by William Shakespeare's edict, "This above all—to thine own self be true." If people do not live their lives authentically, whatever they do will seem meaningless, and contribute to their feelings of anxiety, boredom, and despair.

The Russian novelist Fyodor Dostoevsky once wrote a psychological study of the skeletons in the deepest, darkest closet of the human mind. "I am a sick man ... I am a spiteful man, I am a most unpleasant man," the irascible voice of the nameless narrator in his novel cries out. *Notes from Underground* is the passionate confessions of a suffering man, the ruthless self-examination of a tormented soul. The philosopher Friedrich Nietzsche was very impressed with Dostoevsky's explorations of the mind, claiming that "Dostoevsky is one of the few psychologists from whom I have learned something." Another philosopher, Jean-Paul Sartre, agreed and found in Dostoevsky's "underground man" a forerunner and spokesperson for existential philosophy. For Sartre, the chief importance of the book and the character was their clear acknowledgement of man's essentially irrational nature. *Notes from Underground* is an outstanding example of Dostoyevsky's psychological skills, depicting a character motivated by many contradictory impulses. More than anything else, he demonstrates that human actions are difficult to calculate. Humans are driven by complex and irrational emotions, and make choices based on them, capable of the noblest and the basest actions at the same time.

Like Dostoyevsky, I like to show people as they are, with all their foibles and follies. I want to deal with real people and to reflect on real issues. I don't want to follow the mandarin route, even though some of the topics I discuss may necessitate excursions into more esoteric fields of research. In these chapters I want to show people that they are not alone in their confusion. I want to explain to them that their problems are shared by many others. To be precise, I want to be more helpful to the executives who come and ask me for help.

I realize that there are limits to my role as a teacher. A Chinese saying goes, "Teachers open the door but you must enter by yourself." Learning can be difficult. I can help executives by showing the way, but—as I indicated earlier—in the final reckoning, they have to help themselves. We all can help ourselves, but we have to discover how to do it. However, we cannot change what we do not acknowledge. In the words of Dr. Seuss: "You have brains in your head. You have feet in your shoes. You can steer yourself in any direction you choose." It is up to us to make things happen.

Every act of conscious learning necessitates the willingness to suffer an injury to one's self-esteem, which means being aware of our defensive reactions. Things are usually not how we want them to be. That is why young children, before they become aware of their own self-importance, learn so easily. As adults we have greater difficulties. The poet Samuel Taylor Coleridge once said, "Advice is like snow; the softer it falls, the longer it dwells upon, and deeper it sinks into the mind." My hope is that these musings will fall softly enough.

Instead of cluttering these pages with references, as I would usually do in a more formal book, I've kept my text relatively simple—an approach that may scandalize my academic colleagues. I suspect that if I were to tackle these issues in a more traditional, scholarly way, I wouldn't touch my readers in the manner I want, to help them increase their understanding of these important topics. So I've deliberately taken a more informal approach. I hope that readers will excuse me for putting the usual rigor aside.

The ideas presented in these pages are my personal meditations on life and death, reflections based, however, on very vivid personal stories told by executives. Not only am I influenced by their stories, in making sense out of these narratives, but I also cannot help but be affected by years of reading in the fields of psychoanalysis, social psychology, developmental psychology, family systems theory, cognitive theory, neuropsychiatry, evolutionary psychology, and psychotherapy. And although, as I said, my meditations haven't emerged in a vacuum, I take full responsibility for any idiosyncrasies that are included. In writing this book I also realize that among these idiosyncrasies, I should list a Western-oriented bias. After all, I'm a product of the "developed" world that has colored my *Weltanschauung*. Thus some of my musings may not be as relevant in another cultural context.

Looking through these chapters, I have asked myself why I was moved to write these at this point in my life. It might be because I've reached the age where you become more aware of the tragic transience of things. You know that you were born and you know that you are going to die. The question becomes how to make the most use of the time in-between that is yours. There is a time in life to let things happen, and a time to make things happen. I believe that we stay young by focusing on our dreams rather than on our regrets. These chapters are my personal attempt to look forward, and capture my own dreams.

PART ONE: MEDITATIONS ON SEXUAL DESIRE

1

IN THE SHADOW OF MORTAL SIN

It's so much better to desire than to have. The moment of desire is the most extraordinary moment. The moment of desire, when you know something is going to happen, that's the most exalting.

Anouk Aimée

Sex is hardly ever just about sex.

Shirley MacLaine

I know nothing about sex because I was always married.

Zsa Zsa Gabor

Vanitas Vanitatum! Which of us is happy in this world? Which of us has his desire? or, having it, is satisfied?

William Makepeace Thackeray

There is a well-known Zen story of two traveling monks who were trying to cross a river. When they were almost across, a young woman called out to them from the bank they had just left. She said she was afraid to get into the water because of the current. "Could one of you take me to the other side?" she asked. One of the monks hesitated, but the other returned, quickly placed her on his shoulders, took her across the river, and put her down on the other side. She thanked him and went on her way.

As the monks continued their journey, one of them was troubled. Finally, unable to keep quiet, he broke out, "Brother, our Zen master has taught us to avoid any contact with women, but you picked that one up on your shoulders and carried her!"

"Brother," the second monk replied, "I set her down on the other side: it's *you* who is still carrying her."

At the core of this story is the question of desire. What's desire? Why do we desire? Why do we desire what we do? What are the consequences of desire? And how do we cope with desire? Simple

3

questions to ask, but answering them is another matter altogether. Desire is like quicksand; it's everywhere but hard to get a purchase on it.

Turning to the American Heritage Dictionary in search of a definition, we find that desire means a request, a longing, or being the object of longing, a sexual appetite, or passion. The dictionary also tells us that desire is a craving for something that brings satisfaction or enjoyment, or an intense wish—generally repeated or enduring—for something that is beyond our reach but may be attainable at some future date. Thus desire also has a component of fantasy. We imagine having what we desire. Sometimes our fantasies about what we desire go so far that they replace reality.

But why don't we take a test to see if we can pin down what we mean by desire? What about your own desires (as in sexual desire)? If you're asked to describe your wildest sexual desire, what would it be? Can you describe it clearly, or do you find it hard to envision what it is like? Does thinking about scripting your desire make you feel uncomfortable? Do you find the desire itself elusive? Are you trying to desire something you can't imagine?

This little exercise makes us realize how difficult—if not uncomfortable—it is to articulate our desires. The exercise poses another paradox: once we have obtained what we desire, we may no longer desire it; the desired object becomes less attractive. The unreal is more powerful than the real, because nothing is as perfect in fact as it's in our imagination. Only intangible ideas, concepts, beliefs, and fantasies linger on. This explains why down the ages so many people have maintained that it's better to desire than to have. Is it possible that the unique moment in time when we're closest to realizing our desire will actually be the most "exalting," as Anouk Aimée (quoted at the start) maintains? Is this what the poet James Russell Long means when he says, "The thing we long for, that we are. For one transcendent moment?"

One of the greatest ironies about desire is that when we obtain what we desire, our sense of satisfaction is ephemeral. It seems that fantasizing about desire—incomplete though that is—is more attractive than reality. It may be preferable to stay at fantasy level. At least we have a measure of control over what happens in our own fantasy. Perhaps our best love affairs are the ones we've never had. In comparison, reality can be a bit of a cold shower—not at all what we thought it would be. Recognizing potential disappointment may encourage us to remain in our fantasized state.

Whatever frustrations come our way when dealing with desire, it is an ever-present force that keeps our lives in motion. It's like oxygen: we are not always aware of its presence, we may take it for granted, but it's always there. However we experience desire, the pleasure seems to lie in the act of desiring itself, the passing moment. As Robert Louis Stephenson observed, "It is better to travel hopefully than to arrive." The playwright George Bernard Shaw was of a similar opinion. He noted, "There are two tragedies in life. One is not to get your heart's desire. The other is to get it."

Desire is the essence of humankind. To be alive means to be able to desire. It's an emotional, not a rational force, and hard to control—it has a life of its own. We can't decide *when* we're going to desire and we don't choose desire; desire chooses us. As a well-known practitioner of sexual desire, Casanova, once said, trying to explain his love of bed-hopping: "*Hélas!* We love without guidance of reason, and reason isn't anymore involved after we have ceased to love."

Surprisingly, it's only in recent decades that we've had a better understanding of what desire is all about. Recent work by neuroscientists and developmental, cognitive, psychodynamic, and evolutionary psychologists has been instrumental in decoding some of the biological and developmental mechanisms that determine desire.

But here I have to add a caveat. Desire can be discussed from many different angles. In this chapter I'm going to concentrate on one of humankind's most important desires: sexual desire—the essential spark that ignites the human sexual apparatus. I argue that all human activity—including many management decisions—is prompted by this desire. In our very unpredictable world, there is going to be one constant, and that is sexual desire. It's our sexual motivational need system that links non-being to being. It is sexual desire that makes the world go round. Furthermore, although there is now an extensive literature on homoerotic sexual desire, in this chapter I deal with heterosexuality. Homoerotic desire deserves more than the sort of cursory treatment that I would have to give it if this book is not to be too long.

THE LEGACY OF ADAM AND EVE

To understand humankind's attitudes toward sexual desire, we need to look at how its origins have been explained. We might as well start with the story of Adam and Eve as told in Genesis, the first book of the Old Testament in the Bible. Is this a prototypical sexist tale, suggesting that if you make a woman out of a man, you are bound to get into trouble? Why were Adam and Eve evicted from the Garden of Eden? What was their transgression? Were they ejected because the serpent tempted them to eat a forbidden fruit? Was it really all about an apple?

The "facts" of this well-known story are quite nonsensical, so there must be more to it than meets the eye. What does the apple really stand for? We don't have to be rocket scientists to work this out. Given the nature of the punishment, the forbidden fruit must symbolize a pivotal human activity. One reasonable explanation of this story is that it is all about sexual desire. Adam and Eve's fall from Paradise can be interpreted as a simple tale about two people who lust after each other but are not allowed to consummate their passion. No wonder they transgress. But there's more to it than that. It's also a cautionary tale, containing the warning that all sexual desire comes with a price. Loss of innocence—sexual exposure—accompanies expulsion from the Garden of Eden.

Ironically, in contrast to this harsh moral tale from Genesis, the ancient Greeks and Romans worshipped the pleasures of the flesh. They were anything but repressed in viewing the body as a vehicle for pursuing and indulging sexuality. The Greeks and the Romans had nothing of that guilt-ridden self-consciousness about sexuality that has characterized the Judeo-Christian tradition. The explicit erotic art and literature of the period is a real giveaway. It was a period in history when Western society had erected very few barriers against sexual desire. And Western culture wasn't alone in its liberal attitude toward sexual desire. The same is true about many other cultures, as the Hindu erotic sculptures at the Khajuraho temple, and Chinese and Japanese erotic art and literature demonstrate.

But in Western society this era of sexual freedom did not last. After the relatively free and easy period of classical antiquity, dark days fell on Europe when Christianity became the dominant religious and social force. Christianity conveyed an antihedonistic message, equating sexual desire with sin. For many centuries, the Zeitgeist was dominated by the notion that sexual desire was responsible for dragging people into hell. The *leitmotiv* of the church fathers—quoting the gospel of St. Luke—was that "we are all sinners living in a vale of tears." Humankind's preoccupation with the pleasures of the flesh was superseded by concerns for the afterlife. As we will see, it was only after the end of the nineteenth century that sexuality resumed a prominent, more explicit, less guilt-ridden role in the social landscape.

During the Middle Ages sexual desire was seen as evidence of sin. The temptations of the flesh were something to be avoided. Guided by the story of Adam and Eve's fall, the early church fathers viewed human beings as weak and susceptible to sexual temptation. Moreover, they considered all sins to be addictive, and the terminal point of this addiction would be eternal damnation. Women in particular were symbols of extreme temptation. The church fathers believed that given a choice between pain and pleasure, women would choose the hedonistic road, leading to hell. After all, according to their reasoning, it was Eve who seduced Adam. Her sexual charms distracted him from rational thought, with disastrous consequences.

From a clinical point of view, the church fathers' emphasis on the seductive powers of women symbolizes an archaic, masculine fear of women in general, and the female sexual organ in particular. Deep down, the vagina becomes a symbolic representation of the ambivalence men have about the intrusive and withholding mother, the great mother of mythology—the mother who can protect but also can destroy, the woman as Medusa.

Not only were women dangerous creatures, but men would also have confusing associations about the major differentiator, the vagina, the focus of many masculine fantasies (a process that starts with comparisons made during children's play). This explains why stories of devouring, castrating women are so ubiquitous in mythology and folk tales. Reflecting on the content of these stories, it appears—at least to the male mind—that looking at, touching, or entering the female orifice is fraught with hidden fears. In the male unconscious, sex can become equated with dying, every orgasm turning into a "little death." Thus to the male imagination, the mysterious hidden womb becomes a symbol not only of fertility but also of blood and danger. The vagina becomes an organ of wonder and intimidation, a special part of the body that attracts and repels—many female rites and rituals among primitive tribes support this. No wonder that for the Christian ascetics, the mouth of Hell and the vagina evoked similar symbolism. It was a source of great anxiety. Sexual desire became fraught with apprehension.

An obvious strategy to control the expression of sexuality was to denigrate our sensual nature. Sex was dark, dangerous, and filthy. Women's genitals were not only gateways to sexual pleasure but potentially the executioners of men. To enter the vagina would imply establishing contact with an incomprehensible, pleasurable but also dreaded reality. It explains the enduring myth, present in numerous cultures, of the *vagina dentata*, the vagina with teeth. This myth symbolizes primitive masculine fears about castration anxiety, whereby the man—during sexual union—would not only be concerned about being weak or impotent, but would also fear the loss of the penis. And men not only have to deal with castration anxiety: added to this imagery of fear of annihilation by incorporation are unconscious

7

fantasies of "returning to the womb." Men often fear dependency upon women, as if tenderness and closeness would once again render them helpless infants under the domination of their mothers. This "symbiosis anxiety" causes some men to separate love from sexuality and to view intimacy as a trap.

Obviously, the early church fathers were no psychoanalysts or psychiatrists. Depth interpretations—the understanding of symbolic language—were not their forte. Intuitively, however, they were astute in recognizing this lingering male fear of the *vagina dentata*. Pointing out Eve as the culprit, they reasoned that it was man's great error to let his sexual urges escape the power of his will. To them, the tale of Adam and Eve was an illustration of the disastrous consequences of allowing the genitals to respond to fleshly desires rather than intellectual control. This admonitory tale—which they took quite literally—persuaded them to handle sexual desire with great caution. Given the weakness of the flesh—the body was viewed as a prison of the mind and soul—a superhuman effort was required to deflect people's attention from sensuality. It was their duty to remind their flock that there was a better life to be found in the hereafter, not in the present. Paradise was the great alternative. Humankind's hedonistic tendencies were unacceptable. It was their duty to make clear to believers that sexual desire brought only misery, just as it had brought Adam's fall from grace.

Of course, we may wonder whether the church fathers ever thought about what a world absolutely free from what they considered sin would look like. Wouldn't it have created a terrifying vacuum? What would they have to talk about? If everyone led holy lives, there would be very little for churchmen to do. Certainly it would diminish their role in playing Cassandra. Without sin, the church wouldn't have much work!

SEX WITHOUT THE FUN

St. Augustine of Hippo, the fourth-century North African bishop and scholar, was more of a rationalist and argued that sexual desire might be acceptable, but within strict limits. It wasn't easy for him to come to this conclusion, as he himself had to deal with his lust for his mistress and his devotion to his son. In his *Confessions*, a classic book on Christian mysticism describing his conversion to Christianity, he wrote how he prayed regularly to God, saying, "Give me chastity and continence, but do not give it yet." Eventually, however, he succeeded in reaching this enlightened state, at which point he declared that the sole purpose of the unholy activity of sex was procreation. St. Augustine advised that when a man and a woman were ready to have a child, the man, by exerting his will over his body, should summon a functional but lustless erection in order to have sex. St. Augustine regretted the necessity of the act, however, and made it clear that the participants should not enjoy themselves. A married couple needed to "descend with a certain sadness" to participate in sexual intercourse. Augustine presented the use of the genitalia for any other purpose than procreation as unnatural, describing sex for pleasure as an intrinsically evil act. Of course, the preferred state of humankind was chastity.

St. Augustine was enough of a realist (having fathered a child of his own) to realize that the male body could mock the will in the form of spontaneous erections, wet dreams, impotence, premature ejaculations, or other forms of loss of control during orgasm. Unfortunately, he was not enough of a realist to realize that of all the sexual aberrations, chastity may be the strangest.

We laugh at St. Augustine's admonitions nowadays, but we have to look at sexuality in its social context. Not only did people have to contend with the damming words of the church fathers, there were also a number of other factors that needed to be taken into consideration about sex. In the first place, for many people (with the possible exception of the libertine aristocracy and the erotic underworld represented by people such as Casanova) family life was characterized by real lack of privacy. With whole families sharing rooms and beds, the probability of there being onlookers during sexual intercourse would not contribute much to erotic self-fulfillment. In addition, one of the factors that influenced sexual practices for many centuries (in contrast to social habits during the Greek and Roman period) was the fact that people didn't wash. They generally believed that contact with water was dangerous, and would give them a cold or open their pores, making them vulnerable to infection. Most people stank. Sexual desire was also seriously compromised by the scabies, lice, and flies that plagued everyone, causing chronic itching. And if that wasn't sufficiently off-putting, sex was accompanied by the very real fear of the high death rate associated with pregnancy. We have to remember that, in those days, between 10 and 15 percent of women died in childbirth. Like the awareness of AIDS today, this prospect cast a dark shadow over every act of sexual intercourse.

St. Augustine set the tone of attitudes toward sexual desire for many centuries to come. His long shadow fell over many of his scholarly successors. Influenced by him, the church fathers kept preaching that original sin, starting with Adam and Eve, was passed on from parent to child, generation after generation, through the sexual act. Their message was that in Adam's fall, we all sinned. The prevailing literature, following St. Augustine's writings, was full of illustrations of people who wrestled with sexual desire and lost. Saints were presented as edifying examples of people who triumphed over lust, the intemperate craving for the pleasures of the flesh.

For example, Pope Gregory the Great, who ruled in the sixth century, listed lust as one of the seven deadly sins. Echoing Augustine, Gregory stated that "Legitimate carnal union ought to take place for the sake of creating children, not for satisfying vices." Lust was viewed as a deadly sin as it made people look at others as means to an end for the selfish pursuit of their own pleasures. It derailed their minds from God. The selfish pursuit of lust—ignoring the real duties humankind had on earth—would prevent entry into Paradise. Like his predecessors, Gregory worried that lust would get out of hand; he found it helpful to introduce this classification of sins as a way to educate and protect the disciples of the church from this uncontrollable, basic human pursuit. His list of the seven deadly sins and their punishments became a useful set of cautions to ensure that people's lives were governed by rules derived from divine authority. These seven sins were termed "deadly" because people believed that they could do terrible damage to the soul. Generation after generation was indoctrinated into the church's negative attitude toward sex, a continuing process that may have contributed to humankind's ambivalence about sexual desire as well as to sexual disorders.

Seven hundred years after Pope Gregory's classifying scheme (the ghost of St. Augustine still in pride of place), Dante Alighieri elaborated on this notion of sin in his masterpiece *The Divine Comedy*. In one of his three epic poems, *Purgatorio*, Dante also ranked each of the seven sins, placing the higher levels closer to Paradise and the lower levels closer to Hell. In the case of lust, he explored the relationship between the constructive force of attraction toward the beauty of a whole person and the destructive force of intrusive sexual desire. In painting his view of sin, Dante was more nuanced, however, than the sterner church fathers. To him, there was a fine line between love and lust—the lustful in hell were the people who subordinated reason to misguided desire. In this category he put lechers, adulterers, and similar offenders who failed to control their most basic impulses.

It is clear from *The Divine Comedy* that Dante was not quite sure where to place lust. On the one hand, lust's location in Hell—farthest from Satan—marks it as the least serious of the sins; on the other hand, lust is the first sin in Dante's list, recalling the common association of sex with original sin, that is, with the expulsion of

Adam and Eve from the garden of Eden. Figuratively, however, Dante arrives at a creative solution to punish the lack of self-control of the lustful. These unfortunate souls are eternally battered by powerful winds, unable to control their direction. In Purgatory, the penitents who had been prone to lust have to walk through flames to purge themselves of their lustful or sexual thoughts.

This negative portrayal of desire continued after Dante. His epic poem is one more reminder, however, of how highly regimented life was during the late Middle Ages and early Renaissance. At its epicenter was the unchallenged power of the Catholic Church, and the sanctity of marriage was central to its doctrine. Condemning desire as lust and the enjoyment of other physical pleasure as gluttony was part of Christianity's general effort to promote the afterlife over this life. The purpose of fasting and celibacy was to gain victory over the flesh. The pleasures of this world should be forgone, for the sake of pleasures in the next world.

Unfortunately, the church fathers viewed the sexual function in isolation from the psychological processes at work. They refused to acknowledge that human beings are more than the sum of their physical parts. What they didn't want to see was that desire can be an invigorating, life-affirming force, and, what's more, fun. Of course, the early church fathers weren't familiar with evolutionary, developmental, psychodynamic psychology or family systems theory. They were determined not to acknowledge the importance of human sexuality in humankind's biological makeup. They didn't see the link between sexuality, gender, personality, and human development. They also failed to make a distinction between sex and making love. And although the church fathers were willing to accept sex within marriage as a minor sin, that was the limit of their tolerance and as far as they were willing to go. To them, Eden's forbidden fruit was sin, which they equated with sex, thus maintaining Adam and Eve's expulsion from the Garden of Eden as a dreadful example of the consequences of indulging desire.

With their limited and negative attitude toward physiology, the church fathers stood no chance of considering that it might be better to work with our biology rather than against it. Quite the reverse: from their powerful position, they kept the upper hand, rejecting our physiological heritage. The church remained the major influence on people's attitude toward desire for many centuries to come, and religious theology was quoted authoritatively on the subject of sexuality. Eventually, however, early sex study pioneers such as Richard von Krafft-Ebing, Havelock Ellis, or Alfred Kinsey, and psychoanalysts such as Sigmund Freud, Theodor Reik, and Erich

Fromm, helped to change popular opinion of what sex was all about. These people suggested that there is more to sexuality than mere physical, genital activity. They recognized the psychological dynamics. Most importantly, they helped people see that sexuality should be viewed as a normal part of the human experience. In fact, Alfred Kinsey maintained, "The only unnatural sex act is that which you cannot perform." And to quote Sigmund Freud, "Analyze any human emotion, no matter how far it may be removed from the sphere of sex, and you are sure to discover somewhere the primal impulse, to which life owes its perpetuation."

It is difficult for us to realize now, but at that time (and many of these people, including Kinsey and Fromm, didn't publish until after World War II) it was an uphill struggle to change the cultural mindset about sexual desire. There was an enormous amount of resistance to these pioneers' ideas. But they persevered and stood up to the critics who labeled their contributions shameful and insisted their studies should be stopped. Notwithstanding their heroic efforts, the old religious persuasion persisted that God created the human torso, head, arms, and legs, while the devil added the genitals to the mix. The history of sexual desire has been a struggle between the way our genes have wired our brains, and the social behavior enforced by society. It's a story about the hurdles society puts up to prevent sexual desire being actualized.

GENE-DRIVEN SURVIVAL MACHINES?

Fortunately, in contemporary society sex is no longer regarded as a sacred act to be enjoyed only within the confines of marriage, for the purpose of procreation. From the middle of the nineteenth century onward, attitudes toward sexual desire underwent a major transformation and became much more liberal. The pendulum began to swing the other way and Pope Gregory's fearful list became increasingly irrelevant. The historical barriers—social, cultural, and medical—to the free expression of sexual desire were fading, encouraging increased experimentation with sexual desire.

This change in attitude was facilitated by the fact that people were moving from the countryside to the city in increasing numbers. They were no longer subjected to the stifling controls on their privacy that were part and parcel of village life. This population movement was accompanied by improved sanitary habits, better health care, and more convenient and reliable methods of contraception. In addition, both Protestant and Catholic churches had developed a

12

more tolerant attitude toward sex as also a form of pleasure. The ghost of St. Augustine was gradually exorcised. Sensuality was no longer viewed as an abomination before God, but as just another part of the human condition, inspired by God.

However, sexuality truly came into its own in the early 1960s, when birth control pills were legalized, which gave women greater control over their bodies. No longer hampered by the fear of pregnancy, women were much more able to act out their sexual desires. Additionally, with the progress of biotechnology, people no longer *needed* to have sex to assure species survival. Sex could be simply a social and cultural act. Now, in the twenty-first century, sex has almost nothing to do with biological necessity. In our world, hedonistic behavior is on the rise. We're living in a society more geared to the gratification of sexual desire than ever before. From Hugh Hefner's *Playboy Magazine*, founded in 1953, to TV's *Sex and the City*, sex is portrayed as an almost athletic event with record breakers, rules, judges, and spectators. The body has been turned into a sexual playground. Erogenous zones that have lain dormant for centuries are being rediscovered. Sex has moved away from the missionary position; total body sex, involving a variety of bodily functions, is now *de rigueur*.

The sex script between men and women has also changed. New scripts have been added in the form of sperm banks, telephone sex, sex clubs, and video dating services. Articles in magazines like *Cosmopolitan* or *Men's Fitness*, with titles such as "What Makes a Woman Beddable?" or "Hot, Fast Sex: The Quick and the Bed," reflect the Zeitgeist. The number and variety of sexual encounters that a typical Western man or woman has would rival Casanova. Love affairs look somewhat old-fashioned in an age of one-night-stands and orgies. But now sex has become much easier than it was in the past; has it also become less important? The price we pay for easy sex may be a corresponding loss of our capacity for deep love. The emotions associated with sex—such as affection, intimacy, concern, care, and love—play a lesser role in the desire equation, and we are left instead with a cynical society plagued by AIDS, high teen pregnancy rates, and extremely high divorce rates.

St. Augustine and Pope Gregory weren't evolutionary psychologists. Their knowledge of evolution was limited to the story of Adam and Eve. They saw lust as the desire for sexual pleasure run amok. They were not aware of the fact that the human sex drive, unlike our other drives, is quite unique. They didn't recognize that, for humans as for other animals, desire is all about the survival of the species. Human evolution determines much of our behavior, especially when it has to do with our reproductive needs. Much of what we describe as sexual desire is hardwired in our brain. From an evolutionary point of view, sexual abstinence is very bad for species survival. The early church fathers picked a fight that they couldn't hope to win.

People today are stuck with the same sexual desires that drove our primitive ancestors. Evolution rewards life forms that survive, reproduce, and help their descendents get ahead. We're all the descendants of individuals who were driven and motivated to act on their sexual impulses, despite the church's threats about hellfire and damnation. As George Bernard Shaw said, "Why should we take advice on sex from the Pope? If he knows anything about it, he shouldn't!"

Our genetic imprint obliges us to be sexual survival machines, and so we do many things in the name of lust. Our impulse to reproduce has by necessity put a stamp on how we think, feel, and behave. Not only are we driven by what the zoologist Richard Dawkins calls the "selfish gene," most of the time we are not even aware of how our sexual desires work subliminally to influence our behavior. One thing is clear, however; throughout time, people who express their sexual desires most actively (in whatever ways they like) reproduce faster than the more controlled members of our species. Sexual adventurism has always been an intrinsic part of human nature and despite the dire warnings of the church fathers, this human tendency has never really been controlled by social mores.

2

THE CONTRADICTIONS OF DESIRE

Desire is the very essence of man.

Baruch Spinoza

The desire of the man is for the woman, but the desire of the woman is for the desire of the man.

Madame de Stael

We always long for the forbidden things, and desire what is denied us.

François de Rabelais

The starting point of all achievement is desire.

Napoleon Hill

The storyteller Aesop once said: "There are many operational definitions of desire. It is with our passions, as it is with fire and water; they are good servants but bad masters." Aesop was not alone in having difficulty making sense of desire. He expresses what many people experience when trying to answer the questions I asked in the previous chapter. The response of one of my clients was: "To me, sexual desire translates as a search for forbidden fruits. I always seem to long for the forbidden things, and desire what is denied to me. It's like my animal nature is ruling my reason. But it's a very important aspect to me of what life is all about." Another wrote: "To me, sexual desire is like poetry. It means having all those strange, irresistible fantasies inside me. There lives a compelling force in me that insists it is listened to. It may be the reason I get up in the morning. Looking back on my life, the things I have done, desire has very much made me the person I am." One executive had a darker outlook: "Whenever I have to deal with desire, I foresee a tragedy in the making. There have been times when I lost control. To be honest, all the mistakes I have made in my life have been an outcome of desire. For example, I have been married several times. Was it worth it? Now I wonder.

15

Unfortunately, too often I discovered that the price of getting what I want is getting what I once wanted." Listening to him, I thought about Robin Williams's quip, "God gave us a penis and a brain, but only enough blood to run one at a time."

However it is packaged, the evolutionary origins of desire are there for all to see. This doesn't mean, however, that we should ignore its psychological components. Human action is inevitably a product of both. The genetic matrix unfolds within a particular environmental and cultural context. Historical, developmental, cultural, and situational factors have a strong influence on the form desire will take. We're not only driven by instinctual processes. The mind is also an erogenous zone. In principle, all behavior patterns can be altered by environmental forces. Given the human species' lengthy gestation period, every form of human action is by necessity a product of nature and nurture.

The French-Swiss writer, Madame de Stael, quoted at the start of this chapter, hit the nail on the head. Since human history began, men have wanted to have sex with attractive women, while women have needed to ensure that that they would have a sufficient degree of commitment from their partner. Their problem has been how to assess the strength of this commitment. Monogamy is rare in the animal kingdom for a very simple reason. It's not to the male genetic advantage to remain with one female when he can have sex with several and perpetuate his genes to the maximum. To quote the anthropologist Margaret Mead, "Motherhood is a biological fact, while fatherhood is a social invention."

But women have always had a different agenda because for them, especially in primitive times, there was a tremendous risk attached to having sex. The burden and vulnerability associated with pregnancy, a nine-month gestation, and lactation would have been enormous. Given the adaptive problems of survival and reproduction, our female ancestors needed to be extremely careful in selecting their mate, ensuring their commitment to helping them raise their children.

In this context, it's worth noting an interesting correlation between the length of human infancy—about four years—and the length of many marriages, about the same. Worldwide, the divorce rate peaks at four years, conforming to the traditional period between successive human births. Perhaps human pair bonds were originally designed to last long enough to raise a single, dependent child through infancy, unless a second child was conceived. And perhaps the seven-year itch should actually be the four-year itch, as its duration has an evolutionary explanation. In general, it seems that the more children a woman bears her partner, the more likely the couple are to stay

16

together. Of course, when making these observations, we shouldn't forget the strong economic component of divorce rates. Divorce is less likely when the partners are economically dependent on one another.

Taking a nature versus nurture perspective, we can see that DNA becomes shaped by environmental context. But while the human brain can be analyzed in terms of its neural activity, people are much more than their physiological makeup. They are subject to numerous and various cultural influences, which contribute to a multitude of attitudes toward desire. Every individual's sex drive is a complex cocktail, starting with bodily reactions that stimulate symbolic associations in the mind. Some of the ways sexual desire is expressed will be in line with social mores; other forms of expression will be looked at askance.

By now, we should have realized that there's more to desire than just sex. In that respect, the human species is different from the rest of the animal kingdom. It's the price we have to pay for being both hardwired and softwired. This explains the other factors in the sexual desire equation. If, like animals, we view others as mere sexual containers, engaging in mindless, recreational sex, we deny other people's psychological individuality and see them merely in terms of their physiological function. This may give us a temporary high but will also have a dehumanizing impact on both parties. Sexual desire in humans is a complex phenomenon because it links together three emotional systems: sexual feelings, attachment behavior, and love.

That we're not mindless gene-survival machines, but individuals subjected to highly complex feelings, underlines a basic human feature that goes beyond our sexual drive: our need to be loved, cared for, and valued as a person. Sexual desire can metamorphose into feelings of intimacy, care, concern, and commitment, a recipe for a more lasting attachment. When these three emotional systems work together, satisfying, long lasting relationships will emerge. Moreover, this combination of feelings of sexual attraction, attachment, and love has evolutionary advantages in that it increases the likelihood that the couple's offspring will survive and thrive. Unlike other animal species, human beings are a walking paradox: we've to deal with searching for that obscure object of desire, while being programmed for sex.

It is far from easy to find people in whom all three of these feelings come together consistently. It is more usual for there to be a short circuit between the three that makes them work against each other, triggering competing wishes and interests—so that it is possible to be emotionally drawn to one person, in love with another, and sexually aroused by someone else. Human relationships are very complex: we need to figure out what sexual desire, attachment behavior, and love really stand for.

SEXUALITY: THE SNAKE UNDER THE CARPET

In the National Gallery in London is Sandro Botticelli's Renaissance masterpiece *Venus and Mars*. Botticelli's painting is an allegory of the relationship between the sexes. Venus is Love and Harmony, Mars is War and Discord. In the painting, Venus, awake and alert, looks attentively at the sleeping Mars after a romantic and sexual interlude. Mars is sleeping the postcoital "little death," and the goddess of love reigns supreme after having subdued the god of war. Mars, unarmed, sleeps deeply, depleted of his strength, subjugated by the power of love. In the meantime, equally symbolically, mischievous satyrs play his discarded weapons.

This famous painting illustrates "the snake under the carpet"—the conflicting signals about sexual desire given by men and women. Mars, after having satisfied his physical needs, wants only to sleep while Venus looks for more—a conversation, perhaps? Botticelli has painted a wasps' nest at Mars's head, possibly symbolizing the potential for serious and painful conflict in the relationship. Although the painting can be interpreted as the triumph of "cosmic love" (symbolized by Venus) over violence (Mars), it also raises the question of how long this triumph—and relationship—will last.

Interestingly enough, even though we all think about sex a lot, we are also very reticent about it. Even the most intimate of friends may find it difficult to discuss it, beyond mere generalities. It must be emphasized that sexual desire is quite different from sexual behavior. Sexual desire is a psychological experience that isn't necessarily reflected in action, although it can be associated with physical responses, as genital arousal may occur without conscious awareness.

The French writer Victor Hugo once wrote, "From the oyster to the eagle, from the swine to the tiger, all animals are to be found in men and each of them exists in some man, sometimes several at the time. Animals are nothing but the portrayal of our virtues and vices made manifest to our eyes, the visible reflections of our souls. God displays them to us to give us food for thought." This is a highly questionable statement: evolutionary and developmental psychologists would point out that there are some very real differences. However, from a research point of view, much of what has been written about human sexual desire has been derived from reports of pathological human behavior and the study of animals. The mating behavior of primates and other animals has been a rich source of inspiration. Although some biologically oriented researchers believe that behavior is too important to be left to psychologists, this begs the question how realistic it is to extrapolate animal observations to humans. It's presumptuous to apply what we know about animal sexuality to the human experience. Sexual behavior in humans, given their lengthy maturation period, is far more complex than in other animals. From a neurological point of view, a strong indicator of this is the more highly developed cerebral cortex in humans (the part of the brain that plays a central role in many complex brain functions including memory, attention, perceptual awareness, thinking, language and consciousness). This suggests that sexual interaction has implications for human relationships. In addition, there's no evidence that animals can arouse themselves through sexual fantasy. Homo sapiens do not need another individual to be present to be sexually stimulated. As the film star Sophia Loren once said, "Sex appeal is 50 per cent what you've got and 50 per cent what people think you've got."

When we bandy about the term "sexual desire," we assume we're all talking about the same thing. However, there are many different operational definitions of desire. From a fairly detached, neurological point of view, sexual desire can be seen as the outcome of neuroendocrine mechanisms that are experienced as spontaneous sexual interests. For me, sexual desire is about strong chemistry between two people, the lustful, sexually passionate feelings they have for each other. Sexual desire is typically manifested by sexual thoughts, feelings, fantasies or dreams, increased erotic attraction to others in proximity, seeking out sexual activity (alone or with a partner), and increased genital sensitivity.

The sexologist Virginia Johnson introduced the idea of the "human sexual response cycle," the sequence of physical and emotional changes that occur as a person becomes sexually aroused and participates in sexually stimulating activities, including intercourse and masturbation. She described a number of physiological reaction phases which she defined as excitement, plateau, orgasm, and resolution.

Sexual desire was missing from this classification, so another sex researcher, Helen Singer Kaplan, expanded the cycle by adding a sexual desire phase up front. From what we know about attachment behavior and love, however, the female sexual response may not follow this linear model of discrete phases of sexual responsiveness. Instead, a more circular, intimacy-based sexual response cycle may be more realistic, with overlapping phases of variable order.

We can wonder, however, whether the experience of desire is less a forerunner to sex than an afterthought. Sexual arousal isn't necessarily a conscious process, but much more subliminal. The cognitive overlay that the brain gives to the sensation of desire may already be aroused by other physical or subliminal stimuli. Various studies have shown that the body's entire motor system is activated almost instantly by exposure to sexual images. As a matter of fact, the body may be primed for sex before the mind has had a moment to create lustful images.

Although some sexologists take a very mechanical view of sexual desire as an innate motivational need (a drive that serves the biological function of species survival), most people subscribe to the view that these neurological and biological mechanisms are influenced by psychological factors. The appetite for sex is a complex psychobiological process whereby the sexual drive can be diminished by factors such as mental or physical illness, age, and grief. Hormones, the menstrual cycle, pregnancy, the menopause, and drugs also play a role in its activation and decline. In addition, the more cognitive part of the sexual desire equation will be influenced by the desire to feel loved, to feel masculine or feminine, or the wish to please the partner.

Furthermore, as the admonitions of the early church fathers demonstrated, human sexuality differs from animal sexuality in that it can be constrained by taboos. From early life, we're bombarded with injunctions about the dos and don'ts of sexuality. Although these taboos can be inhibiting, the sexual drive is ingenious. Fantasy plays a very important part in human functioning, so there can be a positive side to injunctions against sex: desire may be activated by the excitement raised by transgressing taboos. Part of the sizzle of sex comes from its danger. As the filmmaker Mel Brooks said, "I've been taught ever since I was a kid that sex is filthy and forbidden, and that's the way I think it should be. The filthier and more forbidden it is, the more exciting it is." Entering forbidden territory has always had its attractions. The amount of readily available pornographic literature of nuns and priests having sex is indicative of what may turn people on—desire triumphing over taboo. In fact, and all too often, sexual desire is about humankind in conflict with itself.

The role of novelty: the "Coolidge Effect"

One important factor of sexual desire is novelty. Many studies have pointed out the important part that the "Coolidge Effect" plays in human sexual behavior. There's a famous but probably apocryphal story about US President Calvin Coolidge and his wife, who were visiting a poultry farm. During the visit, they were taken on separate tours. Mrs. Coolidge, passing the pens and seeing a single rooster busily mating with one of the chickens, asked the supervisor whether one lone rooster was sufficient to service the large number of hens in the pen. "Yes," the man said, "that rooster really earns his keep. He works very hard." Mrs. Coolidge asked, "Really? He does this every day?" "Oh, yes," the man responded. "As a matter of fact, he does it dozens of times a day." "That's very interesting," Mrs. Coolidge replied. "Can you tell that to the President?"

Some time later the President, passing the same chicken pen, was told about the rooster—and about his wife's remark. "Same hen every time?" he asked. "Oh, no, a different one each time," the supervisor replied. "Tell that," Coolidge said with a smile, "to Mrs. Coolidge."

While sexual desire motivates much of our behavior early on in a relationship, most studies show that such intense levels of sexual desire are difficult to maintain with the same person over the course of time. For most of us, love at first sight is easy to understand; it's when two people have been looking at each other for a lifetime that it is more of a miracle.

Usually, at the beginning of a relationship everything is new and exciting. It's a time of exploration of each other's bodies, a time of passion, when our sex drive works overtime. But the exciting period of conquest is soon over and after a while routine sets in. Ironically, the knowledge that we can have sex anytime means that we've it less. As a comedian once said, "Your marriage is in trouble if your wife says, 'You're only interested in one thing,' and you can't remember what it is."

ATTACHMENT BEHAVIOR

The comedian Steve Martin had this figured out. He said, "Don't have sex, man. It leads to kissing and pretty soon you have to start talking to them." This would make a good caption to Botticelli's *Venus and Mars*. Sex alone is not enough: more is needed for a man to satisfy a woman.

Sexuality, as I've indicated, is much more complex for humans than other animals. Attachment theory has thrown useful light on the psychological dynamics between the sexes by redefining the position of sexual behavior in the context of desire. Although sex appears to be the essence of a relationship for many, this isn't truly the case beyond the initial period of sexual infatuation. For many couples, sex is often only a small part of adult intimacy. Sex and attachment, however, make interesting bedfellows. Many people use sex as a way to create or substitute for the sense of connection they need. As the movie star Mae West once said, "Sex is emotion in motion." In my work I have seen many clients who have abundant sexual lives, but long for involved, lasting relationships and greater levels of intimacy and commitment. Many people engage in sex just to satisfy the need to be held. As one woman once confided in me: "I now realize that I use my vagina for a handshake!" Often, the sex act can be interpreted as a conversation carried out by other means—which brings us to the question of attachment.

There is a Hindu proverb that says, "Like the body that is made up of different limbs and organs, all moral creatures must depend on each other to exist." The notion of the self-contained person is an illusion. Total self-sufficiency is an oversimplified fantasy—or to be more precise, plainly not true. An absence of social contact contributes to physical and psychological breakdown. Under conditions of total isolation, we simply deteriorate. Given our evolutionary and psychological origins, the symbol of a lone, self-sufficient cowboy riding into the sunset is more than a counter-dependent fantasy: it is an aberration. Our basic attachment needs ensure that we become who we are as individuals because of our connection to other people. We are social animals. Our attachment needs make dependence on another person an integral part of being human. Relatedness is a core aspect of who we are.

The British psychoanalyst John Bowlby developed a theory of attachment behavior from studying the intense distress experienced by infants who had been separated from their parents. According to Bowlby, our primary motivation in life is to feel connected to other people. This connectivity is the only security we will ever experience. Bowlby suggested that attachment behavior is an adaptive response (related to an infant's helplessness) to the separation from the primary caretaker, the person who provides support, protection, and care.

Bowlby observed that infants would go to extraordinary lengths either to prevent separation from their parents or to reestablish proximity to a missing parent. He discovered that if the attachment figure was easily accessible, the child would feel secure and be more likely to explore his or her environment, play with others, and be sociable. However, when the attachment figure was less dependable, the child would experience anxiety and would go at great lengths to maintain a desirable level of physical or psychological proximity with the attachment figure. When a child failed to establish such a connection, it would experience feelings of despair and depression.

Bowlby's observations demonstrated that maintaining closeness is necessary for species survival; the need for physical closeness between a mother (caregiver) and child has an evolutionary goal. In a dangerous, unpredictable world, a responsive caregiver ensures the infant's survival. This means that a child's mental and behavioral script about relationships will become a function of his or her early caregiving experiences. Although Bowlby focused primarily on understanding the nature of the infant-caregiver relationship, he believed that there was continuity and similarity in attachment patterns from infants to adults.

Mary Ainsworth, an American developmental psychologist, extrapolated Bowlby's attachment theory introducing the concept of the "strange situation." Children aged between twelve and eighteen months were observed responding to a situation in which they were briefly left alone and then reunited with their mother. Depending on the degree of attachment security, Ainsworth identified three basic attachment styles. She observed that most of the children appeared to be securely attached to the caregiver. Although they showed signs of distress when left with a stranger, they would seek out their mother when she returned, would hold on to her for a short time, and then would go back to exploring and playing. These infants had developed attachment security because they had mothers who were sensitive and responsive to their needs. Forty percent of children she examined were comparatively insecurely attached. These children experienced a considerable amount of anxiety when separated. In these instances, Ainsworth noted an interesting pattern: when the mother returned, the children would approach then reject her. Ainsworth's explanation for the ambivalent attitude of these children was that their mothers dealt with them inconsistently and unpredictably. The mothers were variably unavailable and very affectionate. The outcome of this inconsistent relationship was that these infants were so preoccupied with their caregiver's availability that they never felt secure enough to explore their world. Ainsworth also observed a third group of children who were characterized by an avoidant attachment style. They didn't seem distressed during separation, and didn't acknowledge their mother during reunion. These infants, however, were able to keep their distress well-hidden. Although they seemed to negate any attachment to the caregiver, internally they were in a state of physiological arousal. Ainsworth noted that these children were usually reared by caregivers who rebuffed all attempts at close physical contact.

Over time the expectations associated with these three attachment patterns turn into self-fulfilling prophecies. As adults, we relate to others following our own internalized relationship script. This affects the way we process information, how we see the world, and our expectations and experience of social contact. We carry our attachment style with us into adult life, a predisposition to how we will behave in later love relationships, influencing partner choice. An adult's comparative security or insecurity in adult relationships is a partial reflection of his or her attachment experiences in early childhood.

There are, of course, important differences between childhood and adult attachment. First, childhood attachments aren't symmetrical; the relationship is usually complimentary rather than reciprocal because a child is more dependent on the parent than the other way around. Second, there is almost always a sexual component involved in adult attachments.

Extrapolating from these childhood attachment patterns, we can see how some adults, secure in their relationships, are confident about the continued presence and support of their partner. They are prepared to depend on others and for others to depend on them. In contrast, others are insecure and anxious in relationships, worrying that others may not love them completely, and easily frustrated or angered when their attachment needs are not met. Other people may resort to avoidance, not seeming to care much about close relationships and preferring not to be too dependent upon other people or for others to depend on them.

Although the maternal-child interface is the basic model of relationship patterns, from a developmental point of view this two-way relationship is followed by the classical triangle of childhood: mother, father, and child. The way this triangle is played out in the family—how the child relates to one or the other parent—also influences how the adult will deal with romantic attachments. This triangle also sets the stage for possibly pathological relationship structures, where partners seem compelled to repeat specific dysfunctional ways of dealing with each other. This developmental triangle can become a fertile source of future love conflicts. George Bernard Shaw once said, "If you cannot get rid of the family skeleton, you may as well make it dance." In each family a story is played out, and each family's story embodies its hope and despair.

WHAT'S LOVE GOT TO DO WITH IT?

What does love has to do with desire? The terms desire, sex, and love are easily confused as people tend to use these concepts interchangeably. Many people equate sex with love. But as I suggested earlier, although sex pulls people together, physical attraction alone cannot bond two people for a very long time. Although sex involves physical intimacy, it doesn't have the emotional depth that we associate with love. Love is the "marriage" of the sexual and attachment elements of desire.

A great many people have had a great deal to say about love. The poet Robert Frost, describing the compelling, driven aspect of love, wrote, "Love is an irresistible desire to be irresistibly desired." People often associate love with mental confusion or illness. When we are in love, our delusions as well as our love make sense to us. To quote the mathematician-philosopher Blaise Pascal, "The heart has its reasons, which reason does not know." Or in the words of another philosopher, Francis Bacon, "It is impossible to love and be wise." Love makes us do crazy things we would never otherwise do. It can even make us unrecognizable to ourselves. It "sweeps us off our feet"; it "leaves us blind, and dazed"; it makes us "act foolishly." Love ejects us forcefully from our comfort zone and, as the Roman poet Ovid warned, "is not an assignment for cowards." The journalist and social critic Henry Louis Mencken took a more cynical view of love, which he described as "the triumph of imagination over intelligence." The filmmaker Woody Allen has been preoccupied with love's relationship to sex: "Love is the answer, but while you are waiting for the answer, sex raises some pretty good questions." His films play on our tendency to fall madly in bed with someone, while we work out how ready we are to fall madly in love. This isn't what the early church fathers meant when they talked about love. They were more interested in the love of the hereafter than love in the here-and-now, which they discouraged. They were clearly unable to differentiate between a lustful and a lovesick person, a predictable outcome of their preoccupation with celibacy.

A lustful person experiences intense sexual desire that can be satisfied indiscriminately with any number of people, while a lovesick person experiences intense sexual desire towards one specific individual. While people may be unsure whether they're in love, they generally know whether or not they're having sex. Some people argue that sex is such a powerful, aggressive drive that we try to harness it by calling it love. Cynics say that calling sex "love" is a great way of repackaging our basic biological needs. It's an attractive way of papering over the wham-bam-thank-you-ma'am approach to relationships, enacted too often by too many men, and an effective way to keep partners together for a while.

When we're in love, sex is one (very intimate) way of communicating with the other, of expressing our feelings. Sex is a body language in which we can express gentleness and affection, anger and resentment, superiority and dependence far more succinctly than we can verbally, where expressions are unavoidably abstract and often clumsy. While in love, sex is more than an expedient act of pleasure; it is a way of building a connection.

All these observations suggest that human sexual intimacy is rarely merely physical. Although a sexual relationship may help us discover the other in a physical way, in unveiling our bodies, we also unveil aspects of our character. Some women have sex for non-sexual reasons: they will do whatever the man wants because they want to obtain some kind of hold over him; they want to possess him. These women may not realize, however, that emotional attachment makes them vulnerable. Sex doesn't necessarily create an automatic, emotional attachment response in men. Although some women may think that sex is the surest way to attach to another person, they are in for a rude awakening. To quote the actress Sharon Stone, "Women might be able to fake orgasms. But men can fake whole relationships." Or as Woody Allen, something of a specialist on the subject, put it, "Sex without love is an empty experience, but as empty experiences go, it's a pretty good empty experience."

The need for mutual discovery often makes it difficult to separate sex from love. The French writer François de la Rochefoucauld said: "It is very hard to give a just definition of love. The most we can say of it is this: that in the soul, it is a desire to rule; in the spirit, it is a sympathy; and in the body, it is but a hidden and subtle desire to possess—after many mysteries—what one loves." Its physiological aspects apart, sexual passion, for both sexes, is largely an emotion of power, domination, or appropriation. It is a state of mind where the word "mine" features prominently.

Love entails feelings of closeness, genuine appreciation, and concern. But as I suggested earlier, attachment behavior helps us understand what passionate love is really all about—finding someone who connects with us and alleviates our attachment fears. We fall in love when an attachment bond is formed. We stay in love by maintaining that bond. We use our repertoire of emotions to signal the need for distance and the need for comfort through contact. Of course, the experience of love is not the same for everyone. For some, love is delusional and needy; for others, it's emotional game playing; and for yet others it derives from the desire to take care of another person. A cynic, like the writer Somerset Maugham, might take a purely functional view of it: "Love is only a dirty trick played on us to achieve continuation of the species."

26

THE CONTRADICTIONS OF DESIRE

ROMANTIC LOVE

We make various distinctions when we talk about love. They include self-love, parental love, familial love, filial love, conjugal love, religious love, love of animals, love of humanity—and romantic love. Romantic love is celebrated in many cultures. Art and literature have been full of examples of romantic love from the earliest times. In the Old Testament—an anomaly in that formidable text—the "Song of Solomon," or the "Song of Songs," is a dialogue between a bridegroom and a bride, expressing reciprocal romantic and sexual attraction. Then there are Ovid's love poems, *Amores*, *The Recognition of Shakuntala* by the Sanskrit poet Kalidasa, *The Rubaiyat* of the Sufi poet Omar Khayyam, and the famous letters of Heloïse and Abélard, one of the best-known records of early romantic love. And these illustrations of romantic love are only the tip of the iceberg.

What differentiates romantic love from desire is that there's often, at least initially, more emphasis on the emotions than on physical pleasure. Another way of looking at romantic love is to view it as an artistic form of sex in disguise, in which the suppression, sublimation, or even transcendence of the sexual drive plays a major role.

Romantic love is a very special state of mind. In the Western world it really came into its own in the twelfth century, reflected by the literature, letters, and poetry of Provençal troubadours. Before that time, the idea of romantic love—a spontaneous attraction between two people, acting as equal parties in a relationship—was given pretty short shrift. Most relationships were more businesslike. Marriage was the work of the church or family, who arranged matches. Love played a minor role in the process. Women had little say in the matter. Generally, marriages were arranged by men to ensure wealth, status, power, and property. But by the twelfth century, this way of looking at relationships was changing and more was made of the idea of falling in love. By the Renaissance, it was an established element of human relationships, part of a greater awareness of the complexities of love as elaborated, for example, by Shakespeare in *Romeo and Juliet*.

The concepts of platonic love—a chaste, passionate form of love, including deep friendship—and romantic love are closely related. Romantic love may even morph into platonic love by abjuring sexuality altogether. Much romantic literature (particularly in the nineteenth century) is a kind of elegy of platonic love. The protagonists talk a great deal about their fantasies, while physical desire is put on the backburner or buried completely. Frequently, love becomes a torment of the soul rather than physical passion. Is this the ghost

27

of St. Augustine stirring? He wrote, "Since love grows within you, so beauty grows. For love is the beauty of the soul."

Reading these diaries, letters, and novels, there's a remarkable element of idealism present; the protagonists in these courtship dances put each other on quite unrealistic pedestals. And along with this infatuation is a kind of willful blindness. This makes romantic love a sort of religion with two acolytes, a temporary state of mind and being whereby the distinctions between the self and the other seem to have melted away. In the process, the merger between the couple in love can become so intense that it's difficult to distinguish between them.

A clinical perspective on this kind of intense and intimate romantic love is that it is the relived experience of the early maternal-child dyad, rediscovered and reenacted in the adult lover dyad, the revival of a very archaic relationship. This is often borne out by the way lovers talk to and touch each other: "love bird," "sweetheart," "honey," "baby," "pumpkin," "cupcake,"—we have heard it all. These terms conjure up memories of the way our mothers treated us as infants. Symbolically, the couple seems to be enacting a mystical union—the long lost, but longed for mother-child relationship of our earliest years. So is romantic love really "the triumph of imagination over intelligence?" George Bernard Shaw might have thought so: "Love is a gross exaggeration of the difference between one person and everybody else."

But romantic love is more than spiritual rediscovery and reunion and we shouldn't be fooled about its asexual dimension. It might appear asexual, but the physical aspects remain only submerged. Sexual inhibition and the pursuit of the hard-to-get fuel the fire of romantic love. Quite apart from the reactivation of maternal-child attachment patterns, romantic love can only blossom when the individuals in question are also deeply physically aroused.

The fusion of sexual and attachment needs

The short-term, fleeting nature of romantic love is a fusion of affection and sexual desire, a compromise formation that survives as long as sexual desire has a limited outlet. It is like a prelude to a marriage campaign, with sexual consummation the ultimate aim. However, once sex happens, romantic love disappears. Après-sex reality shoves its way pretty rudely into la-la land. Children, the mortgage, washing, shopping, cooking: eventually, someone has to take out the garbage.

Romantic love cannot survive the realities of a real relationship, and when this happens the realization dawns that the pedestals on which the partners have placed each other are unstable. The music stops; the magic disappears; and each party sees the weaknesses or hidden flaws in the once romantic ideal.

But even though romantic love sets us up for disillusionment, it is very powerful. When we look back at our life, we discover that the moments when we really lived were the moments when we felt loved or were in love. We never forget where we met, the first time we kissed, the first time we touched. These memories are so strong they're almost visible.

Romantic love can be transforming—not just of the world but of the self. Being in love is a very good way of learning more about ourselves. In a sense, the language of love is the language of vulnerability. Being in love reawakens old attachment patterns, a learning process in itself. When the heat of passionate romantic love has faded into the background, it can transform into a more enduring form of love—affectionate companionship, mutual care, and intimacy. The ability to create secure attachments like this promotes our emotional health and buffers us against life's many stresses.

If we are lucky, sexual passion and romantic love will remain regular features in our lives, but we need to work at renewing them, make an effort to rediscover the other, and not take the other for granted. Continuing maintenance will help us repair the conflicts and misunderstandings that arise in any relationship. If there is love to draw on, it becomes the most powerful arena for healing and for growth. With love as a secure base, both men and women can go out and explore, discover new horizons. In many ways, love doesn't just make the world go round; it's what makes the ride worthwhile.

3

MARS MEETS VENUS

The great question that has never been answered and which I have not yet been able to answer is "What does a woman want?"

Sigmund Freud

You're not just sleeping with one person, you're sleeping with everyone they ever slept with.

Theresa Grenshaw

It's not true that I had nothing on. I had the radio on.

Marilyn Monroe

Desire is fundamental to living a genuinely fulfilling life. It is a key building block in making us who we are. While many of us may not see a direct relationship between personal identity and sexuality, the absence of desire would significantly alter our sense of who and what we are. We're very much sexual beings.

But what influences partner choice? What attracts one partner to the other? What exactly is desirability?

EVOLUTIONARY PSYCHOLOGY AND PARTNER CHOICE

Often, selecting a partner is an act of faith. Some of my executives describe it as the bravest, most risky, and unrealistic thing they have ever done in their life. While the decision is often made on limited information, they still leap in. There's always a solid dose of wishful thinking in the creation of a partnership. When we're in love, everything seems to be possible. We can climb mountains; we can fly; we can do anything. This is the illusionary effect of love. Other people may be puzzled by what is going on, but the lovers involved appear to see what others don't (or fail to see what they do). They have entered their own world. A couple in love, presents us with a paradox: we see two people full of imagination but also two people who can be completely blind.

"Love is blind" is a partial explanation of the puzzling question of what attracts partners to each other. Why is there such a thing as love at first sight? We look at some people sometimes and wonder what on earth they see in each other. It's often an unanswerable question. But then it has been said that one man's folly is another man's wife.

The "Konrad Lorenz effect" is one interesting way of explaining partner choice. Lorenz was an ethologist who did a lot of research into the power of early imprinting. In his work with birds, Lorenz described how newly hatched chicks became rapidly and strongly attached to parents or parental surrogates. He described how newly hatched goslings would imprint on him—because he was their first contact—instead of the mother goose. He demonstrated this by showing that they followed him around wherever he went. Can we speculate that a similar pattern exists in humankind? If it's so, it may answer the vexing question why "love is blind." It could explain the "chemistry," or "coup de foudre" (lightning bolt) of falling in love, implying a sudden subliminal recognition of faces or features that remind us of close family members—most importantly our parents.

Beyond the "Konrad Lorenz effect," there are many other factors that can influence partner choice. The reproductive cycle of the human species is relatively slow—involving a long gestational period and a significant amount of post-natal parental care. (Effectively, human beings, given the size of their brain and the size of the birth canal, are born far too early.) Consequently, men and women have to be selective when choosing their mates. Males want females who look the most likely to perpetuate their genes and females want males who will be around to help them take care of their offspring. Evolutionary psychologists point out the importance of the genetic, physical, and even emotional fitness of both partners.

As I suggested earlier, men and women are programmed differently for sex. It has been said that women need a reason for sex while men just need a place. Men often see sex as an end in itself, just because it feels good. This may also be the case for women, of course, but generally they have a broader agenda for sex, including intimacy and closeness. To the evolutionary theorist the reason for this is self-evident. While it's advantageous for men to be easily turned on by the mere sight of a nude woman—this serves gene proliferation—quick arousal is disadvantageous for women because it interferes with their strategy of careful mate selection.

As I stated earlier, pregnancy makes women highly vulnerable. They need reliable partners to help them through the whole process of bearing, delivering, and nurturing a child. For millennia of necessity, women have always looked for men with staying power and the ability to commit themselves to a long-term relationship. As the movie star Mae West said, "Men are easy to get but hard to keep."

So what are our selection criteria? Unsurprisingly, both men and women go for appearance. Physical attractiveness is important. It suggests good health, the physical and mental ability to be good reproductive stock. Both are equally influenced by body build. Men look for the "hour glass" figure in women, a low waist-to-hip ratio, which suggests greater childbearing capacity. Women are attracted to a tapering "V" figure in men, indicating athletic prowess—athletic men make better hunters. This may explain why men—like a peacock sporting its tail—display their bravado (future potential as a hunter) on the battleground or sports field. Women prefer tall men, while men prefer women shorter than themselves. Both sexes prefer people of normal or slightly lower weight. Generally, extremes in body shape are viewed as unattractive.

Because men put such a premium on physical appearance, women go to great lengths to enhance their attractiveness, an instinctual impulse on which hugely successful clothing, cosmetic, diet, and plastic surgery industries have been built. They resort to a wide range of tactics to improve their desirability, knowing that it will improve their chances of finding a partner. Women have recognized this necessity through the ages, and worked hard at it.

Enhancing physical attractiveness is only one weapon in the female armory. Women have learned that pretended helplessness creates a protective response in the opposite sex. Mae West—a woman who was anything but helpless—once quipped that "Brains are an asset, if you hide them." In the mating game, it can be advantageous to project a non-threatening level of intelligence. The singer and actress Dolly Parton agrees: "I'm not offended by all the dumb blonde jokes because I know I'm not dumb, and I also know that I'm not blonde." The dumb blonde may be an overworked stereotype, but it is also a tried and tested signal of sexual accessibility. The comedian Groucho Marx might have leered, "Women should be obscene and not heard," but he touched on a truth. Too many women still worry about the adage, "I think therefore I'm single."

Physical appearance is only one aspect of the mating game. To women, a man's social position, material possessions, and ability to provide (demonstrable ambition and industriousness) are also important factors in partner selection. Women have always been on the lookout for men with good financial prospects. In our evolutionary past, women benefited tremendously by being connected to men who were good providers. Women strive to raise the odds of securing social, material, and economic resources for themselves and their children. And a perception that this pattern is still valid today is well and truly alive among men. According to the satirist Patrick O'Rourke, "There are a number of mechanical devices which increase sexual arousal, particularly in women. Chief among these is the Mercedes-Benz 380SL convertible." These materialistic concerns also explain why women generally select men older than themselves: income tends to increase with age. In contrast, men prefer women younger than themselves not only for reproductive reasons but also to show them off to other men as status symbols.

Nevertheless, the ability to be a good provider has to be coupled with other positive attributes such as dependability, emotional stability, a romantic attitude, empathy, and kindness. Kindness is an especially important factor to women because it suggests a willingness to place a partner's needs before their own and more importantly it implies kindness to children. Men who demonstrate kindness to children are less aggressive, a very attractive attribute given the frequency of wife beating.

Fidelity is a major factor in successful relationships. For women, fidelity indicates the exclusive commitment of sexual resources to one single partner. From an evolutionary psychology perspective, this means commitment to one single partner's genes. This perspective explains why men abhor promiscuity in their wives—they want to be certain of their paternity. It also explains the intensity of male jealousy, which can even lead to homicide. Again, the adaptive function of sexual jealousy—dysfunctional as it may seem—is to prevent infidelity and assure paternity: jealous males are more likely to pass on their genes. On their part, jealous females, who successfully drive away other females, will have greater protection and more resources available to them.

A CHARACTER IN SEARCH OF BEING A CHARACTER

The reasoning of evolutionary psychologists about partner choice would be sterile without psychological imagination. What do psychologists, psychotherapists, and psychoanalysts have to say about partner choice? What explanations do they give for why people select each other? Can we discern specific patterns in partner choice?

Psychological studies tell us that we tend to look for people we perceive as similar to ourselves, or to our ideal selves. The expectation is that the other will provide something we think is lacking in us and that we will provide something in return. To complicate matters, we may have an unconscious recognition of disowned, denied, or projected parts of the self in the other. Of course, many of these beliefs are imaginary. We would be unable to "love" if we knew the other person completely. A bit of mystery is necessary for love to work. It makes the other such a good recipient of our projective identifications.

Projective identification is an interpersonal process whereby a part of the self is projected onto someone else. The individual deals with emotional conflict or internal or external stressors by falsely attributing his or her own unacceptable feelings, impulses, or thoughts to another. But unlike a case of simple projection, in projective identification, the person who does the projecting actively pressures the recipient to think, feel, and act in accordance with his or her projections. That is, one of the partners actually induces in the other partner the very feelings that were originally mistakenly believed to be there, making it difficult to clarify who did what to whom first. The recipient of the projection then processes or transforms the projection so that it can be re-internalized (re-experienced and understood) by the person who does the projecting. This process creates a situation where the boundaries or definitions of the self and other become blurred. Projective identification is a way of creating physical closeness to the person to whom these delusionary ideas are projected. Through this kind of interpersonal dance, couples may use each other to "repair" the perceived injuries of childhood.

To illustrate this point, I had a client who told me that during her childhood she had been subjected to the whims of an abusive, alcoholic father. She remembered her father beating her mother during his alcoholic rages, and her feelings of total helplessness, at a loss of what to do. She couldn't wait to leave the house when she was older. Ironically, as an adult, she seemed to have fallen into the same trap as her mother, marrying an abusive man. I inferred from her story that she had selected a partner very similar to her father and that behavior she didn't like about her father (and herself) was projected onto him. Her partner recognized these characteristics in himself—in a subliminal way—and acted accordingly, worsening an already very stressful situation. Without realizing it consciously, in her partner choice, she had opted for similarity given her desire to undo a painful childhood situation. In light of the psychological dynamics that were taking place, this woman's selection of a husband could be seen as an attempt (a failed one) at a cure for the hurts of childhood.

The old joke goes that marriage is a situation where a man and woman become as one; the trouble starts when they try to decide which one. There are two kinds of unconscious contract between partners, one neurotic and the other developmental. In the case of the first, there is an unconsciously shared collusion—as in the previous example—to retain certain splits and projections to deal with shared anxieties. One of the partners deals with emotional conflict or internal or external stressors by transmitting these unacceptable feelings, impulses, or thoughts to the other, who receives them but doesn't really try to deal with them. Instead, they accept it as part of their reality. Both parties remain stuck in a neurotic collusion.

Any two people who are closely tied to each other are in danger of cross-pollinating their ideas and perceptions—not always constructively—and the interaction can rapidly turn into *folie à deux*, where the delusional ideas expressed by one partner are absorbed and repeated by the other, who desperately wants to believe in the person in whom they have invested so much and on whom they depend. "Of course you are right, dear; whatever you say, dear," is the common response of the supportive spouse. The other then takes this as confirmation of their delusional beliefs, and clings on to them even more strongly.

We sometimes discover that the dynamics of a couple's relationship are based on the dynamics of their parents' marriage. Contrary to their conscious wishes, the partners seem to have entered a neurotic mesh, trapped into the same type of relationship, engaging in some form of repetition compulsion.

Under the developmental contract, there'll be a degree of understanding about the repudiated aspects of the self, with the will to arrive at better integration. The relationship with the partner becomes an opportunity for personal growth. The partners don't want to repeat previous mistakes; partner choice is determined by the wish to make a new beginning.

Being "as-if"

The psychoanalyst Helen Deutsch first suggested the construct of the "as-if" personality, demonstrated by individuals who leave others with an impression of inauthenticity, unable to discern what they really stand for. But in spite of their apparent superficiality, as-if personalities seem to enjoy normal relations with those around them. On the surface, they appear perfectly well adjusted. What makes these people different, however, is the possession of a false self; they have very little emotional depth. Deep down, one might say, they're shallow. Whenever I listen to these people, I'm given the impression of characters in a movie who feel they have very little or no control over the plot they are acting out. They see themselves as puppets, manipulated by invisible strings. At times, they refer to themselves as feeling fraudulent—con artists, soon to be exposed.

I've encountered many more women than men with as-if personalities. The women tend to be besotted with flavor-of-the-week partners. For example, if they have a relationship with a painter, they will talk only about art. When they move on to a businessman, they show a great interest in the stock market. When they drop the businessman for the surgeon they develop a sudden interest in everything to do with the medical profession. This pattern can go on and on. Here's how one of my clients described her life: "To be really honest, I'm not living according to what I like to do. My own needs seem to be completely secondary. How I work, how I think, how I dress, even my hobbies always seem to be dominated by the men in my life. I guess I've a talent for picking up their signals. It makes them feel good. I know what pleases them. I give them what they want. But there are times when I feel suffocated, totally trapped."

This woman, at least, was not operating completely on automatic pilot. She had some sense of what was happening to her. She realized that her role-playing would undermine a durable relationship between equal partners and she wanted to do something about it, change her way of behaving. But if she was an exception in wanting to change, she was no exception as an as-if personality. She was caught in a soap opera with herself as principal actress, too dependent on the men in her life, opting out of decision-making and involved in completely unbalanced relationships. She was limited to a life of role-playing. Although she did not genuinely share her partners' interests, she was good at concealing her true feelings in order to please them.

Apart from the personality strands that contribute to as-if behavior, female inequality also accounts for the muddle many women find themselves in. Economic dependency on men is one explanation for the tendency for women to exhibit a false self in relationships. But when caught up in this *pas de deux*, they begin to confuse their identity with that of their partner. Consciously or unconsciously, these women hope that tying their identity to that of their partners will compensate for their sense of powerlessness, self-alienation, and inner division. The fantasy is that by behaving in this way, they will attain power and significance. To make this come true, they project idealized fantasies about the self on to the other, making the other into some kind of hero. In some instances, dependency goes so far that these people are unable to tell their partners where or what they would like to eat, decide how to dress, or what to do. With no stable sense of self, they substitute empty lifestyles for real life and shy away from putting their energy into personal growth and self-fulfill-ment. The original source of this behavior, deep down, is the first mother-child dyad—in this instance, a flawed relationship that did not facilitate true individuation.

Too many women have based their identity on being an inspiration for "great" men. To the cost of their own identity, they ciphered them-selves out, seeing everything through their men's eyes, reaffirming their men's point of view, rather than expressing any opinions of their own. By behaving in this manner, they became grown-up chil-dren clinging to their men, hoping that their partners would manage for both of them. They regressed to an infantile child-parent depen-dency relationship. Sex was part of this primitive scenario, reviving the archaic memory of fusion with the other and for some, erasing the fragile borders of the self even more. Sex destabilized the bound-aries that separated one individual from the other.

"SOME DAY MY PRINCE WILL COME"

At the end of Walt Disney's movie *Snow White*, the handsome prince, riding the requisite white horse, wakens our accursed heroine with a magic kiss and takes her away from it all—including her wicked stepmother and a life of drudgery, lost in a forest looking after several strange little men. The suggestion is that they will live happily ever after. But will they?

We have all gone to bed as children with this freshly told fairy tale bubbling in our mind. It gives us the germ of an idea: if we just dream something long and hard enough, destiny or fate will find us and make our dream come true. However, although most fairy tales end with the "happily ever after" clause, the protagonist frequently comes from a broken home. Fairy tales are about happy endings but the stories often start very differently: one of the parents is dead, sick, or missing; there is often an evil step-parent; and the hero or heroine is the victim of considerable cruelty or injustice. Then love comes along and everyone lives happily ever after, despite the origi-nal miserable circumstances.

Partnerships based on romantic love are a nice concept, but as long as we project god-like idealizations onto our partners and demand that they make us happy ever after in a fairy-tale manner, we will never truly love them as mere human beings. Narcissistic object choices are sure to lead to disillusionment and take us into very primitive territory. Symbolically, such choices are based on archaic feelings of longing. Sigmund Freud viewed this kind of relationship as an attempt to return to the symbiotic stage of development, where a child's identity is still not individuated, and the boundary between it and its mother is still confused. The aim of human development, however, is to go beyond this primordial desire. Pining for such only leads to disappointment.

Maybe it would be better not to look for Mr. Right. Maybe we should learn to identify and be happy with Mr. OK or Mr. Quite Acceptable. Using coupledom to recapture a regressive childhood state or to escape the fear of loneliness is a recipe for disaster. Relationships will only work when both individuals are willing and able to see each other for who they are. Effective partnerships require well-structured personalities to weather the ups and downs inherent in any relationship. Romance is fine, but partnerships need to go beyond romantic imagination. A stable relationship is founded on the acceptance of each other's flaws and weaknesses, their positive side and their darker side, because ultimately it is our imperfections that make us human. Romantic love is all very well for immortals; relationships require real life mortals. Partners shouldn't aim for a state of mutual dependence, and regress into coupledom. Successful partnerships are based on the willingness to re-explore the relationship every day. People should enjoy dealing with their differences. A true partnership implies helping one another to reach full status as responsible and autonomous beings who don't get mixed up in some kind of *folie à deux* and do not run away from life.

4

THE SEXUAL IMAGINATION

As for his secret to staying married: "My wife tells me that if I ever decide to leave, she is coming with me."

Jon Bon Jovi

Most marriages would be better if the husband and wife clearly understood that they are on the same side.

Zig Ziglar

Husbands are like fires. They go out if unattended.

Zsa Zsa Gabor

It's clear from evolutionary, developmental, and psychodynamic psychology that men and women do not think alike. To quote the sexologist Shire Hite, "All too many men still seem to believe, in a rather naïve and egocentric way, that what feels good to them is automatically what feels good to women." The evolutionary mating game has set different rules for men and women. Assuming that each thinks the same is to invite conflict. As the actress Bette Midler pointed out, "If sex is such a natural phenomenon, how come there are so many books on how to?" The huge numbers of self-help books on marriage published annually suggest that men and women operate on different wavelengths.

Here's a funny story I once heard. A man walking along a beach stumbled on a bottle. He picked it up and took out the cork. The moment he did, out came a genie. The genie looked at the man and said, "You released me from the lamp. Traditionally I know you're supposed to get three wishes but I'm in a hurry, I'm giving you only one." The man thought for a while, and then said, "I've always wanted to go to Hawaii but I'm scared of flying and I get seasick. Could you build a bridge to Hawaii so I can drive over there to visit?" "What?" roared the genie. "That's impossible. Think of the logistics! How would the supports reach the bottom of the ocean? Think how much concrete I'd need, how much steel! That's a lousy wish.

Think of another one." "Fine," said the guy and tried to think of a really good wish. Finally, he said, "You know, I've been married and divorced four times. My wives all said I didn't care enough about them, I didn't understand them, I'm insensitive. I want to do something about that. I want to know how women feel inside and what they're thinking when they give me the silent treatment. I want to know why they're crying. I want to know what they really want when they say nothing. I want to know how to make women truly happy." The genie looked at him and said, "You want that bridge two lanes or four?"

As this story makes clear, misunderstandings between men and women about sex are inevitable. Men will always look for sex without investment; women want commitment. The journalist Katherine Whitehorn reiterated this important difference: "In real life women are always trying to mix something up with sex—religion, or babies, or hard cash; it is only men who long for sex separated out, without rings or strings." Of course, not all men and women act the same about sex. There are many variations on this theme.

Although men may be driven by the selfish gene—which tells them that going forth and multiplying makes more sense than committing themselves to one person—the survival of their offspring is important and the urge to have offspring to continue their genes is a counterbalance to one-night stands. Men manage the gene and commit because infants and young children are more likely to survive if they've the care of both parents.

BEING POLYMORPHOUS PERVERSE

Although the sex drive is universal, it is not uniform. Sex is biological but eroticism and romance are cultural. Sexual desire can be aroused and expressed in multiple ways, while the sexual act itself can incorporate a broad spectrum of things from rape, to expressions of affection, to creativity.

Humankind has the tendency to be sexually polymorphous. Most people think of the genitals as our only erogenous zone but as some of us may have found out for ourselves, each part of the body can be an erogenous zone. Specific areas of our body have heightened sensitivity that can translate into sexual responsiveness. For example, our oral needs are expressed by our mouth, which is used for eating but doesn't deal exclusively with satisfying of hunger. The mouth can be sexualized in many ways, including sensual kissing and oral sex. Then there is touching. All of us are sensitive to touch. A woman executive once told me, "My ears turn me on like nothing else. They must be one of my major erogenous zones. Having my ears touched makes me dizzy with desire." Her comment illustrates how, depending on the sociocultural exposure we've had while growing up, we internalize a whole array of associated imagery that can kindle our sexual desire and the way we express it.

DIFFERENCES IN SEXUAL MINDSET

Evolution has its own rules to ensure reproductive success and given our prehistoric origins, men are generally more sexually assertive than women. It's part and parcel of their evolutionary legacy. However, this can be a problem to many couples. This is a very common scenario: usually, after a period of sexual infatuation, both men and women complain about their partners' sexual needs. Men want more and women less. The most common explanations given for refusal are lack of energy because of the arrival of children, the "Coolidge effect," and the effect of ageing. Men tend to be more sensitive about their partner's decline in sexual attractiveness than women.

Generally, sexual frustration is more a problem for men than women. Both men and women give a variety of reasons for withholding sex—needing time for the baby, lack of sleep, overwork, emotional distress, traumatic past experiences, situational difficulties (no time together)—but whatever rational explanations are given, lack of sex is a source of great frustration, especially for the partner with the stronger sexual needs. Having sex is important, because the waxing and waning of sexual desire is a signifier of how well the couple functions in other areas.

At the heart of the matter lie men's and women's different perceptions of what sex is all about. A significantly larger number of men than women believe that sexual desire is aimed at sexual activity. A significantly larger number of women than men cite love and emotional intimacy as the goal of sexual desire. It may be cynical, but it's not far from the truth, to say that men talk to women so they can sleep with them, and women sleep with men so they can talk to them. These differences in perceptions—combined with our illusion that others think just like us—mean that men and women are in for trouble. Men complain about their partner's lack of enthusiasm for sex and women complain that their partner fails to demonstrate affection and attention. A shared complaint is that the blossom has fallen off a once romantic relationship. Women in particular are turned off by the mechanical quality that sex can assume.

41

Numerous surveys have confirmed that a significant proportion of women are fairly indifferent to sex for significant periods of their life. The Australian sex therapist Bettina Arndt, referring to herself, described the conundrum many women find themselves in: "When the bombshell of early motherhood first hit, I remember wondering how any woman could possibly entertain erotic thoughts while sleepwalking through the chaos of feeds, nappies, stress and fatigue. I assume my husband and I *must* have had sex at least a few times in that period ... but I must say I can't remember it happening. Perhaps I dozed through it, who knows." Have you ever heard women recount the many ingenious strategies they use to avoid sex with their husbands or boyfriends? Too many wives are just too tired, too busy with the children, to give any attention to their sexual needs. Studies in which men and women are asked to rank their pleasures in order of enjoyment show repeatedly that whereas sex is the favorite for most men, women prefer knitting, gardening, shopping or watching television. As the old male joke goes, "My wife is a sex object—every time I ask for sex, she objects!"

Scans reveal that men and women's brains react quite differently to sexually explicit images. Notably, men show far more activity than women in the amygdala, the brain sector associated with powerful emotions like fear and anger. On average, male sexual desire is not only stronger than women's, but also more consistent. Female sexual desire is more cyclical. According to some studies, many women only attain the heights of sexual desire attained by men during the few days of the month that they are fertile. They're more likely to fantasize about sex, masturbate, initiate sex with their partners, and wear provocative clothing or frequent singles bars around ovulation than at any other time of the month. This doesn't mean that women will not have sex outside their window of reproductive opportunity. But from an evolutionary point of view, it makes good sense for them to have greater interest in sex while they are fertile. In comparison, men are in a state of perpetual readiness. Apart from these specific differences, there are other factors that determine the intensity of sexual desire—experience, culture, and circumstances.

In addition, there are great differences between men and women in the frequency and content of sexual fantasies. Studies have shown that men have twice as many sexual fantasies as women. Even in their sleep, men are far more likely than women to dream about sex. Their dreams can be highly visual, dominated by themes of lust and physical gratification, with women featuring as mere sexual objects. When women dream about sex, individuals and emotions play a greater role.

There is much more variety and much less predictability in women's experience of sexual desire. There are even women who report that they have never experienced sexual desire, and wonder what the fuss is all about. Other women, however, can be preoccupied with sex but even among them, the level of intensity is different, less strong, and persistent than it is with men. Furthermore, particularly in relationships that have lasted for decades, women rarely experience episodes of spontaneous sexual desire. When they do, the desire is reactive, a response to stimulation from their partner. Desire follows sexual arousal, rather than the other way around.

Unless a couple finds ways to rejuvenate their relationship, these differing attitudes toward sex can contribute to breakup or extramarital affairs. The peak period for women to have extramarital affairs is at the end of their reproductive years. This may be the expression of a conscious or unconscious wish to switch partner before their fertility ends. Men, for whom sex is a less emotionally draining activity—as the worldwide distribution of prostitution demonstrates—engage more consistently in sex outside marriage. The usual explanations for infidelity are boredom and lessening physical attractiveness. Predictably, extramarital sex replaces regular sex with their partner.

Men easily confuse a demand for love and intimacy for a demand for sex. This explains the difficulty a man has being just friends with a woman he finds attractive. The sexual dimension is always present. When in doubt, men assume that a woman is sexually interested. This faulty assumption, combined with the female tendency to flirt, can become a very heady, volatile cocktail. Sexual pushiness can easily mutate into sexual aggressiveness and rape. Men underestimate how disagreeable sexual aggressiveness is to women. Our misconceptions about the other sex's sexual attitudes go some way to explaining why most women, at one point in their life, have been the subject of sexual improprieties and men's frequent lack of understanding of rape victims.

Of course, all these studies beg the question whether men are meant to be monogamous: they seem to be propelled by genetically ordained impulses over which they have less control than they think. According to evolutionary psychologists (as I mentioned earlier), men are genetically programmed to distribute their seed into as many females as possible. Although that drive is constantly present, society has taught them that giving in to these impulses blindly will have serious consequences. As the actor John Barrymore once said, "Sex is the thing that takes up the least amount of time and causes the most amount of trouble."

SEX AND THE PASSAGE OF TIME

Humor is a window to the unconscious, and much popular humor about aging reveals the preoccupations of many people: "You're getting old when getting lucky means you find your car in the parking lot"; "I'm at the age where food has taken the place of my sex life." As men and women age, they become much more alike, including in the intensity of their sexual desire. The frequency of sexual thoughts and fantasies lessens gradually over a person's (especially a man's) lifetime, although sexual imagery endures even into very old age. A number of physiological factors explain how the sexual drive is affected in both men and women over time. In both sexes, the levels of serum testosterone decline gradually during the life cycle with a fifty percent drop between ages twenty-five and fifty—however, men have ten–twenty times the testosterone levels of women of the same age. The menopause also reduces women's sexual desire, mainly because of a significant reduction in the production of estrogen hormones as well as the common and sometimes uncomfortable symptoms that come with these changes. Medical problems, including mental disorders like depression, can affect sexual desire and functioning, while some medications have a significant effect on the sex drive.

Frequently medical and physiological problems are intertwined with psychological ones. For many women, contributing factors to a decline in sexual desire include problems of interpersonal relationships and partner performance, power struggles, or feelings of deep resentment toward the partner. For example, a woman may no longer be interested in sex if her partner is totally devoid of romantic feelings, never takes her out, never thanks her for a nice meal, and has a wham-bam-thank-you-ma'am attitude to sex.

Sexual relationships can also be affected by very restrictive upbringing about sex, or negative or traumatic sexual experiences. Men and women with a history of sexual abuse may have trouble trusting their partner enough to relax and to become aroused. There are more pedestrian reasons for lack of sex, such as having very little time to be alone together. Sexual intimacy will also decline when both partners have a demanding job and are too tired and stressed out to make sex a priority. Many dual career couples have told me that sex takes a backseat when compared with what is expected from them at work.

Some women feel a complete lack of desire for sex for some time after giving birth. Fatigue, anxiety, and depression play a part in this. Some women become completely wrapped up with the newborn

44

baby, which fulfils many of their emotional and physical needs, allows very little time with their partner, and displaces many of their sexual impulses. Once again, an explanation can be found in evolution-ary psychology. It was important for the survival of our Paleolithic ancestors that most of a mother's energy should be devoted to the new baby. Avoiding sex is also a very effective way of avoiding a fur-ther pregnancy: the mother can recover properly from the first birth, and the new baby doesn't have to share the mother too soon with other new siblings.

HOW MUCH SEX IS ENOUGH?

Some people like sweets, others like playing soccer. If someone told me he or she didn't plan to eat sweets or play soccer ever again, so be it. Although I like both, I would see no reason to make an issue out of his or her decision or look for some deep psychological interpre-tations. But sex is a different matter. If the same person told me that he or she never had sex, and didn't plan ever to have it, I would get worried. I would formulate some hypotheses about why this should be the case; I would try to figure out what the underlying problems might be. I might even express my concerns directly, telling him or her that this lack of interest in sex was peculiar and might be indica-tive of a problem. I might go so far to suggest he or she should see a psychiatrist or a psychotherapist. I would be equally concerned if the same person told me that he or she was totally preoccupied by sex; that sex was on his or her mind continually; or that he or she needed to have sex a number of times a day. I would wonder whether this behavior was normal. I would see him or her as an addict. Again, I might suggest it would be helpful to see somebody.

Lack of desire

As I've indicated, many factors can contribute to not wanting to have sex—all of us have times when we just don't feel up to it. Usually, spending some romantic time with a partner, sexual thoughts or stimulating imagery lead to arousal and the return of a healthy sex drive. But for some people it is different. Whatever the stimuli, they're just not interested. However, a low sex drive—as I have learned from my therapeutic experience—is something that people find difficult to talk about. It can be a very bewildering experience, and trouble-some issue, if your partner shows no interest in sex despite your best efforts. But it's also embarrassing to broach a subject that, for many people, is full of shame.

Because of this, many who suffer from sexual disorders don't reach out for help. Still others do not even realize that they have a problem. They have never been particularly interested in sex. Other issues in the relationship have always seemed to be more important to them. However, when couples in conflict have a problem with sexual desire—when it is absent or fading in one partner—it will affect other parts of their lives. And without guidance, they may attempt to deal with the problem in ways that can destroy the relationship.

One executive I coached—a very successful entrepreneur—seemed to have it all. She was highly effective in her job. She was very attractive. She was married with three beautiful children. Her partner, one of the founders of a private equity firm, appeared to be an extremely charming, attentive individual. The couple was seen at many social meetings, jetted off to exotic locations for vacations, and held interesting dinner parties. Their relationship, however, floundered in one intractable area. To use her words, "After a while, he just didn't seem to need any sex. Months would go by without him touching me. Eventually, I learned to live without it."

How little sex is too little? What measurement should we use? Sometimes, when a partner complains of not having enough sex, the problem may actually be an unusually high sex drive. A decrease in sexual desire may be one thing, but total lack of interest is another matter altogether. Unlike men's common sexual complaint—erectile dysfunction—women's biggest sexual problem is caused by a combination of mental and physical factors, which cannot be cured simply by resorting to a pill, like Viagra. In fact, according to some studies, forty-three percent of women and thirty-one percent of men report that they experience problems in this domain.

Experts agree that there's no daily minimum requirement for sexual activity. The classic study, *Sex in America*, the most comprehensive sex survey ever done in the US (based on ninety-minute interviews with more than 3000 randomly chosen adults, published in 1994), reported that one-third of the couples surveyed had sex just a few times a year. A recent Kinsey report said that twenty-six percent of non-married men and twenty-four percent of non-married women had sex only a few times over the preceding year. The figures for the married men and women were respectively thirteen percent and twelve percent. Although the studies report frequency of sex, not desire, it's more than likely that one of the partners of these couples was suffering from an affliction called hypoactive sexual desire disorder (HSDD).

It is estimated that this disorder affects approximately twenty percent of the population, mostly women. HSDD is defined as persistent or recurrent deficiency and/or absence of sexual fantasies/thoughts, and/or desire for, or receptivity to, sexual activity, which causes personal distress. Synonyms for HSDD include sexual aversion, inhibited sexual desire, sexual apathy, and even sexual anorexia. The affected person has a low level of sexual interest and desire that is manifested by a failure to initiate or to be responsive to a partner's initiation of sexual activity. Many of the people who suffer from this disorder have a paucity or total absence of sexual fantasies. In many, the disorder goes unremarked. HSDD becomes a diagnosable disorder, however, when it causes marked distress or interpersonal instability.

Another major disorder is sexual aversion disorder. People with this suffer from a persistent or recurrent phobic aversion to genital contact with a sexual partner, which causes personal distress. The aversion may be concentrated on a specific aspect of the sexual experience or be more general. For example, some people experience general revulsion (including panic attacks) to any sexually related activity, including kissing and touching. This causes marked distress and interpersonal difficulties.

There's a whole range of similar disorders, including female sexual arousal disorder, male erectile disorder, female and male orgasmic disorder, premature ejaculation, and sexual pain disorder, all of which need attention and frequently professional help.

A growing body of clinical literature links sexual abuse with decreased sexual desire. Depression is one of the most common reactions reported by adults who have been molested as children and may account for the decreased sexual desire they experience. Sexual abuse is much more common for women than men, and we see a higher percentage of women who suffer from inhibited sexual desire. Aggressive overtures from their partner can be experienced by them as a repetition of an earlier trauma, and become responsible for a vicious circle of sexual withdrawal and aggressive sexual attacks.

Too much desire

Hyposexuality refers to too little sexual desire, while hypersexuality refers to people who overdo it. Sexual expression is a natural part of a well-rounded life, but if we've an overwhelming need for sex and are so intensely preoccupied with it that it interferes with our job and our relationships, we may have a problem.

Hypersexuality is difficult to assess, because how much sex is too much? When is a person overdoing it? There is no satisfactory answer to this question. Sex drive varies widely in humans, and what one person considers normal might be considered excessive by some and low by others. It doesn't help that men have usually set the standards for sexual desire. Many men view hypersexuality as a sign of masculinity. They don't feel insulted when they are called a Don Giovanni or Casanova. Women, however, dislike this kind of labeling, seeing it as an accusation of promiscuity. It is interesting to note that men have a tendency to exaggerate the number of their sexual conquests, while women underquote.

Hypersexuality, or satyriasis, or nymphomania, describes insatiable sexual appetite. People suffering from hypersexuality engage in sexual behavior at clinically significant levels above "normal" sexual frequency, in an attempt to satisfy an impairing, uncontrollable need for frequent genital stimulation. Hypersexuality is a compulsive and joyless condition, where people have promiscuous and recurrent sexual intercourse with different partners, without much satisfaction, and without emotional engagement. Female sufferers often do not experience orgasm. Hypersexuality becomes a disorder when this behavior causes distress or has social repercussions—sufferers become so preoccupied with sex that they cannot function properly in other domains.

Some specific behaviors are associated with hypersexuality, including compulsive masturbation, compulsive sex with prostitutes, anonymous sex with multiple partners (one-night stands), multiple affairs outside a committed relationship, frequent patronizing of sexually oriented establishments, habitual exhibitionism, habitual voyeurism, inappropriate sexual touching, sexual abuse of children, and rape. Fantasy sex, prostitution, pedophilia, masochism, fetishes, sex with animals, and cross-dressing may also be part of the repertoire of the sexual addict. Any one of these behaviors in and of itself does not constitute an addiction (although some are deemed illegal or considered deviant).

Of course, individuals may be labeled sex addicts simply because they're more sexually active than the person doing the labeling, or because they enjoy themselves in ways the labeler doesn't appreciate. A hypersexual person isn't just someone who has more sex than you do. Even from a clinical point of view, the condition and its diagnosis are frequently debated.

In the past, in keeping with the belief that women were less highly sexed than men, many physicians assumed that hypersexuality occurred infrequently in males, while almost any woman who seemed to enjoy sex could be diagnosed as a nymphomaniac by some medical specialist or other, especially if she had a sex drive stronger than that of her male companion. The sexually driven woman was a cause of anxiety as well as a target for locker-room snickering. In contrast, few complaints were heard about oversexed men. The standard measurement of sexual normalcy related to the husband: a woman showing less desire than her husband was frigid, while a woman showing more was a nymphomaniac. For some men, a sexually demanding woman embodied fantasies and dangers connected to female sexuality, awakening primeval fears of the *vagina dentata*.

Historically, physicians also assumed that nymphomania was much more severe than satyriasis and the consequences correspondingly worse. A nymphomaniac's fate would be prostitution or the insane asylum, while a satyriasist might go through life without getting into trouble if he managed to have a modicum of control. As the actress Joan Rivers once remarked, "A man can sleep around, no questions asked, but a woman makes nineteen or twenty mistakes, and she's a tramp."

Sexual addictions are rarely ranked among with other socially destructive addictions such as alcoholism, drugs, or cigarette smoking. In fact, generally, they are often not recognized as an addiction or disorder at all. Hypersexuals are "sluts," "promiscuous," "sexually liberated," or "studs," depending on their gender. There is no social equivalent to going "dry" or "cold turkey" for the sexual addict: far from being viewed as a kind of recovery, celibacy is seen as another behavioral aberration.

The causes of hypersexuals' obsession with sex are not necessarily clinically defined. An individual's level of sexual desire may be increased by something as commonplace as additional stress, as sex is an excellent form of recreation and usually induces enjoyment followed by relaxation. On the other hand, the primary problem may be a loss of impulse control, which can follow some forms of brain injury or disease. It may be related to a form of epilepsy, or to conditions like Alzheimer's disease. Some experts believe that psychological and neurological conditions such as bipolar disorder and dementia can cause hypersexuality. For people suffering from bipolar disorders, hypersexuality is expressed during periods of mania, exhibited by tremendous swings in their sex drive, depending on their mood. Sometimes sexual activity is much higher than normal and other times it is far below normal.

There may be deeper psychological reasons for this compulsion for promiscuity. While some people may have a relaxed attitude about sex, hypersexuals betray themselves through their highly compelling, driven, tenacious attitude toward it and their lack of awareness of what they are doing. There is often a history of sexual abuse behind their compulsion to have sex over and over again. In these instances, we could speculate that while traumatic memories are repressed, these people use unconsciously another form of remembering what has happened to them by acting out the trauma over and over again. This compulsion to repeat may be an unsuccessful attempt at healing and the compulsive sex act a convoluted form of communication. But having sex is a mechanized activity, not the same thing as making love. The hypersexual individual may confuse the sex act with the idea of intimacy and mutuality in social relationships and equate it with a constructive intimate relationship.

In Mozart's opera *Don Giovanni*, the Don's servant Leporello endeavors to console Elvira (one of Don Giovanni's conquests) and, in the famous catalogue aria, unrolls a list of Don Giovanni's lovers. Comically, he rattles off their number and their country of origin: 640 in Italy, 231 in Germany, 100 in France, 91 in Turkey, but 1,003 in Spain. If we add the difficulties of travel at the time to these numbers, it's clear that Don Giovanni must have been busy to the point of exhaustion. Seducing women was a full-time job for him: there wouldn't have been much time left for other activities.

The behavior of these Don Juans or *femmes fatales* has a masturbatory quality; they are never satisfied. Consummation remains elusive. At first, their activities seem to relieve stress, depression, anxiety, or loneliness but soon they begin to emphasize their uncomfortable state of mind. Sexual obsession carries a high price: financially, if the tendency involves expensive charges for prostitutes or phone sex, but more catastrophically in other ways—for example, job loss (through inappropriate behavior toward others at work, or accessing pornography during company time), destruction of personal relationships, and the contraction of sexually transmitted diseases.

SEX AS A BATTLEFIELD

There is an old saying that maintains that to keep a man, a woman must be a maid in the living room, a cook in the kitchen, and a whore in the bedroom. The model and actress Jerry Hall recalled her mother repeating this to her and added her own personal codicil: "I said I'd hire the other two and take care of the bedroom bit." Unfortunately, the bedroom can sometimes turn into a battlefield. As the sexologist William Masters noted, "When things don't work well in the bedroom, they don't work well in the living room either."

Although sex bonds many couples closer together, lack of it, or the use of sex as a form of self-sacrifice, can be the wedge that drives them apart. As we saw earlier, problems occur when one partner is significantly less interested in sex than the other. Sex becomes a source of conflict and friction, and can have a negative impact on the relationship. The partner with the lower sexual desire may feel pressured to do something that he or she doesn't feel like doing, causing to resentment, anger, and further decline in sexual desire. In contrast, the partner with the higher level of desire begins to feel unloved, deprived, and desperate and as a result would press for sexual activity even more frequently and vigorously, while the other partner becomes increasingly resentful. Sex turns into a combat zone. From win-win it turns into a zero-sum game where the relationship is the loser.

The writer G. K. Chesterton once said, "Marriage is an adventure, like going to war." A common scenario between couples is that of the disappointed, angry, blaming wife demanding emotional contact from a man who withdraws. The man seems interested only in the sexual dimension of the relationship. Some men can be aggressive in demanding sex, to the point of marital rape. Because they underestimate how unacceptable sexual aggression is to women, this behavior contributes to even greater distancing. Ignorance about sex difference in perceptions aggravates the conflict between the sexes. No wonder Freud called the female psyche the "dark continent."

Sexual aggressiveness and withholding can become the major theme in a relationship, contributing to countless battles. Some couples remain in battles for years, and their relationship takes on a sadomasochistic tone. One of the partners wants sex, the other an emotional relationship. One partner withdraws, the other withholds. These episodes of attack-defend or attack-withdraw are highly corrosive to a relationship. It prevents the couple from being truly emotionally engaged. There is no dialog, only ritualistic activity. When this pattern has been established, the most innocuous incident can become the catalyst for a new fight: the dishes that need washing, the beds that need making, the garbage that has to be taken out, the dog that has to be walked, the kids who have to be disciplined, the financial arrangements that need to be made, and so on. But we are really dealing with issues of separateness and connectedness, safety and trust, power and powerlessness, the risk of letting someone in, and keeping someone out. And this repeated cycle of attack, defend, attack, withdraw doesn't do wonders for either partner's sense of self-esteem and gender identity. It leaves them with strong feelings of resentment. Men feel that their wives are not attracted to them and that any sexual intimacy they gain comes as a result of begging or as a reward for favors. For their part, women feel abused, violated, ignored as a sensitive human being and turned into a mere physical object.

The playwright and philosopher Johan Wolfgang von Goethe once said, "It is sometimes essential for a husband and wife to quarrel—they get to know each other better." However, when the bedroom becomes a field of conflict, some couples get caught in a sadomasochistic collusion. Edward Albee's play *Who's Afraid of Virginia Woolf?* dramatizes this situation. The play draws us into a couple's marital battlefield where they savage each other in two ways: they each hate themselves and therefore cannot accept the love the other offers; and the flaws of each are magnified and used to indict the other for not functioning as a savior. Their interactions, witnessed by a young married couple, shatter any illusions about romantic love. It's reasonable to assume that their marriage lost any element of sexuality a long time ago.

When women, fed up with mechanical sex, fail to recognize or acknowledge that their husbands have a physical need for sex that does not disappear when denied, they are in for trouble. From the man's point of view, his partner's failure to meet this need puts him in a real conundrum: either he lives in misery and deprivation or he seeks fulfillment from another source. The most common road to that other source is an affair. This can evolve into a splitting scenario, when even if the couples don't separate they live separate lives, with little or nothing shared between them.

I'm not suggesting that the blame for the sexual battlefield lies with the female party. Many women would enjoy sex more if their partners had better technique, patience, and knowledge. In some cases, relationships without sex can be just as happy and content as those where the sexuality of the individuals is expressed freely. But although the suppression of sexuality does not necessarily produce overt disharmony or argument, it does hasten the demise of the sense of mutuality within the relationship. Relationships that suffer loss of sexuality do not necessarily end in bitter dispute but may descend into the living-dead state so well described in T. S. Eliot's poem "The Love Song of J. Alfred Prufrock": "I have measured out my life in coffee spoons." Comfortable but deadly routine is an inevitable product of the denial of our sexual nature.

THE QUESTION OF THERAPY

The sexual aspect of a relationship is a signifier of the well-being of the relationship as a whole. Although sex and sexuality are not the be-all and end-all of a relationship, without the proper expression of sexual desire, the relationship may suffer severely. Psychosexual dysfunction is not life threatening, but it can affect other ways in which a couple functions. It can have a negative effect on each partner's sense of self-esteem. It can even affect their life at work.

Fortunately, there are many ways of tackling these problems, including psychotherapy, sex therapy, behavioral therapy, marriage or relationship counseling. A therapist will typically review the individual's sexual identity (i.e. his or her beliefs and attitudes about sex); relationship factors including intimacy and attachment; communication and coping styles; and his or her overall emotional health. Therapy may include education about sexual responsiveness and techniques, ways to enhance intimacy with a partner, and recommendations for reading materials or couples' exercises. These may include discussion (and experimentation) about sexual preferences, and the exploration of each other's fantasies.

Adequate sexual functioning requires self-confidence, freedom from anxiety, mental and physical stimulation, and the ability to focus on sexually arousing thoughts or behavior. Anything that interferes with these conditions can disrupt a sexual encounter. If one or more of these conditions is routinely absent, an inability to perform can become a lasting problem.

Self-confidence—the knowledge you can perform sexually, that your partner finds you sexually attractive and respects your sexual desires—is crucial. Nothing is worse for sexual confidence than a belittling attitude from a partner, which can cause anxiety and contribute to episodes of sexual failure. Sexual failure then becomes a self-fulfilling prophecy, creating performance anxiety, in which the person is afraid that he or she won't be able to become aroused and function normally. This fear is self-perpetuating because anxiety performance interferes with arousal. The inability to become aroused then increases anxiety.

Leo Tolstoy once said, "What counts in making a happy marriage is not so much how compatible you are, but how you deal with incompatibility." In a way, healthy sexual functioning implies falling in love with the same person many times over. The kind of relationship you have will depend very much on the kind of person you are. If you're happy and well-adjusted, the chances are your relationship will be a good one. If you're discontented and bitter about the hand life has dealt you, you will have to do something about your feelings before you can expect to live happily ever after. As I've emphasized in this section, happily ever after involves two people finding shared places in their sexual imagination.

5

THE PLAY OF SEXUALITY

Imagination is the beginning of creation. You imagine what you desire, you will what you imagine and at last you create what you will.

George Bernard Shaw

Every act of creation is first of all an act of destruction.

Pablo Picasso

Creativity is discontent translated into arts.

Eric Hoffer

If sex and creativity are often seen by dictators as subversive activities, it's because they lead to the knowledge that you own your own body (and with it your own voice), and that's the most revolutionary insight of all.

Erica Jong

So, we can have too much or too little sexual desire. But however intense or otherwise desire is, we can view the process of passing on our genes to future generations as our organism's quintessential expression of its will to survive. It's our evolutionary impulse to leave an imprint of ourselves behind when we are no longer around. It's through the "selfish gene" that we hope to attain immortality, and the sex act is symbolic of regeneration and the transmission of life.

Apart from attaining a measure of continuity through our children, humankind has always been searching for other ways to achieve a measure of immortality. (I discuss this in more detail later in Part Four, Meditations on Death.) One very attractive strategy for achieving this objective is through the creative process. Creativity has always implied bringing something new into being, with the expectation that the new creation will outlive its creator. To use the words of the psychotherapist Rollo May, "Creativity is not merely the innocent spontaneity of our youth and childhood; it must also

54

be married to the passion of the adult human being, which is a passion to live beyond one's death."

Creativity suggests change and transformation. It involves breaking out of established patterns to look at things in different ways. Looking at a caterpillar, does it seem probable that it will turn into a butterfly? As Friedrich Nietzsche said, "You need chaos in your soul to give birth to a dancing star." Change implies abandonment of the old. It requires courage to break barriers, face the new, and to go where nobody has dared to go before. The satirist Jonathan Swift once observed, "He was a bold man that first ate an oyster." Creativity can be expressed in multiple ways—the arts, science, and philosophy are obvious outlets—and sexual desire, in a variety of disguises, can be an important driver of the creative process.

Ever since artists began creating art, they have incorporated sexual themes into their work. The art of ancient civilizations was replete with sexual or erotic imagery. The relationship to sex and the human body is quite obvious from some of the earliest examples, the Venus of Berekhat Ram (around 233,000 BC) and the Venus of Tan-Tan (500,000–300,000 BC). Erotic art was one of the earliest expressions of art in history, as human sexuality was celebrated as a fundamental part of daily life. Through this creative work our ancestors were able to portray otherwise submerged desires, showing human relations in all their complexity: seduction, attraction, degradation, self-destruction, and self-development.

Psychoanalysts have always recognized the sexual undertone in many creative works. Sigmund Freud, in his essay "Formulations on the Two Principles of Mental Functioning," commented: "An artist is originally a man who turns away from reality because he cannot come to terms with the renunciation of instinctual satisfaction which it at first demands, and who allows his erotic and ambitious wishes full play in the life of phantasy. He finds the way back to reality, however, from this world of phantasy by making use of his special gifts to mould his phantasies into truths of a new kind, which are valued by men as precious reflections of reality."

I would like to add one caveat to this discussion of the relationship between sexual desire and creativity. We need to be careful not to fall into a reductionistic trap. While sexual desire is important as a driver in the creative process, it doesn't rule out the impact of other physiological and developmental processes, as well as personality traits. Although sexual desire will more often than not play a central role in truly creative expression, a host of other factors need to be taken into consideration.

THE FIRST CREATION: HALLUCINATING THE BREAST

To understand the process of creation, we need to recognize how the psychic conflicts arising from the tensions between our inner word of primitive instinctual drives and the constraining and denying forces of the external word begin in earliest infancy and have ramifications throughout our life. The hallucinated breast—the by-product of a hungry child's frustrated oral needs—can be viewed as the prototypical creative act, a precursor of other creative products. Child psychologists consider this process to be the first construct of mental development, the infant's first (imagined) form of mental activity. Although it's a preverbal activity, the memory of this dream-like operation will be retained and can transform—at later stages of life—into specific acts of creation.

In the normal process of growing up, everyone experiences a natural curiosity about sex. "Where do we come from?" is a timeless question. From early life onward, we're trying to answer this riddle. We may wonder what happens behind our parents' closed door. We are fascinated by the "primal scene," sexual relations between the parents, as observed, constructed, and/or fantasized by the child. The primal scene, given the child's undeveloped understanding, may be interpreted as violent, a primitive form of violation, a challenge to the person's body integrity. Although the primal scene is a puzzling image, it is also a sexually exciting one. Firing the imagination, it is an inspiration for creativity. For the young person, the usual sense of the forbidden associated with the primal scene—the tendency for sex to be hidden—only serves to increase its mystique and encourage its interest. The metaphor of the primal scene will be an important organizer and regulator of creativity. Thus the place of artistic creativity can become a primal scene of sorts. Driven by primal scene imagery, creative people tend to do what they are compelled to do in an artistic way, while discovering the narrative of their own existence.

THE SIREN CALL OF THE CREATIVE INDIVIDUAL

Although sexual desire and creativity have always been closely linked, creative people can be paradoxical in their attitude toward sex. While some can be overly preoccupied by it, others have a dose of Spartan celibacy in their makeup. For them, abstinence accompanies a superior level of creativity.

In spite of these exceptions to the rule, the general public is inclined to assume that creative types—less constrained by the mores that apply to the rest of society—are more sexually driven and will have more sex. Of course, this assumption could be a self-fulfilling prophecy, in that creative people may feel they have no choice but to live up to these expectations. They may even drift toward the artistic life because of its sexual benefits.

But how much of this is fantasy and how much reality? Do creative people really have more sex? Do they have greater sexual desire or just more opportunities to have sex than the average executive? Are creative people more attractive? If so, why? Are they assumed to have greater emotionality? Evolutionary psychologists might put some Darwinian spin on that question.

One explanation, starting with our Stone Age ancestors, is that the artistic among them may have been better at attracting a mate. Extravagant use of language has been associated all over the world with love and courtship, a form of cognitive foreplay. Were some of our ancestors better at expressing themselves than others, verbally or artistically? Does the invitation to "come up and see my etchings" carry an echo of primeval seduction? Should the ability to chat up or otherwise engage another's attention be viewed as an intrinsic aspect of human evolution? Have creative people always had the edge in courtship contests? Or has artistic ability evolved from a form of mating display?

Whatever may be valid from an evolutionary perspective, one thing is sure: creative people attract others and as a result get a lot of attention. This brings us to a further chicken-and-egg question. What comes first, sexual drive or context? People in the public eye may have more sexual opportunities than the less creative among us. Creative people often lead attractively bohemian lifestyles, and are more prepared to act on their sexual impulses and opportunities than others. Their partners may not expect loyalty and fidelity. Society is more tolerant of creative people's sexual behavior.

General admiration is not limited to creative people, of course. We have always admired those who can do something difficult—great athletes, inventors, orators, actors, even jugglers. And how much of our speculation is borne out by reality? Do creative people really have much wilder sex lives than the rest of us? Maybe they just describe them better. Although sexual experimentation can be very liberating, there's always the awkwardness associated with high expectation and low performance.

57

THE BOHEMIAN LIFE

Historically, we have always linked the bohemian life of artists with promiscuity, not least because of the often overtly sexual themes in their work. Paintings, drawings, sculptures, performance arts, film, and other media have always provided opportunities for the expression of sexual desire. Explicitly sexual art is the most direct creative expression of the imagination, and reflects real aspects of life. Paintings of scantily clad women, women admiring themselves in a mirror, or women bound and restrained have never been scarce in the history of art. Some sexualized art themes, like rape, bestiality, and, to some people, even homosexuality, can easily be mistaken for pornography. And this kind of imagery evokes sexual associations, stimulating our imagination. Many of these works of art capture the essence of experiences of great personal significance that reverberate on a larger social context.

Western artists from Michelangelo to Mapplethorpe have consciously or unconsciously tried to deal with sexuality and their art has left nobody untouched. This will always be a truism. We have seen it from the conflation of the sacred and the erotic in Paleolithic art, to the ethereal sensuality of Botticelli's *The Birth of Venus*, to imagery of cruelty and amorous suffering in nineteenth-century Symbolist art. Art can be a social barometer; it is quick to assess its changing mores. Moreover, these artists have often been at the forefront of efforts to effect societal change. Art that was once based on elevated, religious themes or myths (in which sexual themes appeared in disguised form) is now less detached from day-to-day reality. Painters have started to celebrate more explicitly the vicissitudes of private life, including sexual desire and enactment.

Edouard Manet's painting of a nude prostitute, *Olympia* (1863), now considered a classic, is the work of an artist rebelling at the repressive nature of everyday life by flaunting the obscene. When it was first shown in Paris, *Olympia* caused outrage among viewers and critics and the gallery that originally exhibited it was forced to hire two police officers to protect the canvas. A second painting by Manet, executed the same year, *Le déjeuner sur l'herbe* (*Luncheon on the grass*), was received in much the same way. This large, provocative work, depicting two clothed men picnicking outdoors with a naked woman was criticized mercilessly. Consciously or unconsciously, the in-your-face quality of Manet's two paintings challenged the traditional view of painting in France, and society's hypocritical view of women. Olympia's sexuality forces the viewer to see her as a real woman, not a saint or mythological goddess. The strong reactions of

58

the audience suggest that Manet accomplished what he set out to do, by arousing sexual excitement or irritation in the viewer.

A number of artists turned to primitivism, a way of communicating their belief that non-Western societies were fundamentally similar in their irrationality, closeness to nature, proclivity to violence, mysticism, and, most importantly, uninhibited sexuality. These artists, especially Picasso, tried to shake off European conventions by forcing viewers to recognize primal impulses within themselves. Paul Gauguin's Tahitian paintings and the early music by Igor Stravinsky (*The Rite of Spring*) are two other prominent examples of primitivist art.

But these artists not only expressed sexual desire in their paintings, they also acted it out. It was a public secret that many of great painters and photographers were intimate with their models. Enacted sexual desire played an important role in making their ideas a creative reality. Making love to their models was a common practice for many great painters. Pierre-Auguste Renoir was particularly unsubtle about the part sexual desire played in his creative work: "I paint with my penis." Pablo Picasso was obsessed with sexual art: "Art is never chaste. It ought to be forbidden to ignorant innocents, never allowed into contact with those not sufficiently prepared. Yes, art is dangerous. Where it is chaste, it is not art." His art, long recognized for its sensual and erotic content (including sexual violence, voyeurism, prostitution, and impotence), was a revealing indicator of his ardent emotional and sexual life, which was characterized by intrigue, infidelity, passion, and melodrama. His stylistic chronology was closely linked to the succession of mistresses that paraded through his life. Although his famous remark about women being "goddesses or doormats" has rendered him odious to feminists, at the time, women walked into both roles open-eyed and eagerly, for his charms were legendary. In his late eighties (between May and October 1968), he etched a series of 347 prints (known as *Suite 347*) with sexual themes. At the age of ninety, the artist grumbled: "Sex and smoking—age has forced me to give them both up—but the desire remains."

Amedeo Modigliani, known for his nudes, was a famous and insatiable seducer of models. He lived a Bohemian life in Paris alongside Picasso and the other great moderns, drinking and womanizing to the end. Drunken, ranting, and stoned on one substance or another, he was the archetypal artist, shifting between studios, salons, bars, and lovers in Paris from the time he arrived in 1906 until his death (from tubercular meningitis) in 1920 at the age of thirty-five. When he died, a pregnant lover committed suicide.

Gustav Klimt was no sexual slouch, either. He claimed to need affairs with lovers to give him inspiration for his paintings. Women were drawn by his extraordinary magnetism. His studio has been compared to a fantasy harem where naked models strolled around at all times of the day. Klimt fathered fifteen illegitimate children by his various models. Meanwhile, in the Pacific, Gauguin literally screwed himself to death with local girls, eventually dying of syphilis. An overdose of alcohol and sex eventually took care of Henri de Toulouse-Lautrec, famous for his paintings of prostitutes and whorehouses.

The early drawings of sculptor Auguste Rodin exhibit an almost pornographic sensuality and erotic flavor. On the other side of the Atlantic, the American artist Georgia O'Keeffe, a woman born a generation later, transgressed contemporary sexual mores—not only in terms of the highly sexualized photographs which Alfred Stieglitz took of her but also in her willingness to live openly with Stieglitz without marrying him (a sinful activity at the time).

Many musicians were also infamous libertines. The numerous love affairs of Franz Liszt shocked society. He was something of a Casanova, adored the adulation of women, and slept with everyone from countesses and princesses to wide-eyed young groupies. Felix Mendelssohn said Liszt's character was "a continual alternation between scandal and apotheosis." According to one of his closest friends, the composer Richard Wagner started a new love affair in every town he happened to visit, and had a habit falling in love with other people's wives. Another composer, Giacomo Puccini, once described himself as a "mighty hunter of wild fowl, operatic librettos and attractive women." His life was a succession of romances and passionate love affairs. A more recent example is Leonard Bernstein, who had many affairs with men and women. According to his daughter, only his need for a "middle-class sensibility" kept him from living a completely gay life.

Moving to the world of literature, sexual desire is extremely explicit in semi-pornographic writings such as Boccaccio's *Decameron* (1353), John Cleland's *Fanny Hill* (1748), the Marquis de Sade's *120 Days of Sodom* (1785), Leopold von Sacher-Masoch's *Venus in Furs* (1870), and Pauline Reage's *Story of O* (1954). Other more mainstream writers who wrote highly erotic material include Honoré de Balzac, Emile Zola, Victor Hugo, James Joyce, D. H. Lawrence, and Vladimir Nabokov, to name only a few.

Not only did many of these authors write explicitly about sexual desire, they were also fairly blatant about their sexual peccadilloes. Three weeks after Lord Byron died in 1824, The *Times* declared him "the most remarkable Englishman of his generation," a description remarkable in itself when remembering that the newspaper was referring to a man who would have sex with anything that moved, including boys, several well-known ladies, and even his own half-sister. Johann Wolfgang von Goethe wasn't in Byron's league, but had many lovers and more than a passing interest in erotica. In France, the writer Georges Sand took a man's name, engaged in cross-dressing, and asserted her equality with the male writers of the time. She was linked romantically with Alfred de Musset, Franz Liszt, Frédéric Chopin, and Gustave Flaubert. She also had an intimate friendship with the actress Marie Dorval, which led to widespread (but unconfirmed) rumors of a lesbian relationship.

Victor Hugo, the author of books such as *The Hunchback of the Notre Dame* and *Les Miserables* seemed to be sexually insatiable. As he required very little sleep at night, he kept his wife quite busy during his waking hours. He was also a frequent visitor of prostitutes and had a twenty-two year old girlfriend when he was in his seventies. He remained sexually very active until his death.

Anaïs Nin, a French-born author, became famous for her sexually explicit diaries. She wrote vividly about sex and the female self long before these became "women's issues." She was as well known for her many lovers, who included Henry Miller, Edmund Wilson, Gore Vidal, and Otto Rank, as for her sexual works, like *Delta of Venus* (1978). Although Ernest Hemingway's life is marked by boxing matches, bullfights, big game safaris, deep-sea fishing jaunts, bar binges, and the occasional war, he was also known for his sexual adventuring. Between the years of 1920 and 1961, he married four times and had numerous affairs.

Apart from his best-selling detective stories, the writer Georges Simenon is remembered for his prodigious sexual appetite. He claimed that he needed sex three times a day and had slept with 10,000 women, of whom 8,000 were "les filles publiques" (prostitutes). His second wife later disagreed with his math, supplying a more "realistic" estimate of 1200. And so the list goes on.

Academic, intellectuals, and politicians may play in a lower league but are far from being sexual amateurs. It's no longer a secret that Albert Einstein had a great weakness for pretty women: he had many romantic entanglements and at least one illegitimate child. John Maynard Keynes, the economist, kept a numerical record of his sexual activity. From 1906 onward he tabulated his copulations, masturbations, and wet dreams, reflecting the perhaps equal pleasure he derived from sex and statistics. He had numerous affairs with young men. The philosopher Bertrand Russell had two marriages and countless love affairs, writing an extraordinary number of letters to his lovers. A sympathetic feminist, he once wrote that "the total amount of undesired sex endured by women is probably greater in marriage than in prostitution." Another philosopher, Jean-Paul Sartre, viewed himself as a Don Giovanni, exempt from outworn social conventions about sex and fidelity. He and his long-term partner Simone de Beauvoir never married and engaged freely in other relationships.

So, does this catalog answer our question whether a supercharged sex drive is essential component of creative success? I am afraid it remains open. Perhaps we project our own desires on to artistic people and fall into the trap of stereotyping. After all, the modern icon of female sexuality, Madonna, has said: "Everyone probably thinks that I am a raving nymphomaniac, that I have an insatiable sexual appetite, when the truth is I'd rather read a book." And one of the greatest inventors of our own time, Steve Jobs, shows a healthily irreverent attitude toward the whole business: "My girlfriend always laughs during sex no matter what she's reading." For many, the bedroom will always be just a place to sleep.

The puzzle of the relationship between creativity and sexual desire is complicated by the fact that many people cloak their sex life in secrecy. Many a biographer has struggled over the question of the sex life of their subject. Perhaps the only certain conclusion we can draw is that creative men—whatever their sexual orientation (a very high proportion of philosophers, painters, and writers have been homosexual)—have always been attractive to the female sex, something that evolutionary psychologists may be interested to consider.

6

LESSONS FROM THE BONOBOS

Sex: the thing that takes up the least amount of time and causes the most amount of trouble.

John Barrymoore

I wouldn't recommend sex, drugs or insanity for everyone, but they've always worked for me.

Hunter Thompson

Whatever else can be said about sex, it cannot be called a dignified performance.

Helen Lawrenson

Sex is dirty only when it's done right.

Woody Allen

"All you need is love," sang the Beatles, and they may have been right. Love can be a great equalizer between the sexes, but although we all look for love and believe we have found it, love does not always last. Divorce rates have not gone down. Permanent monogamy has been replaced by serial monogamy as people change partners. In our post-industrial society women are increasingly able to achieve equality with men. But how do these changes affect desire and attraction? What can we predict about future male-female relationships? How is the conflict between biology and society evolving?

In answering this question, we can draw interesting observations from the behavior of our closest genetic cousin (sharing more than ninety-eight percent of our DNA), the bonobo or pygmy chimpanzee, a member of the Homininae family, which is found in the deepest jungles of Central Africa. The behavior of this living relic of our shared primeval past could tell us something about the transient quality of male-based evolutionary systems. In contrast to Homo sapiens, bonobo society is female-centered and egalitarian, and sex rather than aggression is used as an instrument of social regulation.

The bonobo is the most peaceful primate species in existence. Their mantra could well be "make love, not war."

Bonobos indulge constantly and promiscuously in both heterosexual and homosexual sex. It is estimated that seventy-five percent of bonobo sex has nothing to do with reproduction. Males and females stimulate each other even when the females cannot become pregnant. Whereas in most other species, sex occurs at specific times of the year, linked to female estrus, among the bonobo it is an integral part of social exchange. Female bonobos, like human females, copulate whenever they want.

The bonobo use sex for anything from a handshake to the intervention of peacekeeping forces. Sex is used to gain power, to bond, to make up, to show affection, to barter for food, to show respect or submission, and even occasionally for procreation. Males use sex to solve antagonistic encounters. Females use sex when they want acceptance in a certain community, when they want a specific food, and to elicit help from multiple males.

Bonobos are innately promiscuous and do not form human-style nuclear families or long-term monogamous relationships. The burden of raising offspring rests entirely on the females' shoulders. As we know, family life among Homo sapiens implies paternal investment, which is unlikely to develop unless males can be reasonably certain that they are caring for their own rather than someone else's offspring. Unfortunately, the exclusivity demanded from women comes with a hefty price tag of jealousy and male aggression. This need for sexual exclusivity has contributed to the historic pattern of dominating and subjugating women. Given the downside of Homo sapiens' societal constructs, we could ask ourselves whether we might do better by emulating the bonobo. Should we use sex to strengthen cooperative bonds between men and women? Should it become the strategy of choice to counteract aggression? Could sex be the way to create a truly non-sexist society? Now, women in modern societies have more control over their bodies than they ever had before, this is a question worth considering.

GREATER EQUALITY BETWEEN THE SEXES

The readjustment of male and female roles in developed society over the last two centuries, and particularly over the last three generations, has been phenomenal. Birth control and morning-after pills have given women sexual independence, and other technological advances mean it is not necessary to have sex with men in order to conceive. Sex is no longer a death-defying act, now that the odds of dying in childbirth have been so dramatically reduced (although male jealousy is still a force to be reckoned with). Women also have more control over their lives thanks to education and work. With work comes money; and with money comes increasing freedom and independence. These changes mean that women are no longer prepared to accept a subjugated position. They want true, not token, equality.

The consequence of this is self-evident. Women's increased independence has affected the role of marriage in society. Although marriage (or partnership) is still important, people are unwilling to remain stuck in a difficult or unhappy relationship. The divorce rate has soared. People no longer marry for life.

Women are entering the workforce in increasing numbers, and not necessarily in lower level positions. More women can be found in senior management positions than ever before—although the situation is still open to much improvement. Misogynists have gone so far as to state that working women are a major factor in marital instability. Not only has work made women more financially independent, the workplace is fast becoming the most common breeding ground for affairs. The workplace has become the new focal point for infidelity. The intimacy of men and women working together seems to speed the demise of dysfunctional marriages. Financially independent women are much less tolerant of marital misery that their less fortunate predecessors. Working women, who have control over their own money, are unlikely to hang on in a relationship when it no longer works.

But despite feminists rallying cries about equality, the human animal is no bonobo. Men and women are programmed quite differently from their chimpanzee cousins. We don't really know whether or not sex is a satisfactory experience for female bonobos. We do know, however, that women are not only less preoccupied with sex than men, but that many of them also find sex less rewarding. Thus while the expectation has been that women's liberation would imply a revision of sex roles, evolutionary developmental processes being what they are, the reality has turned out to be very different. Much of the sexual discontent that preoccupies men and women appears to be the outcome of an unsatisfactory compromise on the battlefield of biology versus society—between the clash of nature and nurture.

So conflict between the sexes is likely to continue, and sex will continue to be the most common catalyst for disagreements between men and women. Furthermore, Homo sapiens' model of trying to assure paternity implies that men will continue to be challenged by jealousy and aggression, even in a society where women distribute their sexual favors more freely and men are faced with the threat biotechnology poses to their procreative role. Men have to learn to accept women on equal terms, and move from a patriarchic culture to one that is more androgynous.

Interestingly enough, if men are able to modify their attitude toward women, it pays off in the workplace, which is moving from a command-control-compartmentalization orientation toward a net-work-coaching leadership style. In general, women are less power-driven than men; they are less narcissistic; and have a more balanced mind-set about work and non-work. When this mind-set becomes the predominant one, it will contribute to the creation of more humane as well as more effective organizations.

INDEPENDENT DEPENDENCE

To be able not only to fall but to remain in love, a person must have passed successfully the early childhood stages of separation and individuation, developed a sense of self, and become a person in his or her own right. For relationships to last, partners need a measure of independence and knowledge of their own identities. The "other" should always be recognized as a free, autonomous human being.

Without a secure sense of self and the capacity to distinguish self from others, romantic love is a pipe dream. Like the effect of drugs, it gives only a very temporary high. Intimacy requires the tolerance of separateness, the ability to go beyond narcissistic fantasies of merger and physical oneness. Intimacy implies that each person must be able to distinguish clearly separate, external love objects from internal fantasies. Antoine de Saint-Exupéry wrote: "Life has taught us that love does not consist in gazing at each other but in looking outward together in the same direction." Fantasies are fine, but they don't mean we have to forget the world outside. Romantic love should not come at the price of sacrificing our individuality.

Staying in love implies mature dependence but requires the retention of our individuality. We don't have to think alike to love alike. Only by loving each other independently are we able to grow and develop as human beings. Love cannot thrive in a state of inequality. No person should use another simply as a means to satisfy sexual desire. Sexuality can only be a gift from one autono-mous being to another. For some of us, creating and maintaining this kind of relationship is a developmental experience, our last chance to grow up.

Someone with an insecure sense of self will never be able to tolerate the essential paradox of a relationship: the ability to be close at a distance. Maturity implies the ability to separate our own self-image from that of the other. We might seek the bliss of merger, but we also like to preserve a sense of individuality and autonomy. Both members of a partnership need space—to express their need for togetherness but also to accommodate a degree of wariness about over-intimacy. That's what a relationship is all about—helping each other to reach the full status of responsible human beings who don't run away from life.

Making "coupledom" work

To make the heady cocktail of "coupledom" even more effective, a couple needs to be able to negotiate each other's narcissistic needs. They should be able to use each other as an emotional container. They should be able to create a mature dependency relationship, not oscillate between merger and disconnectedness. They need to avoid a dysfunctional collusion in which they repeat past hurts, and be able to change. Love may be a feeling but a relationship means work.

A significant contributing factor to a stable relationship is the experience of a successful marriage, for example, growing up with parents whose marriage worked well. Children who receive negative role models from parents who go through messy divorces (or repeated marriage-divorce cycles), or who are caught up in unholy parent-child alliances within the family, may grown up fearful of any relationship. Too many people settle for sex, and fail at love, intimacy, and relationship security. Some people may have become counter-dependent because of unfortunate past experiences. For example, previously married men may have become gun shy, telling themselves that all relationships are likely to end badly. Older men, who have never married, may have become too narcissistic; they may find it too difficult to accommodate another person in a shared life. These people need to get out of their comfort zone. They need to see that they can choose to be stuck in a psychic prison, or they can choose to do things differently.

The British academic and author C. S. Lewis, perhaps best known for his series of Narnia novels, experienced a personal epiphany of this kind. When he was a bachelor in his late fifties, Lewis had published a partial autobiography, *Surprised by Joy*, in which he described his reluctant conversion to Christianity. Soon after, he met an American writer, Joy Gresham, an event that gave the title of his earlier autobiography an air of premonition. His brother remembered: "For Jack the attraction was at first undoubtedly intellectual. Joy was the only woman whom he had met … who had a brain which matched his own in suppleness, in width of interest, and in analytical grasp, and above all in humor and a sense of fun." Lewis fell deeply in love with Joy Gresham. However, she was diagnosed with bone cancer shortly after they met. Despite this, they married and had a few brief years together before her death in 1960. Lewis subsequently published a highly personal account of bereavement, *A Grief Observed*.

Laughter is as an ideal way to shorten the distance between two people. Humor and playfulness will not only help in dealing with the daily setbacks of life: a couple aging together has to face some harsh existential realities.

The development of a really good relationship is not a natural process. It means work. It is an achievement. Lust can be a very temporary high, love is a transient experience, but a relationship has to be built and once made, it needs to be fed, nurtured, and constantly renewed. When lust fades, we had all better hope we have someone around who can tolerate all our peculiarities. As the poet John Ciardi said, "Love is the word used to label the sexual excitement of the young, the habituation of the middle-aged, and the mutual dependence of the old."

FINAL REFLECTIONS

People who have strong relationships are generally healthier, have fewer emotional difficulties, are less likely to engage in deviant behavior, and have children who do well at school. Moreover, people with stable relationships have more and better sex than their counterparts.

Sex without love can turn into a mechanical exercise or even a hostile act. The challenge for human kind will be to find constructive ways to untangle sex from aggression—the bonobos are an extreme example. This will not be easy, given our evolutionary heritage. Addressing it is like a shot to the heart of our male-dominated, patriarchic society. But, from the story of Adam and Eve, religion, laws, and customs have all emphasized that women are here to please men. Greater reciprocity is long overdue. Jacqueline Kennedy once said that there are two kinds of women, "those who want power in the world, and those who want power in bed." Our challenge will be to move beyond these choices. Our challenge is to work for lasting equality.

The sexual revolution of the late nineteenth century wasn't the coming of an orgasmic liberation. What has been liberating, however, has been a massive questioning of the double standards and sexual constraints that characterized earlier eras. Many of the taboos and rituals that contribute to sexual dysfunctioning are relics of the past that linger on. It is ironic, therefore, that just when humankind is emerging from many centuries of sexual repression and persecution, and sexual desire has finally been able to take wing, the deadly AIDS virus is imposing its own kind of repression on us. The story of twenty-first-century sexuality appears to be one of greater self-expression but also of serious self-restraint. It's up to us to make wise choices.

PART TWO: MEDITATIONS ON MONEY

7

THE SIN OF COVETOUSNESS

And again I say unto you, "It is easier for a camel to go through the eye of a needle, than for a rich man to enter into the kingdom of God."

Matthew 19: 24

Money, it turned out, was exactly like sex: you thought of nothing else if you didn't have it and thought of other things if you did.

James Baldwin

All I ask is the chance to prove that money can't make me happy.

Spike Milligan

Dogs have no money. Isn't that amazing? They're broke their entire lives. But they get through. You know why dogs have no money? No pockets.

Jerry Seinfeld

The Treasure of the Sierra Madre, a classic film made by director John Huston in 1948 and adapted from the best-selling novel by the mystery writer B. Traven, is a story of psychological disintegration under the influence of greed and money. The film starts with drifter Fred Dobbs (Humphrey Bogart) impulsively spending the last of his money on a lottery ticket. The year is 1925; the place, Tampico, Mexico, where Bogart's bitter, out-of-work character panhandles money from anyone he happens to run into while cursing his bad luck. Dobbs joins up with fellow drifter Curtin (Tim Holt) to work for an unscrupulous contractor, well known to the locals for his habit of "cheating foreigners and half-baked Americans"—one of several early glimpses into the darker, greedy side of human nature. Another such glimpse is revealed at a cheap boarding house "full of rats, scorpions, and cockroaches" where Dobbs and Curtin meet a lively old gold prospector named Howard (Walter Huston), who offers disturbing warnings about the evil things that happen to the mind of human beings who succumb to the lure of money. Though Dobbs swears that he would never become corrupted by greed, viewers can tell that Howard, with his decades of observing human nature in action, remains unconvinced.

Forcibly collecting their pay from their unreliable boss, Dobbs and Curtin combine it with Dobbs's unexpected windfall from his lottery ticket. Then, with Howard, they pool their resources and mount a gold-mining expedition into the mountains, complete with donkeys, tools, and guns. Dobbs pledges that anything they find will be split three ways, but Howard, who has heard that story before, has his doubts. It doesn't take long before the trio finds a promising place to mine, and after a few days of digging, the gold starts pouring out of the mountain. Within a short time, they have become very rich men.

Suspicion, greed, and paranoia follow hard on wealth, overcoming Dobbs, who suspects his fellow miners of every form of treachery. After the gold bonanza, the men split their treasure three ways, as promised, but Dobbs's irrational behavior threatens to destroy everything they have worked so hard for. As the gold continues to come in, the men gradually turn against each other, and the film moves toward its tragic, ironic conclusion.

Curtin is an idealistic young man, unwilling to compromise his values for the sake of money. His inherent naïveté is a contrast to the greedy, money-obsessed Dobbs. Gold enslaves Dobbs to the point where he is prepared to steal from his partners, assuming that they would do the same to him. The plot highlights the growing antagonism between Dobbs and the other two.

Dobbs attempts to murder Curtin and makes off with all the gold dust, only to encounter Mexican bandits who murder him for his loaded saddlebags, which they assume hold animal hides. When they rip the bags open and find only what they think is dirt, they scatter the gold to the winds. The final scene has Curtin and Howard arriving to witness the gold being scattered. It seems to give them a sense of deliverance. They laugh, as if relieved that they survived the ordeal and can start anew, free from the miserable spell that gold had cast upon them.

In many ways, *The Treasure of the Sierra Madre* is a kind of morality play, demonstrating the degree to which money can corrupt a person's soul. Like a doomed hero, Dobbs can't escape his destiny. In the end, the main figures are back where they started, having to explain to themselves the dark forces that overcame them.

Huston's film is an outstanding treatment of the corrosiveness of greed and the dangers inherent in the pursuit of wealth. For many of us, money touches the very core of our being, and we think constantly about it. Although there are certainly some people who are genuinely unconcerned about money, we often suspect them of protesting too much, and that when they say they despise riches, they are telling only a half-truth: what they despise is the riches of others. In other words, they're trying to manage their envy.

As long as we have enough of it, it's easy to say that money isn't everything. Unfortunately, it does seem that the more money we have, the more we want. The philosopher Arthur Schopenhauer once pointedly said, "Wealth is like seawater; the more we drink the thirstier we become." That's exactly how it was for Dobbs in *The Treasure of the Sierra Madre:* there was never enough gold. And yet most of us realize some time or other, that our true wealth in life is life itself. "You can't take it with you" may be hackneyed but it is also undeniably true. Does anyone really want to be the richest person in the cemetery?

So we're left with a conundrum: while poverty is not to be recommended, it takes more than money to feel rich and satisfied with life. Listening to the stories of many executives, I have come to realize that wealth brings its own problems. Far too often, money starts to possess a person, rather than the person possessing the money. Instead of gaining greater satisfaction through wealth, many people find that the acquisition and possession of money creates even greater dissatisfaction.

A CASE OF WEALTH FATIGUE SYNDROME

As a psychoanalyst and psychotherapist, and as a management consultant, I have met many very wealthy individuals who no longer know how to amuse themselves. They are bored; and I have discovered that when people are bored, they not only bore others, they also bore themselves. Fortunately, they can take comfort in Henry Kissinger's quip that "The nice thing about being a celebrity is that when you bore people, they think it's their fault."

The best cure for boredom is curiosity. But despite having bought every possible toy in the shop, these people are still suffering from a malaise that has been called Wealth Fatigue Syndrome; in spite of their wealth, and whatever they acquire, their conspicuous, obsessional consumption doesn't seem to work. Their wealth, and the things it supplies, does not lead to increased happiness. On the contrary, to quote the philosopher Francis Bacon, "Riches are a good handmaiden, but the worst mistress." What this obsessional pursuit of material goods does is to promote "having" over "being." It confuses—and this is where the advertising industry colludes with it—wants with needs.

From my wealthy but dissatisfied executives, I discovered that having it all, and having it now, is never enough. Houses, yachts, airplanes, cars, plastic surgery—nothing seems to work in driving away the specter of unhappiness and dissatisfaction. Acquisitions only bring temporary relief. These people define their lives through earnings, possessions, appearances, celebrity, and all these things make them more miserable than before. Suffering from Wealth Fatigue Syndrome, it becomes harder and harder to get a buzz. They are constantly searching for bigger thrills.

The Russian billionaire Roman Abramovich seems to present many symptoms of Wealth Fatigue Syndrome. Life began unpromisingly for Abramovich. His mother died when he was eighteen months old. A few years later, his father died in a construction accident. Roman was adopted by his father's brother and raised in Siberia. Through a family contact, he became involved in the oil industry. He studied at Moscow's Gubkin Oil and Gas Institute, and began to make money (rather implausibly, it seems with hindsight) selling plastic ducks from his small apartment. Those plastic ducks were the launchpad for a meteoric career. A natural deal maker, Abramovich was in the right place at the right time when the old Soviet order collapsed and Russia made its first tentative steps toward a free market economy. He became part of an elite group of oligarchs who amassed enormous personal fortunes under Russia's first president, Boris Yeltsin.

Abramovich first became seriously wealthy in the 1990s when he and his fellow oligarchs took advantage of the privatization of Russia's state assets. In 1995 he hit the jackpot when he joined forces with Boris Berezovsky and acquired a controlling interest in a large oil company, Sibneft. At the time, many critics complained that the bidding process was rigged and that the company was worth billions more than the pair paid for it. Whatever the truth may be, the deal made Abramovich fabulously rich.

Some people suffering from Wealth Fatigue Syndrome will spend beyond their means; others possess so much wealth that they can spend freely for many lifetimes. Abramovich belongs in the latter camp. Some people with newly found money like to spend lavishly, indulging themselves in expensive hobbies, like acquiring football or baseball clubs. Having become wealthy beyond his wildest dreams, Abramovich did exactly that, buying Chelsea football club, one of the top teams in the English premier football league, investing serious money to increase its ranking. But even this seemed to provide insufficient amusement. Abramovich had already acquired two Boeing airplanes, several helicopters (some soundproofed, so that he could watch DVDs in flight) and the sort of international property portfolio that most of the world's wealthiest people could only dream of. Now he began to show more interest in his other hobby: yacht collection. How many yachts are enough? Even though he already had three of the world's largest privately owned yachts, there were still others that were just a few meters longer. In the rarefied world of billionaires, size matters and giga-yachts are the ultimate status symbol. This was reason enough for Abramovich to set a new benchmark in this bizarre game of "mine's bigger than yours." His yacht *Eclipse*, under construction in 2007, had a specification that included two helicopter pads and a mini submarine, and at 525 feet was set to become the largest privately owned boat in the world, larger than some naval frigates. Although Abramovich trails the world's richest men, including Bill Gates and Larry Ellison, in terms of personal fortune, in the yachting world, nobody can match his growing fleet. It will be interesting to see where he parks it, as he already has a yacht in the Mediterranean, the Caribbean, Central America, and the Pacific.

Size of yachts is one thing, but women are another matter altogether. Abramovich originally gave the impression of being a true family man, spending time with his wife and five children. According to the celebrity press, he and his second wife Irina seemed to have had it all: the houses, the glamour, and the money. They seemed to live a perfect life. It was a far cry from the old, drab, gray Soviet Union where he came from.

However, Abramovich's perfect life turned out to be a fairytale that didn't last. Although he took his time about it, eventually he dropped his wife for a much younger woman. Commenting on the breakup, his first wife, Olga, interviewed by the *Daily Mail*, commented, "Roman may have the world in his hands, but you can't buy lasting love and happiness. I fear for him that he will never be happy with his lot in life. He will always want more. Despite his money, he needs to reassure himself that he is still strong and virile—and as so often happens, he has done this by finding a beautiful girl so much younger than his wife." Collecting women, however, can be even more expensive than collecting yachts. Abramovich's "quickie" divorce in Moscow can now be ranked among one of the world's costliest marriage splits.

Abramovich may be an extreme illustration of Wealth Fatigue Syndrome but although he may be a larger-than-life example, money affects us all, however rich or poor we are. It plays an important role in our lives, determining our outlook and steering many of our decisions.

In our individualistic, competitive world, it is hard to survive without having money. All of us need at least a minimal amount simply to stay alive, and all of us have specific needs that require money for satisfaction. But if we want to be true to ourselves and maintain our mental health, we need to find ways to acquire and deal with money that are congruent with our subjective feelings of well-being and with our values and belief system. If not, in spite of all our money, we may in for some surprises. Money could turn out to cost too much.

8

THE INNER WORLD OF MONEY

About the time we can make the ends meet, somebody moves the ends.

Herbert Clark Hoover

The only point in making money is, you can tell some big shot where to go.

Humphrey Bogart

Every day I get up and look through the Forbes list of the richest people in America. If I'm not there, I go to work.

Robert Orben

A billion here, a billion there, pretty soon it's real money.

Everett Dirksen

PANDORA'S BOX

Money, as Roman Abramovich demonstrates, can be shown off in extravagant ways, but it can also play a more silent role in our relationships, in our work, and the way we make decisions. However, there are many people who downplay the significance of money in their lives. Some even seem to be afraid of it. A typical reaction, when I ask executives why they work so hard is: "I want you to know that the reason I work 50, 60, or 70 hours a week isn't for the money." When I ask them what their hard work is really all about, I get responses like, "It's about the challenge," or "I am trying to change the nature of the industry," or more dramatically, "I am trying to change the world and make it a better place." It is a rare individual who admits that he or she likes the feel of money; I suspect because to say so explicitly would be rather like expressing an overt interest in sex.

But before we go on, just ask yourself, how do *you* perceive and value money? Do you talk about it? Or do you try to avoid it? For some people, straight talk about money is one of the taboos. They are as uncomfortable when asked about money as they would be if asked to give details of their sex life. What was money talk like in your family? In some families, money is taken for granted and never talked about. In others, it is a powerful symbol of control, influence, or status.

Our impressions about money start at an early age and how we deal with money is very much determined by the way in which our parents dealt with it. What did money mean to your parents? Was money ever openly discussed in the family? Or was it a source of conflict—not talked about? Did concerns about money hang like a dark shadow over the family? Did money concerns affect the family atmosphere? How did money affect the scripts in your inner theater?

The scripts in our inner theater are drafted in response to imprinted motivational need systems—the part of us that is hardwired in our brain—which have an important influence on individual behavior. These need systems become operational in infancy and continue to play a role throughout the human life cycle (though they are altered by age, learning, and maturation). Motivational need systems are the driving forces that make us behave the way we do, the fuel that keeps us going.

The human species has basic motivational needs—physical, sensual, attachment, and exploratory. According to developmental psychologists, the pursuit of money is *not* one of these early, predetermined motivators. This doesn't mean, however, that money will not affect our lives. Although money may become a motivating force later in a child's developmental timeline, it can turn into a major motivator as life goes on. For many of us, it comes to play a hugely symbolic role.

Money becomes progressively a more important symbol as children mature. Obviously, the quickest and most pervasive way for children to learn about money is to be exposed to a lack of it. The chances are high that people who are preoccupied with money experienced a serious lack of it (real or perceived) while growing up. Serious economic hardship due to the illness or death of a parent, or to parents' separation or divorce can leave a significant and lasting imprint that will accompany people throughout their lives.

While our perceptions about sex will, with luck, progress as we get older, money is a different matter. Part of the process of becoming an adult is aligning old perceptions about money with present-day reality. One of our developmental challenges is to pick up the thread of money experiences and add these to the other story lines in our lives. What challenges have you experienced when dealing with money? Can you remember any embarrassing incidents concerning money? Were you ever in a situation when you had no money? Did you ever have to pretend that money didn't really matter? These self-exploratory questions can help us better understand the role of money in our lives.

This exercise may reveal that money is laden with a Pandora's trunkload of emotional material. For some people, the need to make money will be a traumatic experience; it will cause tempers to flare, provoke serious conflicts, confuse priorities, contribute to overspending, saddle us with debt, and have a prolonged influence on family life. Where does all this emotional stuff come from, and why do we become so emotional about money?

Our parents help shape our beliefs about money and the symbolic meanings that money assumes. It becomes an emotional currency within the family. The way our parents handle money colors our perceptions about it. Who gets pocket money, and who doesn't? Who gets more, who gets less? When money is handed out, is it done fairly or unfairly? Powerful emotions and feelings will be generated from these money-based interactions. Emotions of envy, fear, hope, resentment, joy, and disgust, among others, will become psychologically attached to money. This contributes to the huge symbolic value that money can acquire.

The way we perceive money is an intergenerational process. Messages about the meaning of money are communicated across generations within a family, creating a legacy of beliefs and expectations, a set of dos and don'ts. These generational messages are influenced by cultural beliefs. Each culture has a way of looking at money. Statements like "It is easier for a camel to pass through the eye of a needle than for a rich man to enter the kingdom of heaven," or "A penny saved is a penny earned," are indicative of a culture's beliefs. Myths, fables, and fairy tales are full of money content: rich princes rescue beautiful women and live happily ever after. The content of these stories, whether fictional or cultural, and the ways in which they are interpreted and transmitted by the parents, will influence our attitude toward money.

THE SYMBOLIC ROLE OF MONEY

Money by itself is quite meaningless. There is not much use for money on a desert island, for instance. Money has to be considered within a societal context, the only place where it has transactional value. But within a societal context, quite apart from its buying potential, money assumes an important symbolic role. Depending on a child's developmental history, money symbolizes deliverance from misery, escape from a gray existence, freedom from familial constraints, a pathway to independence and security, triumph over helplessness, the embodiment of power, an opportunity to escape hard work, an expression of leisure, or the attainment of self-worth and love. Most of us experience money as a combination of all of these.

One way of assessing what money means to people is to listen to their stories. What kinds of stories do they tell about money? Do these stories play a central or peripheral role in their imagination? Another way is to listen to people's dreams. Like many other things, the significance money has in our waking lives will be symbolically reflected in our dream life. In dreams, money frequently represents the things that are most valuable to us; it's very unlikely to be a mere representation of cash. Dreams about money are often about power, control, dependency, competency, being loved, and even sexuality.

Money can be lost, gained, given, or spent in dreams. A dream about finding money might be saying something about our quest for love or power. Dreaming about losing money can signify setbacks in our affairs; that we are struggling with feeling weak, vulnerable, and even out of control; or that we lack ambition, power, and self-esteem. Many people who dream about money are actually stimulated by the desire for it, the lack of it, or their inability to control the way they handle it. This last is often revealed in dreams where the dreamer is drowning in debt.

Since our dreams are triggered by some form of day residue, it's important to associate the dream theme to a specific event or preoccupation of the previous day or days if we want to understand it correctly. The feeling that we're left with after the dream will also help to make sense of it. For example, waking up from a dream with a sense of bewilderment and anxiety may be a give-away about something that is happening in the dreamer's life. However, we must bear in mind that images in dreams can mean quite different things to different dreamers. The individual's circumstances at the time of each dream need to be taken into consideration. Dreams are always configured within the complex web of the dreamer's interpersonal relationships. The ground rule in dream interpretation is "no interpretation without association."

For example, if you have a dream in which you gain money, it will be interesting to know from whom and under what circumstances. What kind of power dynamics are portrayed in the dream? What themes can you distinguish? What kind of feelings does this dream arouse in you?

Perhaps you dream about handing out money? This may suggest a compulsion to help others, a desire for love and affection, or a need for attention. In contrast, a dream in which you see others giving money away may suggest that you are feeling ignored or neglected. Someone may not be paying you enough attention or showing you enough affection. Dreaming that you've no money may indicate a fear of losing your place in the world; you may think that you lack the ability needed to achieve desired goals; you may feel overlooked or neglected by others. Dreaming about losing money may be a signifier of being unable to control yourself. This lack of control may concern money, but it might also be symbolic of your inability to restrain yourself from over-committing resources, emotionally or otherwise.

Dreaming about stealing money may signify anxiety about danger, or a need to be cautious. More positively, such a dream may also mean that you are finally going after or reaching out toward things of value to you.

On one occasion, a senior executive told me that the previous night he had dreamed that he was looking for money that he had hidden behind a book on a shelf. He was sure it was there but couldn't find it. He kept looking everywhere, becoming increasingly panicky. The feeling of panic remained with him when he woke up.

Associating to the dream, the executive mentioned a lunch he had had the previous day with an old friend; the topic of conversation was a recent class reunion. They talked about how well some of their classmates had done in life. He asked his friend if, given the chance, he would have done the same things over again. As he asked the question, he realized he was directing it more toward himself than to his friend and that it was something that had been troubling him for some time. During the lunch, they also touched upon how many of their classmates had divorced, and were now on their second marriage. The executive remembered that the conversation left him with a sense of concern and worry about how his life had been going.

Interpreting this dream, the loss of money might signify that the executive had a subliminal awareness that he had lost—something. Dreams often help us see things that we are not prepared to see or deal with in daily life. While dreaming, our defensive mechanisms do not work as intensively. Symbolically, losing things in dreams— particularly losing something valuable, like money—may indicate lost opportunities, the pain of lost relationships, even the loss of aspects of the self. The dream may contain a disguised warning that the time has come to do something. As his account of the lunchtime discussion suggests, the executive felt concern that he was losing something he valued in himself. Perhaps he was feeling that he had lost sight of his life's dreams. Or perhaps it signified a lack of confidence about the way his life was turning out.

From what I knew about this executive, he had become overly concerned with day-to-day problems, forgetting the bigger picture. Furthermore, given the topic of the previous day's conversation, the dream may also have contained a warning about his private life. It might have signified that he needed to work on his relationship with his wife, or risk losing her.

In this executive's case, dreaming only made reality seem worse. The challenge for all of us is, however, to limit the surprises, to enter waking and dreaming life with our eyes wide open. We need to be sensitive to the issues at hand, including money matters. Victor Hugo once said, "Each man should frame life so that at some future hour fact and his dreaming meet." So many of our dreams seem impossible, then improbable, and then, unless we deal with the dream content, they become inevitable. Much of dream symbolism appears to be rehearsals for things to come that fill us with anxiety. If we pay attention to such dreams, we will be more prepared and will less likely enter difficult situations with our eyes closed. In money matters—like is the case with many other issues—it pays to pay attention. We may have dreams, we may have nightmares, but thanks to the dreams, we may be able to overcome the nightmares.

9

IN PRAISE OF "FUCK-YOU" MONEY

It is not the man who has too little, but the man who craves more, that is poor.

Seneca

When it's a question of money, everybody is of the same religion.

Voltaire

Money never made a man happy yet, nor will it. The more a man has, the more he wants. Instead of filling a vacuum, it makes one.

Benjamin Franklin

If all the rich people in the world divided up their money among themselves there wouldn't be enough to go around.

Christina Stead

Studying dreams may be the royal road to understanding the symbolic meaning of money, but in-depth conversations with well-to-do executives can also be helpful. I have learned that a significant number of executives are preoccupied with the idea of obtaining what they call "fuck-you" money—that is, money for which they're not beholden to anybody. Woven throughout many of these narratives are childhood experiences of lack of money over which they had no, or very little, control. As youngsters these people felt—and indeed were—powerless to do anything about their dire family circumstances. Watching how their parents struggled to keep things going, pay the bills and put food on the table, they realized the influence money had on their standard of living. As these early experiences were internalized, they became significant inner-theater themes that dominated future behavior.

For some, improving their financial situation can turn into a life-long obsession. Children exposed to their parents' financial strain often vow not to let similar difficulties happen to them. They feel a deeply cherished desire to get their parents to smile again, to lessen their strain, to return to a state of oceanic bliss, a sense of togetherness with a caring parent. As adults, in contrast to the financial helplessness they experienced when they were growing up, they want to achieve financial status that allows them to tell other people to "fuck off." They want to acquire so much money that they're invincible, in control, and can get out of any situation they don't like. They never want to be the victims of uncontrollable forces again. To these people, money represents independence, power, and control. It holds the power to exorcize the ghosts of childhood. These people believe that money is the cure to all their ills. But they fail to realize that "he that is of the opinion money will do everything may well be suspected of doing everything for money," to quote Benjamin Franklin. They view the lack of money as the cause of all misery. They don't recognize its darker side.

IN-YOUR-FACE MONEY

Money, in addition to being a symbol of power and control, also symbolizes winning the game of life. It is an indicator of a person's achievements, bettering others. If we experience a lack of self-worth, wealth is one way of showing others that we are a force to be reckoned with. As evidence that we have triumphed over adversity and adversaries, money gives us the recognition we crave from others, helping us to shore up a shaky sense of self-esteem. It's not just winning that counts, however. Its goes much deeper than that. For many people, flaunting wealth is a kind of one-upmanship. Winning in the money game adds to the charm of the conquest.

In talking, over the years, to many money-driven executives, I've come to realize the degree to which people can be propelled by dark, competitive forces. One executive said to me, in all seriousness, "What good is money if it can't inspire envy and terror in your fellow man?" People with that orientation use money to take revenge, to get even. Flaunting money becomes a vehicle to deal with the real or imagined hurts of childhood. For such people, making lots of money is not only a symbol of success, it is also a deliberate attempt to make others envious. Of course, such behavior often brings out the worst in those who are taunted; enraged by a display of wealth, they may respond with their own form of competitive aggression. In such circumstances, money can quickly cost too much. The flaunting of money to inspire envy reinforces a Darwinian outlook on life and makes peaceful coexistence impossible. As the singer Bob Dylan said, "Money doesn't talk, it swears." Shooting at others, we may end up wounding ourselves. But many people prefer to be envied rather than pitied.

Some people see money as the ideal way to keep score in the game of life. Letting others know how much money we have sets up comparisons. To quote the well-known moneymaker (and TV "star") Donald Trump, "Money was never a big motivation for me, except as a way to keep score. The real excitement is playing the game." We should always be suspicious of people who say that money isn't everything; everything may be exactly what money is to them. But, as Trump points out, money certainly lends itself to score keeping. If the annual Forbes list of the richest people in the world is anything to go by, large figures are a great way to impress others. Gaining a spot on that list—the destination of many a narcissistic journey—is a highly effective, but not very sophisticated, way of gaining the admiration (and/or envy) of others.

Far more of us read the Forbes list with envy than achieve its lofty ranking. And as we read it, chances are we feel twinges if not outright pangs of envy. That emotion—the feeling of discontent and resentment, the desire for the possessions or qualities that somebody else has—is one of the darker responses to money. We quickly learn how insidious it can be. Aeschylus wrote, "It is in the character of a very few men to honor without envy a friend who has prospered." While envy is not an emotion that we readily acknowledge, it plays a key role in our inner lives. It takes on a darker hue when we view its emergence as a symptom of our failure to appreciate our own uniqueness and self-worth. Then, it springs from our ignorance of, or lack of belief in, our own gifts.

Envy and rivalry are symbiotic twins and their relationship plays out particularly well when it relates to money matters. When money has a central role in our inner lives, we not only want to be rich, but we find it imperative to be richer than others. The journalist and social critic H. L. Mencken nailed that aspect of human character in his definition of wealth as "any income that is at least one hundred dollars more a year than the income of one's wife's sister's husband." The writer Gore Vidal was another keen observer of human nature: "Whenever a friend succeeds," he said, "a little something in me dies." Something in us may die, yes—but it may also give us the energy to prove once more to the world that we are not yet a has-been; that we are still in the race.

For many of the super-rich, discovering that they're not named on the Forbes list of the richest people in the world is a personal catastrophe. But it's also the ultimate challenge. They go out into the marketplace to do battle once again, ready to do anything to be part of that elite group. But unfortunately, even those who make it onto the Forbes list are still unlikely to be satisfied. Having attained the lofty heights, they torture themselves wondering whether their ranking is high enough. After all, for all but one person in the world, there is always someone higher up. So the new challenge becomes how to better the person just above you? How can you move ever higher in the ranking? And what can you do to lower the ranking of others? No matter how many upward steps you take, envy keeps twisting its knife in your heart.

Consider the snide remark made by Larry Ellison, one of the super-rich, about the world's richest person: "Bill Gates wants people to think he's Edison, when he's really Rockefeller. Referring to Gates as the smartest man in America isn't right. ... [W]ealth isn't the same thing as intelligence." Anyone setting out to better Bill Gates will become embroiled in a never-ending obsession. The result is a stunted life. The quest for wealth doesn't bring the kind of security and peace of mind that most people imagine money will buy. Like the Holy Grail, they remain compelling but elusive.

WHEN GREENBACKS MAKE YOU GREEN WITH ENVY

The destructive competitiveness that uses money as a scorecard, or as a way to gain recognition, may have had its roots in sibling rivalry. Unchecked sibling rivalry may create a pervasive (and sometimes accurate) idea that "the other" is favored by one or even both of the parents. Because love is not perceived to be shared equally, it becomes a precious commodity. The feeling of being insufficiently appreciated causes what psychologists call a narcissistic injury—that is, an injury to a person's self-esteem—which expressed itself in symptoms such as depression and feelings of envy, competitiveness, rage, anger, resentment, revenge, and vindication. Amassing money becomes a way to show that you count; it becomes a means of vindication; it can even be used for revenge.

A good example of this need for recognition and vindication through the means of money is the character of Scrooge McDuck, Donald Duck's uncle. Disney's creation is an excellent representation of what happens when the pursuit of money becomes an end in itself. In the cartoon series, Scrooge McDuck is described as the world's richest person, having followed a trajectory from a poor shoe shiner in Scotland to a penny-pinching billionaire in the United States. His name is taken from the miserly Ebenezer Scrooge, a character from Charles Dickens' novella *A Christmas Carol*. It is theorized, however, that Scottish-born industrialist Andrew Carnegie, who left his country for America at the age of thirteen, served as a model for Uncle Scrooge.

Scrooge McDuck keeps a portion of his wealth in a massive money bin overlooking the city of Duckburg. Infamous for his stinginess, he loves his money above everything. Symbolically, his love for money is illustrated by his principle pastime, diving into his money like a dolphin, burrowing through it like a gopher, and throwing coins into the air to feel them fall upon his skull.

As a businessman, Scrooge McDuck often resorts to aggressive tactics and deception. Business is the stage where he acts out his competitive spirit. In his pursuit of money, he has amassed significant experience in manipulating people and events toward his own ends. But this behavior has come at a high cost: the lack of true emotional relationships. His relations with his nephew Donald, and Donald's own nephews, is distant. The only thing that evokes any emotional reaction in Scrooge McDuck is his money, as it brings back memories of how it was earned. Besides all the fun and games, the cartoon series of Scrooge McDuck is also a symbolically loaded, dark tale about the emptiness of wealth. Intricately woven in these tales is a strong message that the blind pursuit of money comes at the price of a lack of human connectivity.

The Monte Cristo complex

The Monte Cristo complex was named after the protagonist in Alexandre Dumas' novel *The Count of Monte Cristo*. The theme of Dumas' story is revenge—the need to get even for real or imagined hurts. Edmond Dantés is about to marry his fiancée and become captain of a vessel when he is framed as a pro-Bonaparte conspirator, shortly before the French Emperor's dramatic return to France from exile in Elba. Through the envious machinations of three enemies, Dantés is imprisoned in the formidable Château d'If. Educated by a fellow prisoner, the elderly Abbé Faria, Dantés remains in this French Alcatraz for fourteen years, before he engineers an ingenious escape. He flees to the island of Monte Cristo, where he locates a long-lost treasure Faria told him about, hidden since the time of the Renaissance. In his new identity as the Count of Monte Cristo, Dantés uses his fabulous new wealth to fund his revenge and destroy his enemies, in an attempt to right the wrongs he suffered.

As Dumas' story illustrates, for people who suffer from the Monte Cristo complex, revenge is more than just a fleeting temptation;

it's their major motivational force in life. Getting even is the only thing that matters and money is the means they use to do it. But, as Dantés discovers in Dumas' novel, keeping score of old scores and scars ultimately diminishes you. Can you really get ahead while getting even? "The tree of revenge doesn't bear fruit," according to a Dutch proverb. In *Paradise Lost*, John Milton wrote: "Revenge, at first though sweet,/Bitter 'ere long back on itself recoils." Those who plot the destruction of others often perish in the attempt, and exacting an eye for an eye, as the Book of Exodus exhorts, eventually leaves everyone blind. I have met many executives who, while using money for vengeful purposes, ended up being quite dead within.

HAVING TOO MUCH MONEY

Of course, we can always quote Oscar Wilde, "There is only one class in the community that thinks more about money than the rich, and that is the poor." While growing up with no money can be a problem, it is possible to have too much of a good thing. An English proverb states, "An abundance of money ruins youth"—in other words, having lots of money can be detrimental to the healthy development of a child. This can happen because parents, busy with the acquisition and management of their wealth, alleviate their guilt at not being psychologically available by giving presents and money. In essence, they offer money as a substitute for love. But our children need our presence more than our presents.

Can genuine care and love be replaced by money? Not with any hope of healthy development. Money is a poor substitute for love and care. Children raised on this model are generally left with ambivalent feelings toward their caretakers: they are unsure whether their caretakers really love them, indeed whether they themselves are lovable. The result is depressive feelings and a great sense of insecurity, beginning in childhood and lasting into adulthood. Some of these individuals may come to suffer from a disorder comparable to Wealth Fatigue Syndrome: oniomania (literally, a mania for making purchases). They ward off lingering feelings of depression by seeking out the temporary highs they get from spending money. Buying things for themselves makes them feel better but those good feelings are only temporary Band-Aids. As children, these people felt temporary, artificial highs when their parents gave them money to buy things or gifts, and as adults they feel compelled to repeat that pattern. They spend money to feel better, creating an endless cycle of depression and temporary highs.

Money simply cannot give children the inner security and stable sense of self-esteem needed in adulthood. Ironically, it impoverishes them. If you want to see what children can do, you must stop giving them things. When money flows too freely, it's unlikely that important developmental challenges will be handled in an age-appropriate manner by child and parent. The complex psychological work that a child has to tackle to grow into a healthy, responsible adult may be undermined. Money corrupts, just as power corrupts, because it makes us dependent—and a lot of money corrupts a lot. It may impede the establishment of the deep, meaningful relationships that are the cornerstones of mature, healthy functioning and can result in lifelong problems of self-esteem and depression.

When young people have too much money, other people find it difficult to deal with them in a natural way. Wealthy kids given a privileged upbringing may have no sense of how the rest of the world lives. Their developmental experiences are too different than those of others. These two factors—their own lack of real-world knowledge and the discomfort other people feel in interacting with them—exacerbate the struggle to establish relationships. Moreover, the confusion privileged youngsters experience about how they see themselves and how others treat them may impair their capacity for reality testing (that is, make them less attuned to their circumstances and the reactions of others) and make them suspicious about human nature.

Having too much too soon can also impact negatively on motivation. Young people do not learn the value of money when it is always available and fail to understand the energy needed to obtain it. If they never learn what it means to earn money, they may never appreciate the value of hard work. The effects of this go beyond mere finances: young people who have too much money lose the urge to strive, to experiment, to reach out, and to try out new things.

The tale of King Midas, a parable of greed and redemption, is often told to children to help them put money into perspective. According to the story, one day Midas saw an old man asleep under a tree in his private gardens. He recognized the person as Silenus, the teacher and faithful companion of Dionysus, the god of wine. Taking pity on the old fellow, King Midas let him go without punishment. When Dionysus heard this, he rewarded Midas by granting him one wish. The king thought for only a second and then said "I wish that everything I touch will turn into gold." Dionysus tried to caution him about making this kind of wish, but Midas didn't listen. He insisted. And so he was granted the wish.

Midas went on his way rejoicing in his newly acquired power, which he hastened to put to the test. Initially, he was thrilled and turned everything he could touch into gold, including the beloved roses in his garden. His attitude changed, however, when he was unable to eat or drink: his food and wine were also changed to priceless but inedible gold. He finally realized the real depth of his mistake when he turned his daughter into gold. What once was viewed as a marvelous gift, did quite the opposite: it made Midas extremely unhappy. The blessing he had received was really a curse. He could not eat, sleep, drink, or touch anything because everything turned to gold and he missed his daughter terribly.

Finally, Midas went back to Dionysus and told him that he wanted to remove his golden touch. Dionysus laughed when he saw the change in the king but decided to take pity on him and told him to go and bathe in a nearby river. Midas was afraid to get into the water for fear that it would turn into gold and kill him. Instead, he took a jug and washed himself down, filling the jug repeatedly. To his great relief, little by little the gold of his body washed away. Midas took jug after jug of water back to his palace to wash his daughter, servants, horse, and the whole building. He did not stop until he had restored everything to its normal state. After this adventure, Midas was poorer that he had been, but richer, he felt, in the things that really counted in life.

The moral of the story is obvious—"gold" can come in many forms, including happiness, love, and meaningful relationships. It was only when the people and things dearest to him turned into gold that Midas realized the limitations of his way of looking at the world; and it was only by dint of a great deal of hard work that he restored the true value of the things he loved best.

Money should be earned. Real work teaches the value of money, which is why it is important for parents to instill the value of work into their children and make money part of an integrated experience. Without this guidance, children may develop an unrealistic idea of entitlement and assume that everything can be bought and sold for money. They need to realize that the most important ethical and cultural values have no price tag.

As the story of Midas dramatically exemplifies, some people may have lots of money but, when it comes down to it, be very poor. Unfortunately, when money talks it doesn't always talk sense. This places a formidable responsibility on parents to ensure that money talks to their children in the right way. If you want your children to keep their feet on the ground, you need to put some responsibility on their shoulders. The more we shelter children from disappointment, the more devastating future disappointments will be.

Most importantly, your children will see what you're all about by how you live, not what you say. There's nothing more influential in a child's life than the moral power of quiet example. It's pretty hard, however, to start children out in the right direction if that isn't the way you are going yourself. Strangely, we only get a better understanding of what we believe when we start to instruct our children. Do we worry about our children so much because we're afraid they'll grow up like us?

10

YOUR MONEY OR YOUR LIFE

I have mental joys and mental health,
Mental friends and mental wealth,
I've a wife that I love and that loves me;
I've all but riches bodily.

William Blake

The first wealth is health.

Ralph Waldo Emerson

If you make money your god, it will plague you like the devil.

Henry Fielding

Money is a bottomless sea, in which honor, conscience, and truth may be drowned.

Eugene Arthur Kozlay

I have already pointed out the paradoxical nature of money: instead of providing freedom, it imprisons those who covet it; instead of being a possession, it possesses those who hoard it. The lesson to be drawn is that the only wealth that really matters involves things that money can't buy.

"MONEY CAN'T BUY ME LOVE"

Although most of us cheerfully sing along with the Beatles song that claims "money can't buy me love," some of us try to make the purchase anyway. Some people consciously associate money and love; others do so unconsciously. They think that money can buy anything, including a beautiful woman or a handsome man. But while money can trigger a relationship, it can't buy love. Without love, the whole deal is counterproductive: how much does the "purchaser" really care about the person he or she is "buying"? Showing off a trophy wife is just another form of one-upmanship. Money is prone to the same fetishism as sex. Some people believe that the more sex— or money—they have, the more fulfilled they will be; eventually they realize that no amount will ever be enough to satisfy their craving. The problem lies not in having too much or too little, but in using money to replace the things that really count in life.

Money can't buy youth, either, although men and women concerned about the decline in their physical attractiveness often use money to compensate for aging, hooking up with a youthful partner who makes them look and feel better. For these people, "buying" a partner is a stop-gap to fight off depressive feelings.

Whether they are looking for love or youth, some people are prepared to go to any lengths, and spend a fortune, to acquire the right person. There is a certain amount of collusion in this process, however. There are generally women willing to play along, attracted to rich and powerful men and, increasingly nowadays, young men attracted to powerful, wealthy women. As the former US Secretary of State Henry Kissinger said, with some authority, "Power is the ultimate aphrodisiac."

But can collusion ever be the basis for a meaningful relationship? Only very, very occasionally. The late shipping tycoon Aristotle Onassis must have struggled with the issue, for he said, "If women didn't exist, all the money in the world would have no meaning." He knew what he was talking about, having acquired Maria Callas and Jackie Kennedy. Thus while money can't buy happiness, it certainly allows you to choose your own form of misery. And although money can't buy love, it improves your position in the sexual race.

FORFEITING SATISFACTION

Confused? If both poverty and wealth fail to bring us satisfaction, what can? Actually, poverty often does a better job than wealth. While contentment can make poor people rich, discontent can make rich people poor. There is a Turkish proverb that says, "A fool dreams of wealth; a wise man, of happiness." Only someone who does not have any money imagines that money will make him or her happy. The tycoon John D. Rockefeller, a rich man by any standard, said himself, "It is wrong to assume that men of immense wealth are always happy." In fact, a great fortune, like poverty, can become a form of slavery.

People of great wealth often suffer more than others from boredom, depression, and other psychological ailments. Most satisfaction studies have shown that once the basic necessities are met, money doesn't really bring happiness. As the Greek playwright Euripides put it, "When a man's stomach is full, it makes no difference whether he is rich or poor." There is a limit to the number of steaks you can eat in a day.

What is this elusive happiness that we struggle to buy our way into? Sigmund Freud argued that it is the belated fulfillment of an early childhood wish. Anecdotal evidence seems to support that claim: listen to people's stories and dreams, and you'll often hear "feeling good" spoken of in terms of childhood simplicity and togetherness with early caretakers. Very young children do not want money. They want to be cuddled, they want their parents and other loved ones with them, they want to play and explore, and they want to be listened to. Given that, from a developmental point of view, the pursuit of money is an acquired rather than an inherent need, we shouldn't be surprised if suddenly coming into a lot of money doesn't do much for one's feelings of satisfaction, beyond a transitory, exhilarated mood state. For example, studies on happiness show that lottery winners, after a temporary high, return to normal very quickly.

The things that induce lasting feelings of satisfaction are far less tangible. People talk about feeling the joy of achievement, the excitement of creative efforts in working with others, the sublimity of religious celebrations, the rightness of a sense of unity with nature. They talk about enjoying their daily work routine and feeling useful and fulfilled on the job (and yes, as a bonus, sometimes making a great deal of money). And finally—perhaps most importantly—they talk about the warmth and closeness of intimate moments with family and friends.

FORFEITING INTIMACY

Money may buy you a nice dog, but only love will make it wag its tail. Our true wealth lies in the people who care about us, and about whom we care. As I already emphasized in Part One, on sexual desire, attachment behavior is one of humankind's most basic needs. I remember seeing a cartoon that portrayed a balding executive sitting behind a desk, saying, "Okay, I've made it. Now I need love." Sadly, the realization may have come a little too late for him.

In the context of intimate relationships, when money speaks, the truth is often silent. The very rich are always subject to the danger that the people they deal with will tell them only what they think they want to hear. Psychotherapists and psychoanalysts attribute this to the *idealizing transference*—that is, the universal human tendency to admire powerful people. (Here I realize, however, that I'm giving only a partial explanation as we cannot rule out conscious self-serving motives.) Whatever the motivation, money and candor don't go well together. When people bearing big smiles or gifts approach the very wealthy, the recipients always wonder, "Are these people true friends, or are they trying to take advantage of our wealth or power?" As the TV personality Oprah Winfrey once observed, "Lots of people want to ride with you in the limo, but what you want is someone who will take the bus with you when the limo breaks down."

Worse still, the rich sometimes buy into the idealizing transference and self-serving motives themselves. If enough of the sycophants waiting to ride in the limo tell a wealthy man he is the epitome of wisdom, beauty, or skill, he may start believing them, despite evidence to the contrary. This impaired reality-testing can negatively influence the quality of any interpersonal relationships that remain. There is a Yiddish proverb that encapsulates a neat reality check for this: "With money in your pocket, you are wise and you are handsome and you sing well too." And finally, to quote Miguel de Cervantes, "The foolish sayings of the rich will pass for wise saws in society."

FORFEITING TIME

One crucial non-money item is time. So here's another paradox: being rich means having money, being wealthy means having time. If we waste our money, we may end up out of pocket, but if we waste our time, we forfeit—irretrievably—a significant part of our life. Lost money can be replaced through new efforts, but lost time is lost forever. While we are busily pursuing money and material success, we are in effect mortgaging our life. And the payments are onerous: we give up hours and days and months and years of our life to sustain our mortgage. Money can buy you everything except the chance to do it again. And we give up our energy as well. Many people, by the time they have money to burn, discover that their fire has burned out. Their sense of playfulness and imagination is no longer what it was, and they are dull even to themselves.

The very busyness of business obscures the fact that, in life, the journey is all and the end nothing. Unfortunately, many of us come to this realization only when it is too late. We don't understand, or we forget how important it is to be present at critical moments in our family or friends' lives—moments that will fuel our memories in the future. Those moments will never come again, no matter how rich we are. "Your money or your life" holds a deeper truth than the well-known highwayman's threat. Like the characters in *The Treasure of the Sierra Madre*, too many of us equate dollar bills with life. But if we stopped from time to time and took a hard look at ourselves and our circumstances, we would soon realize that dollar bills don't represent what really matters in life. While it's good to have money and the things that money can buy, it's also good to evaluate our priorities once in a while to make sure that we haven't lost out on things that money *can't* buy.

As Ambrose Bierce said in his *Devil's Dictionary*, "Mammon is the god of the world's leading religion." Unfortunately, in this wild dance around Mammon we may sacrifice everything that is essential to life: generosity, compassion, empathy, kindness, fairness, honor, justice, ethics, and esthetics. Moreover, while busily dancing around Mammon, we may forget that while ordinary riches can be stolen, real riches cannot. We all possess infinitely precious things that cannot easily be taken away from us. If we ignore that reality and focus on material wealth over precious intangibles such as time, we will reap what we sow—in other words, if we make money our god, chances are it will plague us like the devil!

FORFEITING INTEGRITY

Those who believe that everything can be done through money are frequently ready to do anything for money, compromising their integrity. Do honesty and material wealth need to be mutually exclusive? Can great fortunes only be acquired dishonorably? A review of the careers of many of the world's super-rich suggests that commerce is rife with immoral, if not villainous, acts. The writer Dorothy Parker expressed this behavior pattern well when she pronounced, "If you want to know what God thinks of money, just look at the people he gave it to." We tend to be much more careful of our money than of our principles.

One of the most dramatic examples of how money can affect an individual's integrity is the story of Kenneth Lay and Enron. For many years Ken Lay seemed to exemplify the American dream. He had a very poor upbringing in rural Missouri; his father was rarely in regular work and Lay contributed to the household income by delivering papers and working as a farm laborer. His parents were determined that their three children should have the education they had missed out on and Lay won scholarships to the state university. He studied business, was an excellent scholar, and was persuaded to stay on to do a masters degree. However, he disappointed his supervisors by insisting on leaving academic life: "I've got to get out and make money." Lay started his career as a corporate economist in Exxon but academia still held appeal: he took time-out to do a doctorate in economics at the University of Houston and worked for a while as a federal energy regulator. He went back into business as head of a Texan gas company that, following the merger of two local firms in February 1986, became Enron. The new company took off during the dot-com-driven stock market boom of the 1990s. By the end of that decade, Enron had been named "America's Most Innovative Company" by *Fortune* magazine for five consecutive years and was on *Fortune's* "100 Best Companies to Work for in America" list in 2000. At its peak, Enron was worth about $70 billion, its shares trading at about $90 each. It had become the seventh biggest company in the US and the world's largest energy trading firm. Lay, as chairman, became one of the best-paid executives in corporate America, making more than $217 million from stock options, and another $19 million in salary and bonuses. He was fêted both in Texas and nationally by influential and powerful people in politics and business (including both presidents Bush) and used a substantial amount of his personal wealth to support a wide range of charitable causes, including those not considered glamorous enough to attract other wealthy benefactors. But while Enron's top executives were counting their riches, the company was bleeding cash.

On December 2, 2001, Enron declared bankruptcy. Thousands of investors—including most of the company's employees—lost billions of dollars as Enron's shares plummeted in value. Twenty thousand people were left jobless when the company's corrupt management (including false profit projections and the use of offshore companies to hide huge losses) was exposed.

Lay continued to protest his innocence as investigators uncovered evidence of the scale of Enron's corruption. He had been lied to and cheated by people who worked for him; he had been working too hard to notice the problem; he was well intentioned toward the company and its people; he had done nothing wrong. On May 25, 2006, Ken Lay and former Enron CEO Jeffrey Skilling were convicted of fraud, conspiracy, and other charges. Lay vowed to clear his name but died of a heart attack before he could be sentenced to what would surely have been a lengthy jail term. Skilling was given more than twenty-four years in prison.

Instead of being remembered as a generous philanthropist (which he was), Ken Lay will always be associated with one of the biggest corporate scandals in US business history. His story is one of hubris and white-collar crime, and tells how a number of smart and powerful men were blinded by greed and brought ruin upon themselves and thousands of innocent victims.

Greed's regress

Is there such a thing as "enough" money? We might think so, but the Ken Lays of the world suggest otherwise. One of the tragedies of human existence is our restlessness: we accommodate ourselves rapidly to the things we set out to accomplish, then become accustomed to and bored with them.

Evolutionary psychologists argue that natural selection has conditioned us to adapt swiftly to new situations and then strive for a little bit more. Satisfaction with a stable state is not conducive to our survival as a species. We need to be kept on our toes. Following this line of reasoning, some of us end up on a hedonistic treadmill, endlessly motivated by the desire for pleasure and the avoidance of pain. And that treadmill never stops, because human desire is insatiable.

And yet can't we accept these findings from evolutionary psychology and still concede that at some point enough is enough? Why is the concept of "enough" so hard to understand? When are we rich enough? When are we successful enough? When are we good enough? Why can't we pick a moment of comfort and satisfaction and decide that we're stepping off the treadmill? The needs of the wealthy seem to mount constantly, as we have seen in the case of Roman Abramovich: first the successful executive wants a sports car, then a house on the Riviera, then a yacht, then a private plane, then multiples and epitomes of those things. Whatever they have, it's never enough. They are always looking out for more; there's always someone who seems to have a better deal. They can't get off the treadmill, and they don't even want to try, from fear of depression. And yet this preoccupation with possessions keeps them from truly living and examining what they are doing with their lives.

If we really believe that our journey is more important than our destination—something with which most people concur in principle but ignore in practice—then we need to focus on our journeying rather than our finances. We need to do things that we enjoy doing and concentrate on the small pleasures of the day. If we focus on finite material achievements, we will experience only a very temporary sense of fulfillment. Acquiring and spending are only very short-term antidepressants that need to be taken continuously. Thus we become like Sisyphus, pushing boulders up the hill, over and over again. Instead of reveling in a glorious sunset or enjoying a family dinner, we stay late at the office doing things we dislike, to be able to buy things we don't need, to impress people we don't care about. How's that for irony?

FORFEITING HEALTH

Money cannot compensate for lost time and lost integrity; neither can it offset lost health. It is only when the rich get sick that they really understand the impotence of wealth. Money can buy us good medicine and good doctors but not good health. It can buy us a comfortable place to sleep but can't ensure sleep itself. It can help us get material comforts but not true feelings of well-being. Ironically, far too many people spend their health gaining wealth, just to spend their wealth trying to regain their health.

That's not to say that the money we have amassed can't have an ameliorating effect as we grow older. When our energy is no longer what it used to be, and our health grows precarious, it is good to have some money set aside. That money not only lets us enjoy our leisure and retirement time, it also helps bolster our sense of self-worth and power. It will give some form of solace when beauty fades. The playwright Tennessee Williams was particularly forthright about this: "You can be young without money but you can't be old without it." Whatever age we are, however, we need to be cautious that money does not overrule the other facets of our lives.

When money is seen as a solution to every problem it can itself become the problem. Instead of finding freedom through money, we become prisoners of money, because it cannot bring us the control or the vindication we may be looking for. Instead, we may have forfeited the essential things in life in our pursuit of it.

11

THE ZEN OF MONEY

When a fellow says it ain't the money but the principle of the thing, it's the money.

Artemus Ward

One must be poor to know the luxury of giving!

George Eliot

Why should people ever take credit for charity when they must know that they cannot gain as much pleasure out of their guineas in any other fashion?

Arthur Conan Doyle

If he had unlimited money at his disposal, he might go into the wilds somewhere and shoot big game. I never know what the big game have done to deserve it, but they do help to deflect the destructive energies of some of our social misfits.

Saki

There is a Zen story that recounts how a famous Zen master was invited to a banquet. He arrived dressed in his beggar's cloths. The host, not recognizing him, chased him away. The Zen master went home, changed into his ceremonial robe of purple brocade, and returned. With great respect, he was shown into the banqueting room. Once there the Zen master took off his robe and laid it carefully on the place where he had been asked to sit. "I have no doubt," he said, "that it is my robe that is expected, as you turned me away from your door when I first arrived,"—and left.

We often respond to the façade, or external presentation of a person, rather than the real person inside the clothes or behind the fancy title. But none of us is wealthy until we possess things that money can't buy.

Since it is highly unlikely that our preoccupation with money will simply go away, we need to learn how to live with the quest for money without losing ourselves to it. We need to realize that in money matters, it's all a question of balance. If too much money can be as demoralizing as too little, how can we juggle our need for it and our fear of it?

Of course, the simplest way of dealing with money matters is to change our need system—that is, to modify our desires. After all, wealth is a relative thing. People who want less may be far richer than people who forever want more. Interestingly, an emphasis on wanting little, on having a simple life, is a common theme in many of the world's religions. Real freedom, according to many doctrines, consists in having no material desires; people are much freer—and indeed wealthier—when they do not have a penny to their name.

This has also been a common theme in Western philosophy: "He is richest who is content with the least," (Socrates); "The greatest wealth is to live content with little," (Plato); "Wealth consists not in having great possessions but in having few wants," (Epicurus). Apparently, we are wealthiest when our minds are satisfied. Can it possibly be true that the greatest single source of wealth we have is between our ears? The pioneer auto manufacturer Henry Ford, who saw the birth and early death of several companies before he hit upon his design for the Model T, thought as much: "If money is your hope for independence you will never have it. The only real security that a man will have in this world is a reserve of knowledge, experience, and ability." It is our capabilities and the wisdom we possess that make us rich. According to Socrates, the best way for people to live is to focus on the acquisition of wisdom and truth. Material production and consumption are not serious ends in themselves, but at best a mere means to achieve something of far greater magnitude. Socrates argued that the challenge of a fulfilled life is to concentrate on building friendships, on creating a sense of true community, and on searching for meaningful pursuits.

The truth of Socrates' assertions is easy to test: if you were told that you had only six months to live, would your reaction be, "I have to make more money" or "I have to spend this time with my loved ones"? It's been said that the best thing that can happen to someone is to have a mild coronary in middle age. That sort of medical emergency provides a compelling opportunity to take a serious look at life. Most people respond to that opportunity by concluding that the greatest wealth is being content with life as it is, appreciating the small pleasures as they come along.

LETTING GO OF MONEY

Another question that has preoccupied philosophers is what should we do with wealth once we have it? The general answer seems to be, put it to work and let it do good in the world. To quote the role model of reflective practitioners, the philosopher-emperor Marcus Aurelius,

"The only wealth which you will keep forever is the wealth you have given away." Much later, two well-known businessmen expressed a similar opinion. "Money is like manure," the billionaire J. Paul Getty observed. "You have to spread it around or it smells." Another tycoon, Andrew Carnegie, came to a similar conclusion: "Surplus wealth is a sacred trust which its possessor is bound to administer in his lifetime for the good of the community."

In 1888, when Alfred Nobel's brother Ludvig died, a French newspaper mistakenly ran an obituary for Alfred, under the heading "The merchant of death is dead." The obituary went on: "Dr Alfred Nobel, who became rich by finding ways to kill more people more quickly than ever before, died yesterday." Nobel's response was one of deep shock: the inventor of dynamite found that he did not want to be remembered as a "merchant of death." The incident motivated him to live his life very differently.

When Alfred Nobel died in 1896, and his will was opened, the world was shocked in its turn. Nobel left nearly all of his enormous wealth to establish five prizes (for physics, chemistry, physiology or medicine, literature, and peace) to "those who, during the preceding year, shall have conferred the greatest benefit on mankind." The Nobel Prize represented the greatest accolade to which anyone could aspire in these fields from its inception.

A more recent example of a remarkable way of dealing with wealth has been presented by Warren Buffett, the billionaire investor of Berkshire Hathaway, who has pledged to give eighty-five percent of his Berkshire stock to five foundations. The largest part of his donation will go to the world's biggest philanthropic organization, the $30 billion Bill & Melinda Gates Foundation. Stating his intention to give his wealth away, Buffett commented, "I'm not an enthusiast for dynastic wealth, particularly when six billion others have much poorer hands than we do in life." In addition, he expressed his hope that other wealthy people "would pick up on this model; I think it's a sensible model."

Alfred Nobel and Warren Buffett demonstrate that the highest use of wealth is not to make more money but to make money do more. Of course, we may wonder whether some of these men—given the ruthless way they acquired their wealth—assumed an altruistic mask to disguise less lofty motivations, such as narcissistic self-aggrandizement. It's certainly true that giving money to worthwhile social causes brings more plaudits than buying expensive cars, lavish yachts, private airplanes, or opulent villas. But even if a desire for recognition is the underlying cause, it is an effective motivator.

Unfortunately, very few people know how to give money away wisely. Strange as it may sounds, philanthropy can be practically and emotionally difficult. Identifying the right causes is not always easy—giving is a very different game from acquiring. There will be some unscrupulous people out there, hoping to get at the money, and there is an emotional dimension as well. Giving away a lot of money might mean dropping off the "world's richest" list. The communications billionaire Ted Turner knows exactly how that feels: "As I started getting rich, I started thinking, 'What the hell am I going to do with all this money?' ... You have to learn to give. ... Over a three year period, I gave away half of what I had. To be honest, my hands shook as I signed it away. I knew I was taking myself out of the race to be the richest man in the world."

In the end, however, all of us want be judged by the way we live, not by our standard of living, and measured by the way we help others, not by our wealth. As I have stated repeatedly, wealth is a state of mind. Anyone can acquire mental wealth by thinking rich thoughts. If we consider ourselves prosperous, we will be. If we see ourselves as continually hard up, that's exactly what we will be.

Until we are happy with who we are, we will never be happy with what we have. Our thoughts and imagination are a great source of wealth, as are our friendships and familial ties, and our ability to take pleasure in the small things of life. I truly believe that the spiritually wealthy are the wealthiest of all—far richer than the richest billionaire, in a commodity that is far more valuable than money. It is our *Weltanschauung*, our outlook on life, which counts, as the following story illustrates.

One day a wealthy businessman took his daughter on a trip to Bangladesh. The purpose of the trip was for her to experience how poor people lived and thus gain an appreciation of her own wealth. They spent a couple of days and nights traveling in the countryside, staying with a poor family in one of the villages. When they returned to Europe, the father asked his daughter what she thought of the experience. She said it had been a fantastic trip.

"Do you now understand how poor people live?" her father asked.

"Sure," said the daughter.

"So what did you learn from the trip?"

"I realized that we have only one dog, while the family we stayed with had four—and cats and cows to boot. We have a large swimming pool but the children who lived in the house where we stayed had the sea that never seemed to end. Behind our house we have a garden where I can play, but these children could play in a whole forest. We buy our food in the shopping center, but they

105

were able to grow their own food. We have a car that seats all four of us, but they had a bus that had room for the whole village." The father's surprised look turned to dismay when his daughter added, "Thanks, Dad, for showing me how poor we are."

Something considered worthless or taken for granted by one person can be the prized possession of another. We need to understand that all our money problems, worries, and shortages largely begin and end with the person staring back at us from the mirror. Although I'm by no means ignoring the fact that real money worries do exist, for many people, worrying about money is simply a state of mind. We are truly rich if we are happy with what we have and what we do. Infinitely more important than money is sharing our human wealth—our time, energy, passions, and intimacy. Those intangibles are the only real security we have in an insecure world. They're our essentials on the journey through life and all we really need to enjoy every moment of that journey.

To sum up, the words of one of England's best-know literary figures, Samuel Johnson, seem prophetic:

> To purchase Heaven has gold the power?
> Can gold remove the mortal hour?
> In life can love be bought with gold?
> Are friendship's pleasures to be sold?
> No—all that's worth a wish—a thought,
> Fair virtue gives unbribed, unbought.
> Cease then on trash thy hopes to bind,
> Let nobler views engage thy mind.

PART THREE: MEDITATIONS ON HAPPINESS

12

LOOKING FOR WILD STRAWBERRIES

One is never as unhappy as one thinks, or as happy as one hopes to be.

François, Duc de la Rochefoucauld

There is no cure for birth or death except the capacity to enjoy the interval.

George Santayana

Happiness does not depend on outward things, but on the way we see them.

Leo Tolstoy

If I keep a green bough in my heart, the singing bird will come.

Chinese Proverb

"Animals are happy as long as they have health and enough to eat," observed Bertrand Russell in his essay *The Conquest of Happiness*. "Human beings, one feels, ought to be, but in the modern world they are not, at least in a great majority of cases." People can be happy only when they feel "part of the stream of life," he observed, "not a hard separate entity like a billiard ball which can have no relation with other such entities except that of collision." In other words, people need people. If we want happiness, we won't find it looking in the mirror; we need to look out the window.

Unfortunately, all too many people are like Russell's billiard balls. Unable to reach out to others, they're islands unto themselves, self-focused and withdrawn, mirror-gazers rather than window-watchers. Eventually, through rampant individualism, they create a veritable prison for themselves, a self-imposed cage of unhappiness. Trapped in neurotic thoughts, they make not only themselves but also others miserable. And they have no idea how to free themselves or how to be good to themselves.

TAKING TWO JOURNEYS

In his film *Wild Strawberries*—an autobiographical tale in disguise—the famous filmmaker Ingmar Bergman tells the story of an old man, Isak Borg, who embarks on two journeys, one from Stockholm to Lund to receive an honorary doctorate, the other into his inner world. To all outward appearances Isak Borg is a very successful man, a respected medical doctor and scientist. However, his personal life reveals a very different picture. His relationship with his aged mother is devoid of warmth, while that with his father (who is apparently out of the picture) is all but nonexistent; Borg's marriage, which was adulterous and unhappy, has ended in a divorce; and Borg has a very distant relationship with his only son. Worse, the son is showing a relational pattern very like his own: an icy formality has grown up between father and son. It is no surprise to learn, in the introduction to the film, that Borg's outlook on life has become increasingly bleak. He is pessimistic about the entire human race. Distraught at the way his life has turned out, he has withdrawn from most human interaction.

During the journey from Stockholm to Lund, Borg—accompanied by his daughter-in-law (who, like Dante's Beatrice, plays a guiding role)—is confronted with various scenes from his past. Many of these revolve around critical incidents and elicit unhappy memories. To counter the feelings these memories stir up—and to avoid being overwhelmed by anxiety and misery—Borg tries to recall happy memories. He tries to return to his "patches of wild strawberries," symbols of the sweetness of life—memories of the fleeting moments of bliss and happiness that we all cling to. As the journey progresses (and Borg is influenced by a number of character-building experiences), his outlook on life begins to change. He becomes happier, more playful. He tries to reach out to people. Unfortunately, this transformation occurs when the clock of his life stands almost at midnight.

Reflecting on happiness tends to send a person on a trip down memory lane. Writing this chapter on happiness has taken me back to my own "patches of wild strawberries," but it's also returned me to the many thorn bushes I've encountered in my life's journey. There are echoes in my own background of both Bertrand Russell's essay and Ingmar Bergman's film. Not surprisingly, then, writing about happiness has been a conflicted process for me. While I've found great pleasure in both the aesthetic aspect of writing (the creation of something tangible) and the pragmatic aspect (the creation of something meaningful), that satisfaction has at times been overshadowed by the personal journey into the self that thinking about happiness inevitably triggers.

110

Happiness is a hard topic to pin down. Feelings of distress are much easier to tackle than so-called positive feelings. They're much more definite, more concrete. Though hard-nosed businesspeople may find it unfortunate, happiness isn't quoted on the stock exchange. It's not something to which a specific value can be attached. It's far less tangible than that—far too elusive. Happiness sneaks up on us, and it slips out of our hands just as quickly. It's often a totally unexpected gift. And yet slippery though happiness may be, its pursuit remains one of the major preoccupations of humankind. I'll try to shed some light on the topic by looking at it from various angles.

Although happiness is rarely mentioned as a goal on a résumé or a corporate report, the topic is nonetheless hard to escape professionally. Over the years, in my role as a researcher, teacher, and consultant, I've studied and given many lectures on the human life cycle, career development, leadership, organizational and personal transformation, and individual and organizational stress. I've listened to many presentations by executives agonizing over the vicissitudes of their careers. Furthermore, as a psychotherapist, psychoanalyst, leadership coach and consultant I've worked to help people make sense of their life's voyage; I've tried to be a guide in their internal and external journeys. And in each of these roles, over many years, I've seen the question of happiness pop up again and again as a key theme. People the world over, from the top-floor corner office to the assembly line, ask, What can I do to become happier? What can I do to improve the quality of my life? What's gone wrong in my work and relationships? Are there ways I can "repair" the conflicts I've created? Nothing triggers the imagination of an educator more than questions to which he has no cut-and-dried responses.

111

13

THE ELUSIVE CONCEPT OF HAPPINESS

And what is Life?—an hour glass on the run
A mist retreating from the morning sun
A busy bustling still repeated dream
Its length?—A moment's pause, a moment's thought
And happiness? A bubble on the stream
That in the act of seizing shrinks to naught.

John Clare
("What is Life?" *The Englishman's Fire-side*)

Two happy days are seldom brothers.

Bulgarian Proverb

Consider the following. We humans are social beings. We come into the world as the result of others' actions. We survive here in dependence on others. Whether we like it or not, there is hardly a moment of our lives when we do not benefit from others' activities. For this reason it is hardly surprising that most of our happiness arises in the context of our relationships with others.

Dalai Lama

The French philosopher Jean de la Bruyère once said, "For man there are only three important events: birth, life, and death; but he is unaware of being born, he suffers when he dies, and he forgets to live." Obviously, de la Bruyère had a well-developed predisposition toward unhappiness. He didn't "enjoy the interval." My objective here, unlike his, is to concentrate on the interval in an effort to better understand what happiness is all about.

The desire for happiness is a universal human characteristic. It was so well developed in the ancient Greeks that they formulated a self-realization theory centered on happiness: *eudaimonism*. Literally, *eudaimonia* means "good spirit" (*eu* plus *daemon*), a word that's usually translated as "happiness." In his *Nicomachean Ethics*, Aristotle examined a range of human experiences. According to him, the highest experience for humankind—and the only true passion—is the attainment of happiness. His definition of happiness is the state of the soul in accordance with virtue. Aristotle saw the search for personal well-being as the most important striving for humankind—the supreme goal of all human activity. *Eudaimonia* is attained, he said, by having a well-ordered lifestyle and engaging in those activities for which one is best suited. He realized that the attainment of happiness is never easy, however: "One swallow does not make a summer, neither does one fine day; similarly one day or brief time of happiness does not make a person entirely happy." As a matter of fact, according to his definition, happiness could only be assessed after a person's death.

But the search for happiness didn't end with the Greeks. It has persisted through the centuries. Even in America's Declaration of Independence—a formal political document—we find the statement that one of humanity's "unalienable rights" is "the pursuit of Happiness." Ironically, Thomas Jefferson (the document's primary author) was a deeply melancholic man who didn't know much about the pursuit of happiness. (And of course we realize that the pursuit of happiness is something quite different from its attainment.)

Many psychologists have tried to make the meaning of happiness more concrete by using terms such as *self-actualization, peak experience, individuation, maturity, sense of flow*, and *subjective well-being*. To most students of the topic these labels imply a sense that life as a whole is good, fulfilling, and meaningful. Unfortunately, *eudaimonia*—whatever label we give it—appears to be only an ideal. Many circumstances, for example illness, injury, lack of education, lack of demand for the activity we want to take on, or inflexible government policies, may prevent us from engaging in what suit us best. And yet despite the ubiquity of such hindrances, for most of us today the pursuit of happiness is the ultimate goal of existence; it gives us hope and a reason for living, motivating us to go on in spite of life's hardships.

So why, despite the almost universal reverence for happiness, does it remain a mysterious concept? Why are we so cavalier about using the word but so hopeless at describing it? Is it because we haven't yet found the answer or because there *is* no answer? Some individuals who have written on happiness believe that it's a subject that shouldn't even be explored. For example, the British writer Gilbert Chesterton noted, "Happiness is a mystery like religion, and should never be rationalized." He preferred not to probe any further, because he felt that the inquiry wouldn't lead anywhere. The American writer Nathaniel Hawthorn said, "Happiness is as a butterfly, which, when pursued, is always beyond our grasp, but which, if you will sit down quietly, may alight upon you."

SEARCHING FOR "PARADISE LOST"

But mystery or no mystery, sporadic efforts at deconstruction have been undertaken. For example, some people have argued that happiness isn't a place or a condition but a state of mind, something that comes from within us—a figment of the imagination, if you will. (That widely accepted view of happiness as a product of our inner world may have contributed to the way it has become cloaked in mystery.) Psychotherapists, on the other hand, have been known to compare happiness to the "Paradise Lost" of early childhood—a vaguely remembered oceanic feeling of total togetherness with mother. (They see evidence of this in the interchange between mothers and infants and in the sense of bliss, or total engagement, revealed in children's eyes when young ones snuggle up to their mother). Many of my patients have spoken of trying to recapture a fleeting memory of a mystical union they once knew—a memory that can be captured for a brief moment only. This perception has been institutionalized in the biblical story of humankind's fall from Paradise. It was Adam and Eve's expulsion from the Garden of Eden that not only brought sin into the world, but also necessitated the quest for happiness.

Some psychiatrists and neurologists, however, have a more cynical view of the subject. They argue that happiness is nothing more than a physiological reaction, a product of body chemistry, or the result of neurotransmitters set into motion. That viewpoint prompts a debate over whether the happiness induced by drugs such as Prozac is real. If the emotion feels the same, and derives from the same chemical source, is it really the same? Is that all there is to happiness? Should we leave it at that?

Regardless of the approach they favor, most people who have studied happiness don't see it as a long-term visitor; only occasionally, they say, does it make its home with us. And yet quite a few people, if asked, would say that they're basically happy—though sometimes more, sometimes less. Perhaps, then, we should compare happiness to the sun breaking through on a cloudy day. Though the rays are seen only sporadically, we know that the sun is always there. And if we try to chase the sun, we discover that it's moving away from us. Frustrating as this may be, it gives us something to strive for.

Ironically, the fact that happiness is never complete or constant is one of its virtues. A state of unbroken happiness would be monotonous at best, a nightmare at worst (like being in a state of perpetual orgasm). In fact, people who profess a constant state of happiness are likely to be diagnosed as hypomanic or in denial by psychiatrists, psychotherapists, or psychoanalysts. In other words, there's such a thing as being too happy. Ups and downs are required to give our experiences color. Dark is needed to highlight light. As Dante Alighieri said in *Inferno*, "No sorrow is deeper than the remembrance of happiness when in misery." Many of us have discovered that there's no pleasure without pain, just as there's no joy without sorrow. Carl Jung concurred when he noted, "Even a happy life cannot be without a measure of darkness, and the word *happy* would lose its meaning if it were not balanced by sadness. It is far better to take things as they come along with patience and equanimity." Paradise without hell would be unimaginable. We need polarities; we need contrasts. There's a good reason Dante dwelled so long in *Inferno* but moved relatively quickly through *Paradiso*.

Having established that happiness is both elusive and ephemeral, what else can we say about it? What are its constituent components? We can't answer that question definitively because happiness means different things to different people. It's a very subjective experience; we all have our own fantasies about what happiness is (or should be). Some people use the label *happiness* to describe a state in which they're no longer plagued by desire (even though not every past wish has yet been fulfilled). Others refer to happiness as the feelings attached to special moments retained in memory—a smile from a loving parent, a successful moment at school, a first love affair, the birth of a child, a reunion of the family, or a get-together with friends. Those of a scientific bent describe happiness as a sense of satisfaction with life as a whole, the absence of negative emotions or psychological distress, a sense of purpose in life, and feelings of personal growth. In all these definitions, though, a positive state of mind is crucial.

POSITIVE PSYCHOLOGY

There is even a relatively young branch of psychology that studies the strengths and virtues that enable individuals and communities to thrive: positive psychology, or the science of well-being. One of the leading figures in the positive psychology movement is the psychologist Martin Seligman who noted in 1998, in his inaugural speech as president of the American Psychological Association, that rather than devoting attention to negative experiences, psychologists should change focus, instead studying people for whom everything was going well.

Positive psychology can be described as the scientific pursuit of optimal human functioning. Its purpose is to explore how individuals derive a positive sense of well-being, belonging, meaning, and purpose in life. Rather than focusing attention on lives that have gone desperately wrong, the idea is that psychologists should change tack, focusing instead on people for whom everything is going well.

Disciples of this school of thought argue that while psychologists know virtually all there is to know about depression, very little time has been given to deciphering the secrets of a happy life. Positive emotions (joy, elation, contentment, pride, affection, happiness) should receive as much attention as feelings that counter happiness (guilt, shame, sadness, anxiety, fear, contempt, anger, stress, depression, and envy). They suggest that the focus needs to be shifted from mental illness to mental wellness. Thus while psychoanalysis once promised to turn acute human misery into ordinary suffering, positive psychology promises to take mild human pleasure and turn it into a profound state of well-being. Furthermore, according to advocates of positive psychology, studying people's well-being opens the door to understanding the prevention of ill health and the promotion of good health. They argue that there is a set of human strengths that can serve as buffers against mental illness: courage, optimism, interpersonal skill, work ethic, hope, wisdom, creativity, honesty, and resilience.

Just as dwelling on negative events can lead to depression, dwelling on things that have gone well can help pick you up. How you see things can matter more than what actually happened. To be seriously happy, according to positive psychologists, we have to set our sights on a good and a meaningful life. To do this we need to identify our signature strengths—the things we are really good at—which could be anything from perseverance and leadership to a love of learning.

Some critics have argued, however, that positive psychology has a very culture-specific outlook, fitting the American emphasis on self-reliance and self-expression particularly well. Others join the choir of critics saying it is nothing new, just a rehashing of older positive-thinking movements. In addition, positive psychologists stand accused of ignoring the fact that depressed, or even merely unhappy, people have real problems that need to be dealt with. It has even been argued that positive psychology has some characteristics of a sect, and cannot demonstrate much scientific research to support its claims.

Whatever criticism positive psychology evokes, there is something to be said about the study of optimal human functioning and the building of a field focusing on human strengths and virtue. It is a worthwhile endeavor to pay more attention to the effects of autonomy and self-regulation, the role of optimism and hope in influencing health, and how creativity can be encouraged.

14

THE HAPPINESS EQUATION

There are three kinds of lies: lies, damned lies, and statistics.

Mark Twain

That action is best, which procures the greatest happiness for the greatest numbers.

Francis Hutcheson

The reason people find it so hard to be happy is that they always see the past better than it was, the present worse than it is, and the future less resolved than it will be.

Marcel Pagnol

If you can't convince them, confuse them.

Harry Truman

Issues of definition aside, most of us agree that obtaining happiness isn't easy. When I ask people if they're happy, I often get evasive and conflicting responses. Many, though, describe their lives as distinctly unhappy. Philosophers, rarely the cheerleaders of the world, are among this cohort. Henry Thoreau believed that "most men live lives of quiet desperation," while Jean de la Bruyère claimed that "most men spend the best part of their lives in making their remaining years unhappy." The lexicographer Samuel Johnson was no optimist either, remarking that "human life is everywhere a state in which much is to be endured, and little to be enjoyed." The psychiatrist Thomas Szasz was even gloomier, alleging that "happiness is an imaginary condition, formerly attributed by the living to the dead, now usually attributed by adults to children, and by children to adults." The filmmaker and writer Woody Allen dresses his dark outlook in lighter colors: "More than any other time in history, mankind faces a crossroads. One path leads to despair and utter hopelessness. The other, to total extinction. Let us pray we have the wisdom to choose correctly."

Are they correct in making these gloomy statements? Or do their words reflect the dark *Weltanschauung* of only a selected few?

117

Do writers, artists, and psychiatrists naturally have a more depressive outlook toward life? Perhaps they do. Surveys about happiness produce optimistic numbers that are hard to ignore, however. In surveys of subjective well-being (conducted in many different countries and subcultures), most respondents score themselves well above the neutral point on a scale of life satisfaction. In other words, they generally score themselves as being more happy than unhappy.

Of course, we can always question the results of such studies, since they're self-reporting. Many processes, unconscious as well as conscious, are at work when people self-report, giving skewed responses. For example, the "social desirability factor"—the human urge to be accepted by peers—might lead someone to exaggerate their happiness to maintain their social acceptability. It's fair, then, to wonder whether people really are happy when they say that they're happy. Researchers who have tried to tackle the question have generally found inconsistent validation of self-reported happiness when family members and close friends are questioned. In my own studies of mood states, however, I've found that a high percentage of people are very good at misleading those who are close to them, both at work and at home.

HAPPINESS FOR THE PURPOSE OF SURVIVAL

Reservations about self-reporting aside, why are the results so rosy? Why do people choose happiness over unhappiness, even when life is hard on them? At the most basic level, perhaps it's a survival mechanism. If we want to survive as a species, we need to avoid the withdrawal and apathy that negative mood states engender. Brooding and navel-gazing don't make for effective action; on the contrary, they impede our efforts to look after ourselves, provide for our family, and serve our community. Because we're social animals, the networks we build are important to building and maintaining society. Our human world functions best when people are able to reach out and engage with others in social interaction. Man alone is much more vulnerable than man as a group. Given all the adversities that we encounter, a team, a group, a clan, a tribe, a nation has much greater efficacy than an individual alone.

In 1999 I spent some time in the rain forest of Central Africa hunting with the pygmies, who are a relatively primitive tribe. During my time with them, it became clear to me that their success as a people was very much influenced by their positive outlook toward life. The pygmies were dependent on each other for survival. They hunted together; they gathered roots and fruits together; they built shelters together; they took care of each other's children. All these activities were done to the accompaniment of cheerful banter—the fruit of a constructive, optimistic outlook on life. From my observations, pygmies are happy people. They have a knack for reframing experiences in a positive way, and they love to laugh and sing. Jokes and laughter were common methods of resolving problems between members of our hunting team. The pygmies' willingness to express positive emotions (and their outright enjoyment of those emotions) makes conflict resolution much easier in all phases of pygmy life. In fact, I discovered quite quickly that a silent pygmy camp—a camp without expressed happiness—is a camp that has problems.

Some social psychologists use the label "the Pollyanna Principle" (named after the heroine of a children's book who always has a sunny disposition) to describe the tendency of humankind to process pleasant information more efficiently than unpleasant. The French expression *la vie en rose* (in English, seeing things through rose-tinted spectacles) is a succinct description of this tendency. When I ask people about their past, in my initial interviews with them, they frequently portray an idyllic picture of childhood. This picture is quickly shattered, however, when I probe deeper and begin to uncover the reality. Cynics say that nothing is more responsible for the "good old days" than a bad memory.

CORRELATES OF HAPPINESS

Interestingly enough, according to evidence from studies on identical twins, the state of subjective well-being that we call happiness appears to be heritable. In other words, there seems to be a genetic component to the ability to be happy, although estimates for the size of the influence vary widely (with the highest at about fifty percent). Whatever the true percentage may be, current thinking is that genetically based personality dispositions (traits and temperament) predispose people to be more or less happy. This heritability factor may explain why the baseline for happiness remains relatively stable throughout their lifetime for many people (with variations on a day-to-day or even an hour-to-hour basis). The temperament bestowed on us at birth seems to play a significant role in the happiness equation.

The French author François de la Rochefoucauld reached the same conclusion without benefit of scientific research: "Happiness and misery depend as much on temperament as on fortune." Does this mean that we might as well give up trying to improve our feeling states? Fortunately not—life is not that deterministic. Because there's no specific gene for happiness, genetics is only part of the picture. While we may be genetically hardwired with certain traits, as I have argued before, this wiring in our brains isn't a static condition. Our developmental and current life experiences make a significant difference to our state of mind. Most scholars who have researched this topic (geneticists included) agree that life circumstances have an influence on subjective well-being. A large measure of what determines the way we feel, think, behave, and act is a result of our upbringing and social and cultural forces. In other words, while genetics plays a part, happiness and unhappiness are also learned behaviors. Many contextual factors play a role in whether we are happy or not.

In addition to showing that people have a tendency toward happiness, survey studies confirm that money doesn't bring happiness. As I explored in Part Two, rich people aren't necessarily happier than people with more modest means, and we don't need to be wealthy or famous to be happy. That said, however, happiness is independent of income level only for those whose basic needs have been met. Among the poorly fed and provided for, there seems to be a positive correlation between income and happiness. The slight increase in happiness that we see when income rises at the lower end of the income range levels off, however, at the higher levels. At all levels, what seems to matter more than absolute wealth is the person's perceived wealth. Feeling rich requires having desires that we can afford. All of us are wealthy to the extent that, rather than seeking to have what we want, we seek to want what we have.

Furthermore, happiness has a slight positive correlation with social status and level of education, perhaps because these factors often raise income levels. Job status and satisfaction have an even stronger positive correlation with happiness. People of working age with no job at all are unhappier than people who are employed. Numerous studies have shown that unemployment contributes to an array of psychological disorders ranging from apathy and irritability to various somatic stress symptoms. These studies also suggest, however, that retired people on the average are happier than people who are still working (that excludes retired people who held interesting jobs that provided a great deal of job satisfaction and who now miss the challenge of their previous activities).

Whether we are young or old makes no difference in the happiness equation. Self-reports of happiness favor no particular age. Childhood happiness by no means guarantees happiness later on, and vice versa, despite the genetic component. Our opening reference to Bertrand Russell's experience is indicative of this. Russell seems to have become happier as life went on. Some happy children turn out to be neurotic and unhappy adults, while many people whose childhood was unhappy are happier as life progresses. Furthermore, age can change the intensity of happiness. We are not necessarily less happy when we get older, but our feelings tend to mellow; we have fewer high highs and low lows—in other words, our feeling of happiness stabilizes.

Happiness is as oblivious to gender as it is to age. The peaks and valleys of happiness between genders may be somewhat different—women are likely to experience greater ups and downs in positive and negative feelings and moods—but the average level of happiness is about the same. Men and women differ, however, in experiencing certain forms of unhappiness. For example, women are twice as likely as men to suffer from depression, while men are more likely than women to behave antisocially or become alcoholic.

People seem to have a remarkable elasticity as far as happiness is concerned. Social science research points out that we adapt to new situations very quickly. Objective life circumstances play a temporary role in mood states, but they have little effect in the long term. Extreme ups and downs in happiness or unhappiness are quickly neutralized through a process of habituation and we return to our customary state of being.

Let's take an example. When I'm at my house in the South of France in the summer and eating white peaches on a daily basis, I enjoy it, but not at the same level of temporary pleasure that miraculously finding a peach in my backpack while hiking in the Pamir mountains or the Altai Republic would give me. I've often hallucinated about those white peaches as I've sat at the top of a mountain, exhausted, sore, and dehydrated. But that anticipated pleasure lessens with continuous satisfaction.

The forefathers of modern economics who introduced marginal utility theory understood this phenomenon well. Herman Gossen expressed it in his "first law," describing how the first strawberry one puts in one's mouth is much more satisfactory than the ones that follow. We all know this from our own experience: the second cup of tea or coffee in the morning is never as delicious as the first; as we eat more and more strawberries, we become sated, and we don't experience the same level of satisfaction as we continue eating. What was once a high, memorable experience quietly slips away. New stimuli need to be pursued to arrive at similar feelings. Fortunately, some experiences—eating strawberries, a good meal, sex—become exciting again after some time has passed. Desire can resuscitate itself.

This human tendency to adapt quickly to a new state of being, reverting to our customary emotional baseline, is called "hedonic equilibrium." Some social scientists use the more negative label "hedonic treadmill," suggesting that we adapt to changing circumstances to the point of emotional neutrality. Researchers have long recognized that as soon as someone improves their life circumstances, their satisfaction with the new situation quickly wears off. Initial highs eventually give way to complete indifference. For example, million-dollar lottery winners—after a temporary state of euphoria—very quickly bounce back to normal state of moment-to-moment happiness. Whatever triggers happiness, our individual personality plays an important role in returning us to our original state of emotional equilibrium.

Since we can be satiated by happiness, we might ask how long a person could really be happy in heaven. While theologians usually describe hell in great detail, they have very little to say about heaven. Perhaps that's because descriptions of life in heaven make it sound rather tedious—happiness, happiness, and more happiness. None of the activities that are really exciting—if sinful—take place in heaven.

Although some of us may find it difficult to imagine, even people who experience an extreme stroke of ill-fortune can find happiness. Studies have shown that people who have been in extremely stressful situations tend to be much less unhappy than others make them out to be. Many victims of extreme ill-fortune feel almost apologetic for not being unhappier than outsiders think they should be. Frank Reed, who was held as a hostage in Lebanon for forty-four months in the late 1980s, attributed the way he coped with his ordeal and his swift recovery from it to his "emotional equilibrium." Questioned a month after his release, during which time he had regained 20 lbs in weight and overcome the severe anemia from which he had suffered during captivity, Reed told journalists that he had "never been a person to go through super highs and super lows ... That may have sustained me during the whole ordeal."

Many people are able to reconstitute their lives and find new happiness after serious physical setbacks. The late movie star Christopher Reeve (well known for his role as Superman) is probably one of the best-known examples of such a turnaround. Despite an accident that left him paralyzed from the neck down, he overcame suicidal depression and found new meaning—and happiness—in life by being a spokesman for paraplegics. "There'll be a lot of nice years ahead," he said after his accident. "The only limits you have are those you put on yourself."

Survey research suggests that happier people fit a generic profile: they are married, don't belong to an ethnic minority group, have positive self-esteem, are extraverted, and have a feeling of personal control. They refrain from dwelling excessively on the negative side of things (they are more optimistic), live in economically developed societies (with a stable political system and political freedom), have social confidants, and possess the resources to strive toward valued goals. They may practice a religion; religious people have established social networks and social support (through the church, synagogue, mosque, temple, or other gathering), especially valuable in times of crisis. They may participate in group leisure activities (social clubs, choirs, team, or sports activities), which offer similar support systems, and be able to take holidays, a break from the daily routine.

The question of causality begins to loom large as we consider these factors. What contributes to what? Are happiness and marriage correlated because marriage brings happiness or because happy people are more likely to find marriage partners? How does the interchange work? Is it the external events that make the difference, or is it our outlook on life—our *Weltanschauung?* Do people who find themselves in a perpetual state of unhappiness perceive and interpret situations more darkly than others do? The findings about happiness and self-esteem, extraversion, personal control, and optimism all point in this direction. Happiness may be, before everything, a state of mind—the way we look at the world. In other words, the way we think about the causes of our successes and failures in life really makes a difference.

15

OUR *WELTANSCHAUUNG*

There is only one way to happiness and that is to cease worrying about things which are beyond the power of our will.

Epictetus

Every man is an architect of his own fate.

Appius Caecus

The novelist Anthony Powell said of one of his characters, "He fell in love with himself at first sight, and it is a passion to which he has always remained faithful." Witty as this observation may be, narcissism is no laughing matter. The satisfaction that narcissism brings is very transient, because self-centeredness hinders the outward focus that is essential to good relationships. Bertrand Russell noted that we should "aim at avoiding self-centered passions and at acquiring those affections and those interests which will prevent our thoughts from dwelling perpetually on ourselves. It is not the nature of most men to be happy in a prison, and the passions which shut us up in ourselves constitute one of the worst of prisons." Among the "passions" that can make us unhappy he listed fear, envy, competitiveness, the sense of sin, self-pity, and self-admiration. He concurred with the idea that, first and foremost, happiness is a state of mind. Extreme self-centeredness is a delusionary way of finding happiness. We have to evict the ghosts that plague us. The art of happiness is to neutralize or minimize the internal forces that torture us. We need to break out of our self-imposed prison. As the saying goes, "Smile and the world smiles with you." Happiness is like a magic potion we cannot pour on others without getting a few drops on ourselves.

Not only do we imprison ourselves with our self-centeredness; we also take on the role of torturer (though admittedly one among many). We are experts at seeking out ingenious ways to make our lives miserable. But why do we do that if, as research findings suggest, happiness is largely dependent on our cognitive state—on how we interpret and respond to situations? Where do our ghosts come from?

124

In almost all cases we are prisoners of our past. As the Danish philosopher Søren Kierkegaard once said, "Life can only be understood backwards, but it must be lived forward." Our internal theater—the themes that influence our behavior—is very much influenced by the kind of parenting we were exposed to. We internalize and model ourselves on the behavior of the people who take care of us during our impressionable years.

Developmental psychologists and cognitive theorists have demonstrated that much of our behavior is learned. The proof of the pudding is that when we unmask our torturer, we see familiar faces behind our own—the faces of the people who raised us. Their admonitions still haunt us: *Don't do that! Put on your jacket or you'll catch cold! If you behave like that, you'll become like your uncle, and you know what happened to him! Don't listen to what your friend says—his parents are no good! Your grandmother was a saint, but your grandfather was a good-for-nothing—and you're behaving just like him! Don't play with that girl; she's a troublemaker!* Messages like these are internalized when we're young (since we model our behavior on that of our parents), and they have an effect on how we interpret life-events over the course of the years.

Many of us turn out to be proxies of our parents, sent on "missions impossible." We carry their ghosts with us in the form of feelings of shame, guilt, anger, anxiety, fear, and sadness. These internalized feelings may continue to haunt us later in life, the critical voices of our caretakers still echoing in our heads and influencing our outlook on life.

As an English proverb says, "All happiness is in the mind." The outlook that we carry into adulthood holds the key to our happiness, since events and situations can be interpreted in very different ways. One person may see as positive the same challenge another sees as negative.

A good illustration is the parable of a poor man who was walking through the woods dwelling on his many troubles. He stopped to rest, leaning unwittingly against a magic tree that would instantly grant the wishes of anyone who came in contact with it. The man was thirsty and thought to himself, "Oh, I wish I had a drink." Instantly a cup of cool water was in his hand. Shocked, he looked at the water, decided it was safe and drank it. He then realized he was hungry. "I wish I had something to eat," he thought. A meal appeared before him. "My wishes are being granted," he thought in disbelief. "Well, then—I wish for a beautiful home of my own," he said out loud. The home appeared in the meadow before him. A huge smile crossed his face as he wished for servants to take care of the house. They appeared and the man realized he had somehow been blessed with an incredible power. He wished for a beautiful, loving, intelligent woman to share his good fortune—and there she was. "Wait a minute, this is ridiculous," said the man to the woman. "I'm not this lucky. This can't happen to me." As he spoke, everything disappeared. He shook his head saying, "I knew it," and walked away, dwelling once again on his many troubles.

This tale re-emphasizes that our *Weltanschauung* matters in the happiness equation. If we depend on others to make us happy, we're endlessly disappointed. We have to take the initiative ourselves. Self-pity doesn't bring happiness, nor does giving up. Most people are as happy as they tell themselves to be. It's the way we think about our successes and failures that makes a difference. Do we dwell on our incapacity to do things? Do we blame others for our failure to solve problems? Or do we tell ourselves that we can make a difference? Let's look now at several more specific ways in which outlook and happiness are related.

INTERNAL VERSUS EXTERNAL LOCUS OF CONTROL

Psychologists sometimes distinguish between two ways of looking at the world. They categorize people as being either internals or externals, depending on their action orientation. An extreme internal is someone who thinks that he or she can do anything; nothing is impossible. Such people imagine that they are in control of their lives. Internals attribute events to themselves; they consider themselves master of their own destiny. They tend to be proactive and entrepreneurial. In contrast, extreme externals see themselves as being victimized by the environment; everything that happens is a question of chance or fate. Externals give up before they even start; they don't think that they can accomplish anything. More reactive than proactive, they lack a sense of personal efficacy. And yet giving up is the ultimate tragedy, because a defeatist outlook results in total passivity—a road that bypasses happiness.

In laboratory experiments in which dogs or rats were given electric shocks, those animals that had no way to avoid being shocked eventually suffered from paralysis of the will and became apathetic. In short, they gave up. Even in new situations they wouldn't try to help themselves. This belief that they couldn't make a difference is known as *learned helplessness*. Like these research animals, human beings in extreme situations—a concentration camp, for example—often lose hope. Their experience teaches them that nothing they do makes a difference. These animal experiments suggest that our cognitive, learned outlook matters.

I've seen many situations of learned helplessness in organizations. For example, take the case of a company that for many years had been led by a conservative, autocratic leader. This person favored centralized power and took care of most of the decision-making. No initiative was permitted without his explicit permission; every decision had to pass through him. Eventually, this firm was acquired by a global company that had a very different outlook on business. When the new executives took the helm, they tried to disseminate their particular philosophy to the employees of the company through words such as empowerment, entrepreneurship, and accountability. But in spite of their encouragement to do things differently—to introduce more contemporary management practices—nothing happened. The employees continued in their usual ways, foregoing initiative and deferring to their supervisors on all decisions. Notwithstanding the new circumstances they found themselves in, the employees were frozen in dependency mode. They didn't know how to take a fresh look at managing the business. Some employees were so bewildered by the new corporate expectations that they left the company. Others, because of their lack of effectiveness, were asked to leave. Serious morale problems followed.

This period of confusion lasted for some time. Gradually, however, with the help of a number of newcomers, most of the remaining employees were able to transform their outlook. They discovered that making decisions on their own didn't carry a penalty—the new leadership had been serious when they said that employees were empowered to take action. They discovered that people who stuck their neck out and engaged in entrepreneurial activities were rewarded rather than punished—even when their experiments were less than successful. It took some time, however, for the employees' trained incapacity to disappear. The previous CEO had given the old employees too many "electric shocks" to allow them to believe that they had some control over their lives. Like the dogs and the rats in the research lab, the employees were initially incapable of moving forward.

Thus internals, who have a more positive, active outlook on life, are more likely to experience moments of happiness than are externals. Perceived control—and even the illusion of control—usually has a positive effect on personal well-being and serves as a buffer against stress. Perceived loss of control or learned helplessness—the perception that all our actions will be futile—leads to a sense of hopelessness and is widely seen as a recipe for depression and other psychiatric disorders.

The moral meaning we can draw from such experiences is this: if we want a shot at happiness, we need to be proactive. Emulating internals, we need to believe that we can make a difference. When someone else writes the script—which is how life is in the externals' world—we're not really living, but just playing a part. Sitting down and waiting for miracles won't get us anywhere, while articulating and doing what we want in life may well lead to meaning and fulfillment. We need to follow our convictions. We need to tell ourselves that we're not merely creatures of circumstances; we're free agents.

OPTIMISM VERSUS PESSIMISM

The link between happiness and personality dispositions is evidenced in our level of optimism as well. Do we see the glass as half full or half empty? Psychologists have known for some time that optimism is a good defense against unhappiness. Are we advocates of positive psychology or do we have a more cynical mindset? Are we optimists or pessimists?

Optimists argue that we live in the best of all worlds, while pessimists *worry* that this may be the case. Optimists look at the bright side of things, seeing each defeat as a temporary setback. When faced with a bad situation, they perceive it as a challenge and work hard to turn it around. They have hope for a better future and believe that they can succeed in what they set out to do. Furthermore, they assume others take a positive view of them. Positive psychologists go as far as stating that optimism can be learned, that we can teach ourselves to see a half-empty glass as half full.

Having a positive attitude toward life makes optimists by definition happier than pessimists. And—a point that positive psychologists emphasize—optimism bears fruit: positive things are more likely to happen to people who think positively. They cope more successfully with stressful events, they enjoy better health, and they're more successful. What's more, their optimism is contagious. One person's positive thoughts trigger positive thoughts in others.

In contrast, pessimists see everything through a negative filter. Regrettably, pessimism often becomes a self-fulfilling prophecy. Pessimists may turn others off with their negative attitude, reinforcing their own negative state of mind. While optimists create their own heaven, and enjoy the ride, pessimists are the architects of their own hell, taking on the role of torturer. Believing that bad events are inevitable and lasting, they give up on hope easily. They feel unable to change the course of events in their lives.

Of course, any outlook toward life needs balance. Too much optimism—and there can be such a thing—leads to self-delusion and self-defeating action, while excessive pessimism leads to paralysis. If we are to engage in effective decision-making, we need the ability to distinguish between the things we can control and those we cannot—a distinction that healthy optimism heightens.

If we lack that ability—if we're externals with a pessimistic orientation—we are susceptible to cognitive distortions. As we saw earlier, those distortions are generally learned; they're hangovers from injunctions given by our caretakers when we were at a vulnerable age. Examples of cognitive distortions are the tendency to see everything in black or white, exaggerating or diminishing events, jumping to conclusions, and "labeling" (the inclination to put people into specific "slots").

When I work with pessimistic executives, I try to help them reframe the way they look at life and at specific situations, encouraging them to take small steps to bring about change even when events seem out of their control. I encourage them to look at setbacks as challenges and to try harder rather than giving up. It's my belief—a belief supported by evidence—that we can *think* our way to success and happiness, just as we can think our way to failure and despair. Optimism is the best antidote to helplessness, enabling us to bounce back from defeat.

EXTRAVERSION VERSUS INTROVERSION

Along with optimism-pessimism and an internal versus external locus of control, extraversion plays a role in happiness. Extraverts tend to be more sensitive than introverts to the external environment. Because they react more strongly and more affirmatively to positive emotions in that environment, they seem to find it easier to be happy.

An indirect mechanism further links extraversion and happiness. Extraverts are better able than introverts to search out people and engage positively with them. Given societal demands for social involvement, this trait allows extraverts a better fit in the world. And because outgoing personalities feel more comfortable in social situations, they engage in more social activities. This explains why, in general, sociable, outgoing people have a greater sense of satisfaction with life. As the writer Aldous Huxley once said, "Happiness is not achieved by conscious pursuit of happiness; it is generally the by-product of other activities."

HIGH VERSUS LOW SELF-ESTEEM

Another element of our *Weltanschauung* is our sense of self-esteem. For happiness to visit us we need a positive self-regard characterized by qualities such as self-acceptance and self-respect. Indeed, one of the best indicators of happiness appears to be how comfortable we are with ourselves. People who like themselves find it easier to open up to others. That self-disclosure, and the two-way communication that generally results, helps to create bonds with others. People who engage in open communication have a wider social network and more social support, and engage more frequently in satisfying social undertakings.

People with low self-esteem, on the other hand, are more likely to display socially withdrawn, self-centered, antagonistic, or brooding behavior. While those with high self-esteem see themselves as masters of their domain, believing that they can make a difference, those with low self-esteem tend to engage in scapegoating and other defensive behavior patterns. There is a strong correlation between low self-esteem and psychological disorders, especially depression.

This brings us back to the question of nature versus nurture. Are positive self-esteem, extraversion, optimism, and an internal locus of control largely the result of genetic predisposition—that is, entirely predetermined—or do we have the power to affect our destiny? Fortunately, as we saw earlier, the genetic influence on personality traits isn't completely hardwired. We're left with quite a bit of room to maneuver. We should view the personality dispositions we display in adulthood as an intricate interplay between nature and nurture. While the nature component is strong, there is ample space for developmental influences including—as neurological research is demonstrating—developmental changes later in life. We do have the power to affect our destiny, but we need to want to do it. By reminding ourselves what went well instead of what went wrong in life, we may be able to build a buffer against unhappiness, making us better able to take life's knocks when they come along.

16

DECONSTRUCTING HAPPINESS

Not in Utopia—subterranean fields,—
Or some secreted island, Heaven knows where!
But in the very world, which is the world
Of all of us,—the place where, in the end
We find our happiness, or not at all!

William Wordsworth

Enjoy yourself; it is later than you think.

Chinese proverb

Some cause happiness wherever they go; others whenever they go.

Oscar Wilde

In an old Chinese saying, happiness is said to consist of three things: someone to love, something to do, and something to hope for. There's a lot of truth in this observation. We need love and hope in our lives, and we need activity. Sigmund Freud thought similarly: in his view, the two pillars of mental health are the ability to love and the ability to work. Unfortunately, workaholic that he was, Freud failed to note that play is also an essential part of human nature. We all have an exploratory, motivational side—one that we see in small children as they experiment and try new things. People whose work feels like play are fortunate indeed.

Let's take a closer look at the three elements of that Chinese proverb: someone to love, something to do, and something to hope for.

SOMEONE TO LOVE

All of us need someone to love, someone we can feel close to and confide in. The first love relationship we experience (if we're among the lucky ones) is with our parents. Later, other family members come into the picture: grandparents, brothers and sisters, perhaps

131

aunts, uncles, and cousins. When we grow older, there are friends, a spouse, and children. Sharing experiences with these people is part and parcel of the happiness equation.

Happiness cries out to be shared. It's like an embrace: for many of us the best way to enjoy it is by sharing it. In fact, happiness that's shared is double happiness, while happiness hoarded is empty. The secret of happiness is the ability to find joy in another's joy, the desire to make *other* people happy. To experience true happiness, we need to learn to forget ourselves, because self-centeredness and happiness are mutually exclusive. We need instead to be generative; we need to care about others. Many of us have seen this phenomenon in action: when we bring sunshine into the lives of others, we get some rays in return. Even the littlest things can produce moments of happiness—a smile, a hug, and a heartfelt thank-you. These little gestures can turn into glorious feelings for both giver and recipient.

The reason true happiness frequently only comes through sharing is that (as I have explored in my chapters on sexual desire) the human need for connectedness runs deep. From birth onward, there are many fibers that connect us to the human community. As mentioned before, social networks are critical to a person's well-being. Attachment behavior is a deeply ingrained motivational human need. We have a great propensity to establish affectionate bonds with our mother and other caretakers as a means of establishing a feeling of security. As I earlier suggested in my discussion of attachment behavior, many forms of stress, and disturbances such as anxiety, anger, and depression, are the result of unwilling separation and loss.

Among humans there exists an innately unfolding experience of human relatedness. Humankind's essential humanness is found in seeking relationships with other people, in being part of something. No person can remain an island unto himself or herself, notwithstanding the literary fantasy figure of Robinson Crusoe. The need for attachment concerns the process of engagement with another human being, the universal experience of wanting to be close to others. It also concerns the pleasure of sharing and affirmation. When this need for intimate engagement is extrapolated to groups, the desire to enjoy intimacy can be described as a need for affiliation. Both attachment and affiliation serve an emotional balancing role by confirming the individual's self-worth and contributing to his or her sense of self-esteem. Having close ties to friends and loved ones and being a member of a community of people are essential aspects of becoming a person. They're critical not only to mental health but also to happiness.

Remember, though, that loneliness is not the same as being alone. Being alone is solitude; feeling alone is loneliness. The latter is an indicator of poverty of self. It signals an inability to reach out, to transcend one's personal sphere, and it suggests underdeveloped social skills. Worse yet, loneliness is self-perpetuating: people unable to reach out to others have little hope of breaking their loneliness pattern. And yet a Moorish proverb suggests that, "to die with others is better than living alone."

One of the most intense love experiences that people have comes through close partnership. As I have discussed previously, the most satisfying relationships people are involved in are the truly intimate ones. A relationship such as marriage brings out extremely intense feelings—including happiness. For many people, the intimacy of a true love affair results in many happy memories—memories that reinvigorate during down times.

Researchers on family dynamics have shown that the amount of time couples spend together—their level of companionship—determines marital as well as overall happiness. As Friedrich Nietzsche once said, "The best friend is likely to acquire the best wife, because a good marriage is based on the talent of friendship." When we experience genuine physical *and* psychological intimacy, we go from strength to strength. This intense relationship helps us to develop and grow; it serves as a base for both greater self-understanding and greater understanding of others. Bearing and raising children is often part of this learning process. Children are important as engineers of happiness because they're catalysts, helping their parents transform from a self-centered view to a more mature, exocentric perspective on life. Young children are the greatest narcissists in the world; they "teach" that happiness is often greater when it comes through giving rather than receiving. Thus, having children is a developmental experience that contributes to happiness.

Although the good memories that grow out of an enduring partnership serve as a buffer against the stresses of life, spouses can also play an important containment function, helping each other overcome conflict and anxiety. If there's mutual affection and trust in a marriage, the spouse takes on the role of "container," or confidant. Although having a loving spouse may be the best option, this role can also be taken up by close friends. For many, true happiness is felt while in the company of good friends.

We draw great comfort from our friends when times are tough. Because friends help us work our way through life's obstructions, they're instrumental in creating happy moments. They also serve as a kind of supplemental memory bank, helping us recall experiences and things about ourselves, including happy memories that we've forgotten. They affect our physical well-being as well: research has shown that having someone to confide in reduces stress, appears to strengthen the immune system, and boosts longevity. Talking about intimate things—engaging in self-disclosure—has great prophylactic value. Sigmund Freud, when he started to experiment with psychoanalysis, referred to the process of encouraging people to talk about whatever came to mind (unscreened by the normal conventions of daily life) as "the talking cure."

Unfortunately, friendship isn't particularly easy. It isn't something we can buy in a store or create with a wish or a snap of the fingers. Building a friendship—and that includes a relationship with a partner—requires hard work and determination. We have to make an effort to understand and help others, giving a part of ourselves away in the process. And if we think only of ourselves—if we engage in excessive narcissistic behavior—it's very difficult to establish real friendships.

The groundwork for most friendships is laid early in life, during childhood, high school, and university. Friendships develop so easily in our youth that we take the whole process for granted. But keeping friends—that's another story; it doesn't occur the least bit automatically. Keeping a friendship going, helping it to develop and mature rather than allowing it to stagnate, is a delicate process. Friendships are fragile entities that require care, nurturing, and even sacrifice. Maintaining friendships involves being loyal, affectionate, sympathetic, and ready to help when the need arises. But we're amply repaid for our efforts: having a friend means ready access to a willing ear, an understanding heart, and a helping hand. As a caveat it can be said that a person's character can often be assessed in the selection of his or her friends.

What happens to our friendships as we grow older? Do the crucial links we made early in life remain intact, or do we lose sight of the people who once were our friends? For many people the answer to the second question is affirmative. And yet despite the fact that friendships are often very transitional, they become increasingly important as we age. In middle age and onward, they're needed more than ever before. However, for many of us, the opportunity to make new friendships seems to diminish after the early stages in life. As a result, the friends we lose aren't replaced.

And lose them we do. Sometimes distance separates us; sometimes our interests diverge; sometimes one of us outgrows the other; sometimes we drift apart for lack of effort. Even marriage can be a factor in the dissolution of other friendships. If the marriage bond is particularly intense, all others may pale in comparison. Furthermore, the exclusivity of a partnership may bring out negative feelings such as jealousy. A spouse may look at the friend as a bad influence or find certain of the friend's behaviors disturbing. When the chemistry isn't right between a partnered couple and a particular friend, a difficult choice has to be made. Having young children—with all the caretaking that this implies—may also hamper friendships. Taking care of kids often triggers an inward-looking pattern that leaves little time for the development of new friendships or the cultivation of old.

But not all friendships end deliberately. As we get older, death becomes a more frequent visitor, diminishing our circle of friendship against our will. All these transformations point out the need to be active in maintaining friendships. Samuel Johnson coined it very succinctly: "If a man does not make new acquaintances as he advances through life, he will soon find himself left alone. A man should keep his friendships in constant repair." Since life doesn't stand still, we need to look forward, not just back. We need to be proactive in searching out people with whom we feel compatible, showing an interest in them rather than waiting for them to show an interest in us. If we don't make an effort to establish new friendships, we may find ourselves all alone in old age—a situation that unbalances the happiness equation.

It's important to treat the people we're close to—partners, friends, neighbors, and colleagues—as we'd like to be treated ourselves. Confucius' excellent advice was, "Behave toward everyone as if receiving a great guest." Being fair to others is important as we pass through life, partly because we inspire fairness in return. If we treat people well, it's likely that we'll be treated well by them; on the other hand, if we feel a sense of entitlement and demand special treatment from those around us, it's likely that we'll alienate loved ones, souring crucial relationships.

Giving fair treatment—that is, ensuring reciprocity in our relationships—requires the ability to place ourselves in another person's shoes. That's why true narcissists, with their non-empathic outlook, have a hard time establishing real friendships. They simply can't imagine how it feels to be in someone else's situation. People with certain other personality disorders—those who are narcissistic, paranoid or schizoid, for example—shouldn't apply for friendship either, given their similar problems with empathy.

The reason empathy is such a critical element in interpersonal relationships is that life is a process of social exchange. People make calculations—though not necessarily consciously—about what they get out of every relationship. Given the principle of distributive justice and equity that's at work in every human interaction, what we put into a relationship and what we get out of it have to remain in equilibrium.

SOMETHING TO DO

There's a cartoon from *The New Yorker* that shows an executive coming home from work, entering the house briefcase in hand. His wife looks at him expectantly, as if having asked him how his day went. The caption reads, "What kind of day it was? Well, it was a day like any other day. I loved, I hated. I laughed, I cried. I felt pain, I inflicted pain. I made friends, I made enemies."

As the cartoon suggests, work, the second pillar of happiness, ties a person to the human community. It adds purpose to our living. It stimulates the senses. That's why work is essential for our mental health. People who have nothing to do tend to be unhappy. Paradoxically, the hardest work of all may be doing nothing.

Consider Oblomov, a prime example of impaired work performance. The eponymous hero of this tragic tale of passivity, apathy, and indolence, as told by the nineteenth-century Russian novelist Ivan Goncharov, retains his powerful imagery to the present day. Oblomov is an exemplar of arrested character development, an individual incapable of going beyond a functionally vegetative state. Sapped by passivity and apathy, he found both life and suicide too challenging. Oblomov never really lived his life (or what we think life is supposed to be) at all. He simply stayed in bed. (Of course, one could argue that bed is exactly the place to be if one wants to avoid risk. On the other hand, most deaths take place in bed.) Oblomov replaced real action with daydreams and fantasies, transferring to the reader his own sense of impending doom and futility. While Oblomov's is an extreme case, it warns us of possible consequences of the passivity and inertia that we may fear in ourselves. Work in and of itself isn't the answer, however. Doing work that brings no satisfaction is likewise very draining. As the writer Maxim Gorky once said, "When work is pleasure, life is a joy. When work is duty, life is slavery."

One of the best prizes in life is the opportunity to work at something we like and are challenged by. Unfortunately, far too often and for far too many of us, work is drudgery. Workplaces take on the appeal of concentration camps. While economic necessity forces some people into work that they find meaningless, many of us can afford to be selective. Unless we find ourselves unable to climb out of that first category, we need to stick with the good stuff and trim off the useless branches, focusing on work that we can do well and that makes us feel really alive.

If happiness is a goal, we should also look for work that gives us a sense of purpose. When we feel that what we do makes a difference, our life has more meaning. Work that allows us to feel that we're making a contribution, work that really absorbs us, work that demands our total concentration—is the kind of work that makes for happy moments and creates happy memories to sustain us in difficult times. If we completely lose our sense of time when we're working and if we are not fatigued at the end of the day, these are good indicators that we're doing this kind of work. There is a German proverb that says, "When a man is happy, he doesn't hear the clock strike." As important as meaningful work is, however, it's not as crucial as close relationships. Even the person who spends every day waiting for the five o'clock whistle to blow may consider himself or herself happy with a loving family and good friends to spend his or her free time with.

SOMETHING TO HOPE FOR

Finally, we all need hope in our lives; we need something to strive for. Meaningful work is one of the ways in which we create hope but there are many other routes to take. Hope is a vital element of the human condition, spurring us on and encouraging us to explore and grow. As we go through the process of discovery that each life is, the makeup of our desires—the profile of our hope—is the only real boundary we face. Thus the way we cultivate or abandon hope is an important part of our inner theatre and a key element in the script of life.

Although we tend to think of hope as something ephemeral, it can also be tangible. It can take on many forms—a new love affair, an exciting job opportunity, the building of a dream house, a special trip. There's something for everybody. The images attached to hope are registered with the other good memories that sustain us when times are tough.

Hope gives us a sense of direction in our journey through life—a sense of where we want to go. In fact, without hope, why undertake the journey at all? With despair at the helm, we might end up somewhere we don't want to be. Hope takes the edge off melancholy and despondency and helps us to remember that the sun is always there above the clouds, even if we can't see it.

People who have hope have an easier time dealing with the misfortunes that are part and parcel of life's journey. They look at setbacks as temporary states, not permanent conditions. They get new strength out of the fact that they see each adversity as limited in time. They don't despair. They are persistent; they don't give up easily.

We can reframe the concept of hope by referring to dreams. Because dreams give life meaning, emptiness and despair flourish in their absence. A life without dreams is little more than death. And yet our dreams often seem distant; they hover in the sunshine, tempting but elusive. Often they truly are beyond our grasp. But even if we're never able to touch our dreams, we can look up to them and believe in them, and try to live our life accordingly. Our dreams can spur us on to higher and better things. Without dreams, we might just as well operate on automatic pilot, leading a life without poetry or joy.

The most impressive feats in the world have been accomplished by people who've had big dreams. But to be able to dream, we have to believe in ourselves. We have to have faith that we can be what we aspire to be. When we look at individuals who've made a difference in the world—famous dreamers such as Mahatma Gandhi, Martin Luther King, Jr., Mother Teresa, and Nelson Mandela—we see the evidence of dreams that gradually crystallized over time, enduring despite the obstacles in the way. These dreamers envisioned lofty ways to create a better world and then set about realizing their dreams, one step at a time.

The example of these individuals tells us that we should hold on to the dreams of our youth, or at least retain our willingness to dream the way we did then—to aim for the stars, transcending what others think is possible. "We are all in the gutter," Oscar Wilde said, "but some of us are looking at the stars."

But dreams are delicate flowers, easily crushed. That's the reason many of us find it difficult to talk about our dreams or to share them with others. We are afraid that people will laugh at us, deride us, and consider us fools. Yet that's a risk we need to take. If we dare to share our dreams with a few select people we trust, those loved ones can help us hold on to our dreams. Even if our worst fears come true and our dreams are dismissed as foolish, we need to pursue them relentlessly, because our chance for happiness lies in that pursuit. We're the architects of our own ambitions. We're happy as a result of our own efforts once we know what course to take. Dreams are our possibilities. We need to use all our talent and energy and courage to fulfill those dreams.

Unfortunately, there's a dark side to dreams as well. Excessively high aspirations, as symbolized in these kinds of dreams, can be as great a threat to happiness as a lack of dreaming. When challenges consistently exceed our abilities, we become stressed. If the discrepancy between where we are and where we'd like to be or where we feel we ought to be is too high, we may become depressed and unhappy. If we stop worrying about things that are beyond the power of our will, however, we'll feel much better. It's often better to break big dreams down into manageable parts. Think big thoughts but enjoy the small pleasures. Doing so gives us a sense of control and lets us celebrate small milestones along the way.

For example, if a publisher asks me to write a book and suggests that it should run to about three hundred pages, it seems a daunting assignment. But if I break that assignment into manageable parts and resolve to write three pages a day, the task is more manageable. I feel good about myself each day when I've fulfilled that specific commitment. And earlier than I had expected, the book is ready to be handed to the publisher. Nothing is impossible if we divide it into small jobs. In any case, the process of moving toward our dreams may be more important to the feeling of happiness than reaching that goal.

People without dreams feel disoriented, drifting restlessly through life. Sometimes only an enforced challenge such as a life-threatening accident, a serious illness, or a dramatic outside event, such as a war, can save them. Paradoxical as it sounds, such events give people a new lease on life because they force a hard look at reality. People who have come through such circumstances often reset their priorities, reestablish floundering relationships, and identify and pursue meaningful tasks and commitments. Drifters thus are given a new beginning, and happiness may follow.

One of my students gave me a vivid description of how he was almost crushed under debris following a bomb explosion in a hotel in Lebanon during the internecine war that took place in that country. He had been a rather confused, happy-go-lucky drifter until this experience, which transformed him. Getting out of the rubble relatively unscathed made him really appreciate being alive. He felt as if he had been reborn. Having become a "twice born" (to quote the psychologist William James), he rearranged his priorities. He felt that he had been given a new chance in life and didn't want to waste any more time. He returned to his medical studies, became a physician, and turned into a major AIDS activist, spending most of his time in Africa implementing preventive programs.

Even if we firmly believe in our own efficacy, pursuing our dreams can be daunting. Those dreams can seem so formidable, and our powers so slight. But life is made up of little things. When we tackle our dreams step by step, they're achievable. The sage Lao-Tzu said, "The journey of a thousand miles begins with one step." The greatest things ever done in life have been done little by little. Our initial efforts, paltry though they may seem, can turn into big things later. Those tentative first steps point us in the right direction and color the rest of the journey.

17

STRIKING THE RIGHT BALANCE

I have measured out my life with coffee spoons.

T. S. Eliot

What I dream of is an art of balance, of purity and serenity devoid of troubling or depressing subject matter... a soothing, calming influence on the mind, something like a good armchair which provides relaxation from physical fatigue.

Henri Matisse

Man is fond of counting his troubles but he does not count his joys. If he counted them up as he ought to, he would see that every lot has enough happiness provided for it.

Fyodor Dostoyevsky

Happiness is no laughing matter.

Richard Whately

Even when we have people we love, work that's meaningful, and hope to sustain us, happiness can be elusive if we fail to keep our private and public lives in balance. Achieving balance sounds like a simple goal, but it's easier said than done. The pressures of the workplace can be tremendous. Because the corporate culture of many organizations negates family values, those pressures affect not only the employee but also the family. And as if workplace pressures weren't enough, we're apt to throw in a few self-inflicted ones. We may be trapped in a career maze, for example, obsessed with beating our office competitors to the next step in the career trajectory. And yet when we confuse happiness with success—at least the outward version of success, as represented by wealth, position, power, or fame—we all but guarantee that the various components of our life will be thrown out of joint (though the unbalancing process can be so insidious that we don't realize what's happening).

LIVING A WHOLE LIFE VERSUS A DEFERRED LIFE

The fact that many of us are masters of self-delusion, having a great capacity for rationalization and intellectualization, adds to the disequilibrium between private and public life. We try to fool ourselves into believing that we're well balanced. For example, most people, when asked how much time they spend at home, give an answer that's far from the truth (though they don't necessarily distort the facts consciously). And even those who are aware of the disproportionate amount of time they spend at the office may console themselves by referring to their non-work time as "quality" time. They may try to convince themselves that it's not the length of time they spend at home with the family that counts, but rather the quality of that time. But do they really believe what they say? And would the other members of their family agree with their conclusions?

I often hear executives say that they're working very hard now so that their wife and children will have a better life later. (It is usually men who make this comment.) All too frequently, however, when this famous "later" arrives, there's no longer a wife. She's moved in with someone else, and the children have become strangers. They call another man "Daddy" and don't really know their father any more. All that the dedicated worker gets for following the build-for-the-future, deferred-life strategy is isolation and loneliness. It seems to be so much easier to make a success of oneself than to make a success of one's life. We can get 'A's in all our courses but flunk life itself.

We need to remind ourselves, as we strive for that first kind of success—the kind that, as a Yiddish proverb says, "makes you drunk without wine"—that certain important moments will never come back. We need to cherish those passing moments; we need to seize the day. Life isn't a rehearsal; it's the real thing. If we want to enjoy life, we have to do it today, not tomorrow nor some faraway time in the future. We have to ask ourselves what we really want. Do we want a whole life or a deferred life?

Many investment bankers and consultants at high-powered firms I've worked with have struggled with this choice. Some of them, because of hardships experienced at an impressionable period in their lives, made an early and deliberate career decision never to be poor again. Their main goal in life was financial independence. Through extreme hard work, they succeeded in meeting that target, often acquiring money beyond their wildest dreams. To quote one person, "I earned more money in one year than my father did his whole life."

People caught in this bind are like rats on a treadmill, unable to get off. As they meet the initial need for financial security, new needs— mostly imagined, as I discussed in Part Two, on money—begin to emerge. They want a bigger house, a more exclusive sports car, and a special summerhouse. Their "toys" get more expensive as well. The more they have, the more they want, not realizing that happiness doesn't cost anything. They mutter that they're going to stop working soon; that they're going to pursue the things they've always wanted to do soon. Sometime in the future, when they have more time, they'll take piano lessons again; sometime in the future, they'll go back to university to do art history; they'll take up painting. But that "sometime" never seems to come around. And in the meantime, life is passing them by. Even if their work is exciting, they're leading a one-dimensional life. There's no time for anything but work. Such people have mortgaged the present for the future (or so they hope).

Sometimes we want to live for today but feel that we don't have the luxury of that choice. Perhaps there's an overseas trip that just can't be missed if we want to be promoted, even though it means missing a son's birthday. Or a presentation that has to be given (and given well) if we hope to boost our sagging sales figures but conflicts with a daughter's tennis competition. These are difficult choices, to be sure, especially with a job or career on the line. But the family is on the line as well. Kids grow up and leave home quickly enough. Before we know it, we no longer have any influence in their lives; they make their own decisions without consulting us. And if we were seldom with them in their early years, what will our legacy be? How will they remember us? What will they say at our funeral (and what would we have liked them to say)?

A fulfilling life is meaningless unless it's lived in the present. Far too many of us fail to live for today. And yet if we put all our energy into reaching out for the future, the things that are now within our grasp will be lost. Nothing matches the pain of realizing the full importance of time only when there's very little of it left.

The most important influence on the life of any child is the parents, who shape character and values through personal guidance and unconscious suggestion. How can we help our children grow up as well-rounded adults if we're not there? How can we instill values if we're always at the office? How can we give our children valuable memories if we're too busy to spend time with them? The bottom line: despite all the fantasies about quality time, meaningful relationships imply sustained relationships.

With organizations as demanding as today's typically are, we have to be firm in setting boundaries in order to preserve those aspects of life that are truly important. Perhaps if enough people speak up, in this age of the knowledge worker, employers will have no choice but to make the proper adjustments. And even if we have to take a solitary stand on this issue, our efforts at balancing life are an investment in the future. No one on his or her deathbed has ever been heard to say, "I should have spent more time at the office." Having special moments with family members is critical to the attainment of happiness. Furthermore, being able to look back at these moments with happiness is to enjoy life twice.

OUTWARD SUCCESS VERSUS INNER SUCCESS

Albert Einstein had a formula for success that says a lot about balance—$A = X + Y + Z$—where A stands for success, X stands for work, Y stands for play, and Z stands for keeping one's mouth shut. Like Freud with his formula of love and work, Einstein pointed out some of the essentials that affect happiness.

No person will ever know true happiness without having a few successes to his or her credit. Success creates a feeling of competence, a sense that one is capable of addressing creatively the demands of any situation. A satisfactory self-evaluation depends on meeting personal or group-determined standards. In other words, it relies on comparison against an explicit or implicit goal. However, successful accomplishment of a specific goal or broad dream doesn't guarantee happiness. The destination we reach after months or years of striving may turn out to be a disappointment. That discovery can plunge us into despair, if we let it, or it can prompt us to embark on a new journey—one that will foster meaning and happiness.

True happiness depends on our coming to grips with feelings of inner restlessness and anxiety resulting from self-imposed perceptions of a discrepancy between where we are and where we would like to be—that is, the comparison between our aspirations and our actual achievements. And for many of us that discrepancy looms large. The fact is, we won't all be CEOs; we won't all discover the cure for cancer—and we need to accept that. Our success needs to be measured not by what we've achieved but by the obstacles we've overcome. We need to celebrate the small victories along the way.

As I already emphasized in Part Two, on money, many of us tend to focus on outward success—what we equate with wealth, position, power, and fame; we think that happiness consists of having and getting. But pursuing those goals is like chasing a rainbow. All we see when we arrive is a gray mist. What makes for happiness is inner success—the kind that results from living life to the fullest. Play and listening—in Einstein's equation, keeping your mouth shut—are essential to inner success, because they help us to acquire precious possessions such as friendship, love, goodness, concern, kindness, and wisdom. The success that really satisfies and contributes to moments of happiness often comes to people who aren't looking for it. That's because the road to true success lies off the beaten track.

Not only is the outward success of the beaten track ephemeral, it's downright dangerous. I firmly believe that the unrelenting pursuit of outward success is one of today's chief sources of unhappiness. An obsession with success can have serious dysfunctional consequences, because it snowballs: people driven by success are rarely satisfied, no matter how high they climb—no accomplishment gives lasting satisfaction. Whenever they reach one level of success, they imagine yet another, higher level. The income they once dreamed of now looks like a starvation salary. It comes down to this: people who equate happiness with success will never achieve enough success to be happy. They're like Sisyphus, interminably pushing a rock up a hill. Ironically, Sisyphus's only period of happiness was probably that short moment when the rock was rolling down—when he wasn't pushing, when he had time for self-reflection. But self-reflection would probably have been the last thing he'd have wanted. His conclusions would have been depressing indeed.

The inner restlessness and discontent that accompany the pursuit of external success have ruined many a person. Paradoxically, happiness rests on being satisfied both with what we have and what we don't have. That dual satisfaction is a solid foundation for a feeling of well-being. The happiest people are often those who are content with their present state, and who don't want things they can't get.

18

PUTTING THINGS IN PERSPECTIVE

He will be loved when dead, who was envied when he was living.

Horace

Envy never makes holiday.

Francis Bacon

Fools may our scorn, not envy raise,
For envy is a kind of praise.

John Gay

The neighbor's cooking always smells better.

Maltese proverb

An important ingredient in the recipe for happiness is comparison, though too much of that essential ingredient can spoil the stew. Let's look at the ways comparison can further or hinder our happiness, something in which envy once more plays a prominent role.

Putting things in perspective, regularly reminding ourselves that our life isn't that bad after all, helps to keep unhappiness at bay. This healthy process can involve both intrapsychic comparison (when we compare our present state to a past, less desirable state) and interpersonal comparison. We might, for example, be grateful that when our car breaks down we have the money to pay for repairs (whereas ten years ago we would have had to abandon the clunker). Or we might, when facing surgery, be grateful that we have someone to hold our hand (unlike our solitary elderly neighbor). In other words, when we feel low, we may visualize past stressful situations, or others' stressful situations, to make us feel better in the here and now. Reminding ourselves of how bad things could be in comparison with our comparatively more comfortable day-to-day existence—a universal and constructive way to boost morale—generally raises our spirits.

SOCIAL COMPARISONS

There are both upward and downward comparisons, of course. Things aren't always better than they used to be, and we're not always healthier or better paid or smarter than our neighbor. In general, however, happy people make more downward comparisons than upward. No matter what their situation, they can see others who have it worse, which helps them realize how well-off they really are. They've learned to appreciate the things they have rather than dwelling on what others have—a lesson they probably mastered with their ABC. Perhaps when they complained as children about feeling disadvantaged in some way, their parents gave them examples of other people who were worse off than they were.

While unhappy people inevitably make both upward and downward comparisons in assessing their life situation, it's the upward comparisons they dwell on. Feeling a deep sense of having been wronged, they spend their days searching for confirmation that life has dealt them a poor hand of cards. As a result, their selection of targets with which to compare themselves is biased. By primarily making upward comparisons, they focus on the fact that others have a better deal in life. "Why does my neighbor have a better car than I have?" they ask. "How does my sister manage to go on such expensive vacations?" When occasionally they focus on someone who is worse off than they are, they savor that sensation, but their pleasure is quickly overshadowed by the envy of the many others who are perceived as having gotten a much better deal in life.

People fixated on the idea of having been given a bad deal see one person's gain as another's loss. They look at everything as a zero-sum game. Regardless of what they're in pursuit of—whether it's love, power, or money—they're always able to find someone who appears to be better off, and they see that other person as hoarding what should rightfully be theirs.

All of us feel disadvantaged at times, particularly when we compare ourselves to others a few steps up the ladder in status, looks, income, or power. Our challenge is to work through our mixed emotions. For the purposes of mental health, it's important not to dwell on negative comparisons, nor to become obsessed by a sense of having been wronged. Otherwise envy rears its ugly head once more and threatens to devour us.

Social comparison and envy are part of a single continuum. The former shades gradually into the latter, which brings out the worst in people. Bertrand Russell recognized this when he said, "Few people can be happy unless they hate some other person, nation, or creed."

147

We should ask ourselves, though, if happy is the right adjective to use in such a situation. Russell continued, "If you desire glory, you may envy Napoleon. But Napoleon envied Caesar, Caesar envied Alexander, and Alexander, I daresay, envied Hercules, who never existed."

As I indicated earlier, some people find a kind of enjoyment in other people's misery. Those same people favor upward comparison, which generally triggers an envious, hostile reaction. That reaction isn't entirely other-directed, however. As the writer Hermann Hesse observed, "If we hate a person, we hate something in our image of him that lies within ourselves. What is not within ourselves does not upset us." As Hesse clearly understood, envious people have serious problems centered on self-esteem. They're more unhappy with themselves than they are with those they deride. But they are also masters of splitting and projection and have difficulty dealing with the unacceptable parts of themselves.

I doubt that there's a person alive who, at one time or another, hasn't been troubled by envy—that is, by the painful or resentful awareness of an advantage enjoyed by someone else (such as wealth, power, status, love, or beauty) combined with the desire to possess that advantage. As I already suggested in my essay on money, envy is a universal emotion and it spawns a range of equally painful feelings: frustration, anger, self-pity, greed, spite, and vindictiveness. While acting out of envy may give temporary relief, any of these negative emotions can cause substantial subjective distress. Envy and all its offshoots are dangerous to one's self and others and they take prisoner those who indulge in them.

Not that people deliberately reveal or verbalize such feelings. Envy isn't for public consumption. We prefer to hide it or at least dress it up in lofty imagery. Although envy has a positive side—it can be a great equalizer, reducing differences and reinforcing a sense of equity in relationships—too often it leads people to demand an eye for an eye. The result? One more blind person in a world already full of suffering.

As we know, envy is also one of the seven deadly sins. The Bible is full of stories about envy. The last of the Old Testament's Ten Commandments is, "You shall not covet ...." Literature gives us numerous examples of envy, and one of the best known of these is John Milton's portrait of Satan in *Paradise Lost*. In Milton's poem, Satan is a fallen angel who, seething with envy and wanting revenge, fabricates man's dismissal from Paradise. The universal nature of envy is also attested to in the proverbs of many different societies: for example, in Bulgaria, "Other people's eggs have two yolks"; in Denmark, "If envy were a fever, all the world would be ill"; the Swedes talk about "royal Swedish envy" (warning against provoking envy by being too conspicuous); and in various countries we hear about "tall poppy syndrome" (highlighting the enjoyment people seem to get out of the downfall of "tall poppies").

The most dramatic story about envy that I know is Russian. It concerns a peasant to whom God granted the fulfillment of any wish. There was, however, a catch. Whatever the peasant chose, God would do twice as much for his neighbor. The idea that his neighbor would be better off than he was, whatever he did, troubled the peasant. After mulling over the offer, the peasant finally said, "Take out one of my eyes." The novelist Gore Vidal acknowledged that same dynamic: "It is not enough to succeed; others must fail."

Sometimes envy is packaged (and successfully disguised) as moral indignation. We pretend to be very righteous about people who we claim have transgressed some kind of moral code—for example, denouncing a colleague for living ostentatiously in a world plagued by poverty. However, this sense of righteousness very often masks a desire to be in the transgressor's situation. When people obsess over someone else's "despicable" behavior, they may well be tempted by it. The target of their wrath may represent what they most fear in themselves. Often, this indignation is related to sexuality. A homophobe, for example, might target homosexuals as a way of trying to master his concerns about his own gender identity.

The indiscretions of a number of American televangelists bear this out. They have preached about vice and sin, avarice and greed, while at the same time visiting prostitutes and misusing the money given to them by their constituencies. The book *Elmer Gantry* by Sinclair Lewis (later filmed with Burt Lancaster) is the story of a preacher who is a con man, and is an attack on the ignorant, gross, and predatory leaders who had crept into the Protestant Church. The novel describes how Elmer Gantry, a "God-fearing" man, preached against sin and damnation by day, and then by night engaged in the same activities he had earlier condemned. Moral indignation is often envy with a halo.

Ambrose Bierce, in *The Devil's Dictionary*, touches dramatically on the destructiveness of envy when he describes happiness as an "agreeable sensation arising from contemplating the misery of another." The German language has given us the word *Schadenfreude*, meaning pleasure at the misery of others. But if a person bases his or her happiness on enjoying the misery of others, what does that say about the overall quality of that life? Although the misery of others can bring moments of pleasure, true happiness can't coexist with envy, spite, or vindictiveness. If envy takes a person prisoner, it limits human potential, makes for disconnectedness, stifles the ability to play, and leads to unhappiness.

19

COPING WITH STRESS

Don't remain a dependent, malleable patient:
Become your own soul's doctor.

Epictetus

The trouble with being in the rat race is that even if you win, you're still a rat.

Lily Tomlin

Sometimes when people are under stress, they hate to think, and it's the time when they
most need to think.

Bill Clinton

A heart attack is nature's way of telling us to slow down.

Proverb

Albert Schweitzer once said that happiness is nothing more than good
health and a poor memory. While his comment about poor memory
may meet with objections—after all, who wants to be accused of
being in a state of denial?—monitoring health is undeniably important. If we don't protect our health, the attainment of happiness is an
impossible pursuit. When all is said and done, our physical condition
strongly influences (and in some cases even determines) our mental
state. According to many stress researchers, physical state is a strong
predictor of happiness, particularly for the old. The ego is first and
foremost a bodily ego. It's hard to think clearly when we're in poor
physical condition. As a result, when we're assailed by ill health, our
thoughts and conversation tend to be limited to a discussion about
our various physical ailments. At times, all of us have encountered
people who converse only in somatic language—the language of
bodily concerns.

Being healthy can be compared to burning a candle wisely. If
we take excellent care of our candle, it burns for a long time. If we
start to mess with it, it can go up in smoke in a very short time.

Unfortunately, in my dealings with executives I've met quite a few people with the habit of burning the candle at both ends—anger-prone, Type A people. They experience a sense of great time-urgency, they're restless, impatient, and extremely competitive, and they demonstrate a high level of aggressiveness and free-floating hostility. This constellation of behaviors is a major risk factor in coronary heart disease.

You may know the kind of people I'm talking about. They're like rats on a treadmill or the White Rabbit in *Alice in Wonderland*—always in a hurry and never getting to their destination. Do you recognize the type? Do you perhaps recognize yourself? When these people go to a restaurant, they eat fast, talk fast, and pay the bill fast. They have no time to enjoy their meal. They certainly don't linger over wine or coffee. Their speech is loud, at times even explosive; their facial muscles are tense. Poor listeners, they always try to dominate the conversation. Because they're under constant pressure (whether self-induced or external), they feel guilty when they attempt to relax. In fact, whenever possible they do more than one thing at a time. Even during the night they're not at peace. They may, for example, grind their teeth as an accompaniment to stressful dream imagery—a pastime that's made many a dentist happy.

HEALTH AS A BANK ACCOUNT

Physical health can be compared to a bank account. This is an unusual account, however—one from which we can only withdraw; the bank doesn't allow deposits. Some people tend to be spendthrifts. Unable to save, they squander their health as readily as they do their money, committing suicide slowly. They realize the importance of their health only when there's very little of it left.

Stress researchers sometimes make a distinction between physiological and chronological age. For some—the candle-burners and bank-account raiders—physiological age overtakes chronological age. Since physiological age is to some extent within our control, we need to monitor our health vigilantly—exercising regularly, eating sensibly, drinking only in moderation, and recognizing what smoking and drugs can do to us.

Furthermore, we need to remember that, while old age will come to all of us if we are lucky, our so-called golden years will be brighter if we've managed throughout our life to maintain a low-stress, positive state of mind. People under stress are more susceptible to illness. Findings from the field of psychoneuroimmunology indicate that pleasurable experiences and positive states of mind enhance the immune system. It appears that our body's immune system fights disease more effectively when we're happy. As a result, happier people live longer. Worry, lack of physical and emotional contact, anger, and hostility, on the other hand, are hazardous to our health. Negative moods encourage illness.

Of course, there's more to physical health than taking practical steps toward fitness. Some of us have had bad luck with genetic inheritance, for example; others have had the misfortune to be tapped by a disease that vigilance couldn't have prevented. Still, far too many people mortgage their future, only to regret having done so later in life.

The American humorist P. J. O'Rourke once said, "There is one thing women can never take away from men. We die sooner." We can discern a moral underlying the humor of that remark: men would do well to adopt certain "female" characteristics—among them, emotional intimacy, which most people would concede women are better at than men. As indicated repeatedly, social support—the sense of being liked and appreciated by friends and family members, the comfortable give-and-take of confidants—provides a buffer against stress and promotes happiness. Someone to talk to about intimate matters helps alleviate stressful situations. The people (men and women alike) most at risk from ill health and unhappiness are those who bear their problems alone, unable or unwilling to talk about what's troubling them. Fortunately, disclosure begets disclosure. When we express our fears to other people, they generally share their own concerns in turn, and we come to understand that we're not alone; others struggle with similar issues. For most of us that's a reassuring discovery that leads to peace of mind.

Statistics tell us that people in close relationships tend to have better health-behavior practices. People who care about each other make an effort to monitor each other's health. When there's intimacy in a relationship, the partners tend to drink and smoke less, avoid drugs, have a better diet, and follow their doctors' orders.

Sexual activity, as I described in Part One, can also counter stress. It has a positive effect on relationships and enhances physical fitness. If sex is mutually satisfying, it improves self-esteem, works as an anti-depressant, and counters stress by boosting the immune system. In contrast, sex without love can negatively affect one's health and happiness. As the philosopher Epictetus said, "An active sex life within a framework of personal commitments augments the integrity of the people involved and is part of a flourishing life."

As I indicated before, an optimistic mood state also serves as a buffer against stress, a fact that has been known for a long time. In the Old Testament, book of Proverbs, King Solomon says, "A merry heart doeth good like a medicine." Stress researchers concur with this. Laughter is an essential component of both mental and physical health. People who laugh often really do live longer. In his book *Anatomy of an Illness*, the journalist Norman Cousins explained his theory that his recovery from a potentially life-threatening illness could be attributed in part to his active use of laughter. An increasing number of studies show that humor has a healing quality. Because laughter decreases stress hormones in the blood (such as adrenaline, epinephrine, and norepinephrine), it relaxes us, bringing us into a calmer, more homeostatic state. Laughter makes the body young and lively, exercises various organs, and (like positive mood states generally) increases our immune response.

We can laugh to forget, but we shouldn't forget to laugh. People who can't laugh are psychologically incomplete. Because laughter, that audible sign of transient happiness, is an antidote to anxiety and depression, it makes tough times more tolerable. The ability to laugh at ourselves is of special significance because it guards against arrogance and pomposity. In fact, it's a good test of mental health.

Regular exercise is also essential to both physical health and happiness. We feel better, both physically and mentally, after doing exercise. We're in a more relaxed state of body and mind. When we exercise regularly, we reduce our stress level, enjoy more energy and stamina, strengthen the heart, and have better circulation, lower blood pressure, faster metabolism, and more resistance to life-threatening diseases. Furthermore, regular exercise lessens the odds of becoming depressed or burnt out. The Roman poet Juvenal's adage *Mens sana in corpore sano*—a sound mind in a sound body—still rings true.

20

HOMO LUDENS

He who would learn to fly one day must first learn to stand and walk and run and climb and dance; one cannot fly into flying.

Friedrich Nietzsche

All work and no play make Jack a dull boy.

Proverb

Men deal with life as children with their play,
Who first misuse, then cast their toys away.

William Cowper

Why not go out on a limb? Isn't that where the fruit is?

Frank Scully

One sunny afternoon I was walking over the Pont des Arts, the pedestrian bridge over the river Seine in Paris. There was a special buzz in the air. A sense of excitement and enthusiasm permeated the whole area. People—old and young—thronged the bridge, sitting, standing, even lying down. All of them were painting or commenting on each other's paintings. In the typical French proclivity for wordplay, the event was called *"Faites de la peinture,"* which means more or less "Get painting." But the event's title was also a pun on *"Fête de la peinture"*—pronounced in exactly the same way—meaning "festival of painting." Looking at the scene, I could see that all the people taking part were totally absorbed, cognitively, emotionally, and sensually. And that is what play is all about. While playing, we lose ourselves; interior and exterior worlds merge. We transform as a person. We lose the baggage of daily life. There is a fusion between childhood and adulthood. And on the bridge, the usual separation between children and grown-ups dissipated. They were all "playing" together.

154

THE ROLE OF PLAY

Einstein was correct in pointing out the importance of play in our lives in his equation for happiness. Play is closely tied to creativity and has a regenerative function. It implies a diversification of interests, doing things outside our normal routine. As the saying goes, "all work and no play make Jack a dull boy." We gather happy life experiences (and therefore memories) by having a variety of interests. Leisure activities serve a revitalizing function. As I mentioned earlier, research has shown that people who enjoy leisure tend to be happier. Leisure helps us to look at old situations in new ways. Real recreation (think of it as "re-creation") stimulates aspiration and makes us more innovative and effective at work and in our relationships.

Many people don't know how to manage leisure; they don't know how to play. An executive in one of my leadership seminars was just such a man. Listening to his story, I was reminded of the paintings of Diego Velázquez (one the most important painters of the seventeenth century), which featured children of the Spanish royal family, looking eerily adult. This executive (I will call him Jan) could have stepped out of such a painting. He had been forced into an adult role prematurely because of a depressed mother and a father who had disappeared when Jan was two years old. With no other support figure around, Jan had assumed a responsible role in the family at an early age. In that role he became his mother's confidant, trying to help her overcome her dark moments and sharing her emotional burdens. As he grew older, Jan increasingly took care of household duties. Meanwhile, his childhood slipped away. Like the children in Velázquez's paintings, he never had the opportunity to play or to engage in make-believe.

As an adult Jan focused on his work, becoming a very successful businessman. His colleagues and subordinates described him as quite caring but too serious. Unfortunately, he compartmentalized his caring, saving it for the office. At home he was detached from his wife and son, probably in reaction to having been overinvolved with his mother in the past. Having relegated the childrearing to his wife, Jan remained so distant from his son that the young man became like a stranger to him. When alone with his son, he felt awkward, uncomfortable; he didn't know what to say or how to handle himself. When I first met this man, late in his life, he was trying to pick up the broken thread of his childhood and to make a belated effort at play.

While some people—Jan among them—don't know how to play, dedicating all their energy to work, others play too hard and too much. But does life have to be either/or? I don't think so. We increase the probability of attaining happiness when we learn to find play at work and learn to work at play. Well-balanced personalities don't work all the time. They know how to laugh; they know how to play; they know how to do fun things with others.

When we play—even when we play at work—we return to the world of childhood. We experience once more the feelings of joy, surprise, and anticipation that make up the world of an infant. We feel as alive, as intense, as we did when we were young. We enter a world of fantasy, daydreams, and night dreams, where time doesn't matter. And it's in the transitional world of play—the domain that floats between make-believe and reality, between teddy bears and adult responsibilities—that creative processes take place. It's a world of intuition, free association, metaphors and images, and imagination without limits—in short, a world of infinite possibilities. It's a world of divergent thinking, leading to connections and associations that contribute to new insights. When adults are in this world of play, periods of private, creative inner work alternate with experiences of reality testing, illumination, and reintegration. Minds are like parachutes; they work better when they are open. Getting into such a state of mind enables us to find new ways to deal with questions, issues, sensibilities, and problems that have left us puzzled. While we're playing, and doing out-of-the-ordinary things, solutions emerge that have eluded the traditional work approach. Such creative insights often make for intense moments of happiness.

REGRESSION IN THE SERVICE OF THE EGO

To understand better the underlying dynamics of play and the creative process, psychoanalysts have made a distinction between primary and secondary process thinking. They noted the connection between primary process thinking and creativity. Here primary process thinking refers to primitive mental processes that are directly related to unconscious mental activity. They are characterized by unorganized, non-logical thinking and by a tendency to seek immediate discharge and gratification of instinctual (that is, sexual) urges. Dream work, to give an example, can be seen as a vivid illustration of primary processes at work. In contrast, secondary process thinking consists of the kind of mental activity that's characteristic of conscious and preconscious mental activity, marked by logical thinking and by the tendency to delay gratification by regulation of the discharge of instinctual demands. It's at the primary process thinking

156

level, however, where sexual desire plays a significant role, and influences the creative process.

Psychoanalysts have also introduced the concept of "regression in the service of the ego." It is a form of regression to playful, primitive, and unconscious modes of thought whereby secondary processes will be part of the equation. Creative products will be the outcome of this form of regression. It's a very constructive process of dealing with conflicted material. Starting with the early experiences of childhood, creative people seem to alternate between imagination, fantasy, and a rooted sense of reality. The creative process implies a miraculous coming together of the imagination of the child with its apparent opposite and enemy, the sense of order imposed on the disciplined adult intelligence.

This form of expression is quite different to what happens with "crazy" people. Although such people may find "creative" solutions to their conflicts, their creativity is of a more magical nature. Their "products" have a private meaning, and lack the connection with an audience. The way "crazy" people express their creativity is an example of regression gone awry. Whatever the outcome of their creative products, they do not reverberate with the social context. Symbolic products have been created that are too private, having become too unintelligible.

When we take a closer look at the creative process we might see that much of our creative work is energized by unresolved memories, the "ghosts" in our inner theater. These ghosts, which fill us with wonder and desire, feed our imagination. Children's play takes on an important role in exorcising and metabolizing these internalized ghosts. If parents and caregivers show excitement and interest in children's play, they can perform an important role in managing these "ghosts." By participating, they share the child's transitional space—the place of wonder and illusion between fantasy and reality. Unrestricted, imaginative play is central to the development of creativity in children. It will establish the building blocks for things to come. Very much will depend, however, on how the child copes with the constraints imposed on him or her by societal forces. To quote Picasso, "Every child is an artist. The problem is how to remain an artist once he grows up."

Meeting creative people, we may discover that they can be more primitive and cultivated, more destructive and constructive, a lot madder and a lot saner, than the average person. They are willing to go where others do not dare. This is what creativity in the arts and sciences is all about—going beyond everyday reality, and creating a new reality. It is the ability to see what others can't. As Michelangelo supposedly said, "I saw the angel in the marble and carved until I set him free." Creative people are able to recognize the shapes in a cloud formation, not just the clouds.

It may be a truism to say that every new idea looks crazy at first; genius is little more than the faculty of perceiving things in different ways. Creative people are able to take a fresh look at things others take for granted. This is very much a triumph of originality over habit. It is the ability to connect the unconnected. But although creativity implies a certain amount of fluidity between fantasy and reality, we need to remember that creativity also requires a certain degree of order. Although a playful attitude may be typical of creative people, the truly creative combine playfulness and discipline, responsibility and irresponsibility. Playfulness without its antitheses—doggedness, endurance, and perseverance—is unlikely to produce results. In the creative process, thought comes first; then the organization of that thought into ideas and plans; then the transformation of those plans into reality. The germ of an idea needs to be combined with the perseverance to make it a reality. To quote the painter Francisco Goya, "Fantasy, abandoned by reason, produces impossible monsters; united with it, she is the mother of the arts and the origin of marvels."

Dealing with loss

The painter Edvard Munch once said, "Sickness, insanity and death were the angels that surrounded my cradle and they have followed me throughout my life." Munch was able to utilize these experiences of loss and bereavement creatively. In dealing with the hurts of childhood, some of us—as children—are able to manage, while others may have greater difficulty. These difficulties can be life limiting, as is the case for the mentally impaired. There is often a relationship between creativity and some forms of mental illness, including depression, schizophrenia, and attention-deficit hyperactivity disorder. Many studies have shown that eminently creative individuals have a much higher rate of bipolar disorder, or manic depression, than the general population.

Staying in touch with our crazy side

Given its importance for attaining happiness, each of us should evaluate our ability to engage in play. Do we ever question things that have long been taken for granted at work? Are there things that really fire us up at the office? Do we have any passions outside work? Do we engage in activities that tap other parts of our brain? Are we in touch with our own crazy side? Do we daydream and pay attention to our nocturnal dreams? The more "yeses" we can give to this set of questions, the better off we are. Taking a playful approach to responsibilities at work fosters creativity, while engaging in after-work hobbies and pursuits improves our outlook toward life and reenergizes our spirit, whether we opt for relatively tame activities such as fly-fishing, bird watching, or cultivating roses, or more risky ventures such as hunting, skydiving, or helicopter-skiing.

If diversity of leisure is missing, we may be in for a big surprise when the time for retirement comes and our options are limited by physical and situational changes. I've known quite a few single-minded people, men and women whose only interests were career-related, who found themselves at a complete loss upon retirement. While working, they never thought to seek pleasure outside the office. Their development was totally career-related. When they left the workplace in late middle age, they experienced a sense of abandonment and isolation, becoming disoriented and depressed and experiencing a variety of other stress symptoms. Some even died prematurely; having made no time for leisure, they had to make time for illness.

EXPLORATORY NEEDS

The growth that human beings experience through play is closely related to their exploratory need—the need on which cognition and learning are based. The developmental psychologist Robert White called this need "competence motivation." Although infants are born conspicuously incompetent, they are programmed not only to learn a great deal about their environment but also to find ways to affect and manipulate it. White (and other developmental psychologists) views exploratory behavior as a basic motivational need, the purpose of which is to acquire competence in dealing with the environment. The successes that are attained during that acquisition contribute to feelings of efficacy, which significantly enhance a person's sense of self-esteem.

This exploratory motivational need is shown soon after birth. Child observation studies report that novelty, as well as the discovery of the effects of certain actions, stimulate the brain cells in infants and cause a prolonged state of attentive arousal. Similar reactions to opportunities for exploration continue into and throughout adulthood.

Closely tied to the need for exploration is the need for self-assertion—the need to be able to choose what to do. Playful exploration and manipulation of the environment in response to exploratory-assertive motivation produces a sense of effectiveness and competency, autonomy, initiative, and industry.

Understanding this basic motivational need helps us realize that learning shouldn't be seen as something we do only as preparation for adult life. On the contrary, the learning process should never stop. We need to continue developing our potential, growing and expanding as individuals. We need to be open to new challenges and tasks at different points in our lifespan.

As we look around us, we see a world that's in constant flux, with new things happening all the time. With all these changes, there are myriad discoveries waiting to be made. Ongoing learning means being passionately involved in life—attending to life's movements, sounds, and colors; using our senses of smell, taste, touch, hearing, and sight; cultivating our aesthetic side; and being adventurous.

What we learn in formal educational environments is important. Frequently, though, it's the studying done after school that has the greatest impact. In fact, many things that need to be learned simply cannot be taught. We learn those things by doing—and we remember them as a consequence. The recall factor of experiential learning is much greater than that of classroom learning, because the memories of critical incidents in life remain prominent.

The more we learn, the more we discover how ignorant we are. That's no bad thing: it's important to know how little we know. In fact, we should cherish our ignorance, because it's what pushes us toward further exploration. One of the secrets of a fulfilling life and the attainment of happiness is maintaining intellectual curiosity. But to be curious and learn, we also have to unlearn; in other words, we have to be prepared to take risks, to go out on a limb. As the economist John Maynard Keynes once said, "The greatest difficulty in the world is not for people to accept new ideas but to make them forget about their old ideas."

All life is a process of growth and motion. Human beings are no exception: we need to make a continuous effort to reshape ourselves. We also need to experiment. The more we do so, probing our limits and our surroundings, the more we develop. At times we'll fail at our endeavors. That's guaranteed. But temporary setbacks lead to learning experiences that are retained.

Nothing is interesting if we're not interested. The more things we're interested in, the more alive we are. It's a lonely person who thinks that he or she can no longer learn from others. That presumptuous stance is an invitation to disaster. Just as continuing to learn keeps us young, ceasing to learn hastens aging. In fact, nothing ages a person faster than not thinking, not exercising the brain. Few minds wear out; most rust away. For our survival we need to remain intellectually curious, striving for personal growth.

Our efforts to remain receptive to learning are made easier if we can retain certain childish qualities. Playfulness helps us to see new circumstances as adventures. Imagination allows us to explore the vast, unmapped country within, that secret reservoir of promise and potential that few adults tap. Creativity permits us to use our imagination constructively, making use of childhood experiences recalled at will. Finally, inquisitiveness brings us moments of happiness that stem from discovering new things. More often than not, the challenge isn't to arrive at new answers but to pose new questions. What we don't ask, we'll never know. The words *why* and *how* can't be used too often.

The joy of learning also helps us to become more effective teachers and in that teaching process we learn ourselves. It's important, however, that we teach others how to think, not what to think. Generativity—the willingness to be a mentor and teacher to others, to really care for others—is an even more important factor as we grow older. Seeing young people who've been under our wings do well can bring moments of happiness, while envying the next generation stifles happiness.

François de la Rochefoucauld once said, "The only thing constant in life is change." If we're open to learning, that ubiquitous change can be our teacher. In fact, since being mired in the rut of old habits leads to inflexibility and stagnation, we should not only accept change but seek it out, breaking routines and surprising ourselves and others. We need to let go of the past. We need to keep trying new things and congratulate ourselves when we find ways to break monotony when it threatens, and find ways to be players, rather than spectators, in the game of life. It's better to be eighty years young than thirty years old. We grow old not by living but by losing interest in living.

Far too many of us, jump restlessly from one desire to the next, never being content with how things really are, never taking a holistic view of life. The poet T. S Eliot once said, "We shall not cease from exploration, and the end of all our exploring will be to arrive where we started and know the place for the first time." Let me end with a Zen story that illustrates the ethereal nature of happiness.

Once upon a time there was a stonecutter. He lived in a land where a life of privilege meant being powerful. Looking at his life he decided that he was unsatisfied with the way things were and so he set out to become the most powerful person in the land.

One day he passed a wealthy merchant's house. Through the open gateway, he saw many fine possessions and important visitors. "How powerful that merchant must be!" thought the stonecutter. "I wish I could be like him."

To his great surprise, he suddenly became the merchant, enjoying more luxuries and power than he had ever imagined, but envied and detested by those less wealthy than himself. Soon a high official passed by, carried in a sedan chair, accompanied by attendants and escorted by soldiers beating gongs. Everyone, no matter how wealthy, had to bow low before the procession. "How powerful that official is!" thought the merchant. "I wish that I could be a high official!"

And he became the high official, carried everywhere in his embroidered sedan chair, feared and hated by the people all around. It was a hot summer day, so the official felt very uncomfortable in the sticky sedan chair. He looked up at the sun. It shone proudly in the sky, unaffected by his presence. "How powerful the sun is!" he thought. "I wish I could be the sun!"

Then he became the sun, shining fiercely down on everyone, scorching the fields, cursed by the farmers and laborers. But a huge black cloud moved between him and the earth, so that his light could no longer shine on everything below. "How powerful that storm cloud is!" he thought. "I wish that I could be a cloud!"

Then he became the cloud, flooding the fields and villages, shouted at by everyone. But soon he found that he was being pushed away by some great force, and realized that it was the wind. "How powerful it is!" he thought. "I wish I could be the wind!"

Then he became the wind, blowing tiles off the roofs of houses, uprooting trees, feared and hated by all below him. But after a while, he ran up against something that would not move, no matter how forcefully he blew against it—a huge, towering rock. "How powerful that rock is!" he thought. "I wish that I could be a rock!"

Then he became the rock, more powerful than anything else on earth. But as he stood there, he heard the sound of a hammer pounding a chisel into the hard surface, and felt himself being changed. "What could be more powerful than I, the rock?" he thought.

He looked down and saw far below him the figure of a stonecutter.

PART FOUR: MEDITATIONS ON DEATH

21

YOU DON'T GET OUT ALIVE

Death is a debt we all must pay.

Euripides

People living deeply have no fear of death.

Anais Nin

Death is nothing, but to live defeated and inglorious is to die daily.

Napoleon Bonaparte

Once upon a time, in a small country located in the foothills of the Himalayan Mountains, there lived a king, Shuddodana Gauthama, whose wife was expecting her first child. Before the birth of the child she had a strange dream in which a baby elephant blessed her with his trunk. When she recounted the dream, it was perceived by her courtiers as a very auspicious sign. The infant when born was named Siddhartha, which means "he who has attained his goals." After his birth, Siddhartha's father consulted an illustrious soothsayer, and asked him about the future of his son. The soothsayer proclaimed that his son would be one of two things: he could become a great king, even an emperor, or he would be a great sage and savior of humanity. As Siddhartha was the only heir to the throne, his father did not want him to renounce the world. Eager that his son should become a king like himself, he was determined to shield him from anything that might result in taking up the religious life, that is, religious teachings or knowledge of human suffering. King Shuddodana told his courtiers that his son was not permitted to see the elderly, the sick, the dead, or anyone who had dedicated themselves to spiritual practices. He wanted Siddhartha to grow up surrounded only by beauty and health.

Siddhartha studied science, technology, art, philosophy, and religious studies under the tuition of famous scholars. In addition, he excelled in riding, archery, and fencing. Living in the luxury of his palaces, he grew increasingly restless and discontented, however, curious about the world beyond the palace walls. Finally, he decided to ask permission from his father to leave the palace grounds and get to know the world. The king carefully arranged that Siddhartha would still not see the kind of suffering that he feared would lead him to a religious life, and told his courtiers that only young and healthy people were permitted to greet the prince. But while venturing outside the palace, and despite his father's effort to remove the sick, the aged, and the suffering, Siddhartha saw a couple of old men who had accidentally wandered near the parade route. Amazed and confused, he chased after them to find out who they were. While doing so, he came across a number of people who were severely ill. And finally, by the side of the river, he chanced upon a funeral ceremony where for the first time in his life he encountered death. Deeply depressed by these sights, he decided to transcend old age, illness, and death by living the life of an ascetic. Abandoning his inheritance, he left the palace, took up the lonely life of a wandering monk, dedicating his life to learning how to overcome suffering. From the age of thirty-five onward, Siddhartha became known as Buddha, a title meaning "the awakened one," or "the one who knows."

TRAGIC MAN

As the story of Buddha tells us, we don't get out of life alive. Or to quote a well-known statement by John Maynard Keynes, "In the long run, we are all dead." Humankind faces a terrible experiential burden: there is an omnipresent, half-hidden terror in the form of plain, ordinary, but inevitable death. Death is the shadow that follows us wherever we go. Thanks to the development of our frontal lobes—the last part of the human brain to develop—Homo sapiens has the ability to look toward the future. No other animal has the kind of frontal lobe we have. And although thinking about the future can be pleasurable, the future also includes death. It is a high price we pay for our development as a species.

As humans, we live our entire lives with the knowledge that we are going to die. Like it or not, every moment of our life is another step towards death. Death anxiety is a most profound source of misery. In the words of the psychologist William James, it is "the worm at the core" of man's existence, as the first breath we draw predicates our last. The knowledge of death creates the conundrum that some people are so afraid to die that they never even begin to live. It is as if they tiptoe through life carefully, to arrive, safely, at death. They

166

seem to have never understood Socrates' admonition that "the unexplored life is not worth living." Spending all our time worrying about dying doesn't make living pleasurable. Our greatest tragedy is that we try to find ways to suppress our anxiety about death, annihilation, and definitive separation, but because this anxiety is caused by our wish to live, it makes it difficult for many of us to live our lives to the fullest.

Death anxiety is increased because the recognition of our mortality runs counter to our survival instincts. How can we deal with this existential conflict? What can we do about it? How can we cope?

Our ways of dealing with our knowledge of death varies. Some people will go into overdrive to find ways to suppress it, while others may fall into a state of resignation and depression. These are the people who ask themselves, why bother to live, knowing that all our efforts in life will come to nothing because we are going to die. Why spend the energy? Why not just give up? Some people see a hopeless end, while others see an endless hope. Of these two choices, the second is more constructive.

Whatever route we take, many of us feel compelled to alter or to repress this troublesome awareness in one way or another. These attempts at suppression, however, create a constant supply of repressed psychic energy, which, shaped by cultural and historical forces, may transform itself into a rich kaleidoscope of human creativity and resourcefulness. Thus we can say that the drive for self-preservation (which runs counter to the fear of annihilation and death) lays the groundwork for learning, shaping how we think and what we do. It will affect our thoughts, emotions, and motivations. But this energy isn't only used constructively; it can also contribute to racism, religious fanatism, political intolerance, violence, and many other types of troublesome activities.

22

THE DENIAL OF DEATH

Of all the wonders that I yet have heard,
It seems to me most strange that men should fear;
Seeing that death, a necessary end,
Will come when it will come.

William Shakespeare

Men fear death as children fear to go into the dark; and as that natural fear in children is increased with tales, so is the other.

Francis Bacon

I'm not afraid of death. It's the stake one puts up in order to play the game of life.

Jean Giraudoux

There is nothing certain in a man's life but that he must lose it.

Owen Meredith

Animals don't face the kind of existential conflict that we have to deal with. Generally, we assume that they go through life in their merry, instinctual ways. Homo sapiens isn't so lucky and may envy their situation. Ironically, it's our evolutionary progression, our ability to acquire knowledge, and our capacity for reflection that make death such a fearsome encounter for us. It puts our defensive apparatus on alert; it's the reason behind the heroic efforts we make to push thoughts of death away. But despite these, the alarming reality of our impending death continues to intrude. Periodic reminders that the Grim Reaper is waiting for us are announced to us through the death of loved ones, wars, natural disasters, or a lump in our breast, admonitions that are very hard to ignore. We only begin to understand the truth of death for the first time, however, when it touches someone whom we dearly love.

THE TRIUMPH OF IRRATIONALITY

Although at a rational level we know that death is the inevitable outcome of life, at an irrational level we see things quite differently. The idea of being swallowed into a complete void, faced with the disintegration and decay of the body, isn't easily faced or accepted. Instead, we often act as if death can happen to everyone except to ourselves. One of the heroes of the famous Indian epic the Mahabharata, when faced with the riddle "What is the most perplexing thing in the world?" answers the question by saying, "Man's unfaltering belief in immortality, ignoring the inevitability and omnipresence of death." This riddle is a reminder of our ambivalent attitude toward death. Sigmund Freud described the psychological imagery associated with death in his essay *Thoughts for the Times on War and Death* (1915): "It is indeed impossible to imagine our own death; and whenever we attempt to do so we can perceive that we are in fact still present as spectators." Hence many psychoanalysts argued that at the bottom no one believes in his own death, or to put the same thing in another way, that in the unconscious every one of us is convinced of his own immortality." The Spanish philosopher Miguel de Unamuno concurs and writes in *The Tragic Sense of Life*: "What distinguishes man from other animals is that in one form or another, he guards his dead. And from what does he so futilely protect them? The wretched consciousness shrinks from his own annihilation."

Death reawakens in us basic fears that center on themes of annihilation, loneliness, abandonment, rejection, and separation. With our instincts for survival, it can cause outbursts of panic.

One morning in Huizen, the village in Holland where I lived as a small child, the enormity of death was sprung upon me. I remember happily sitting in a bathtub being sponged down by my grandmother who was singing a song to me. Out of the blue, she asked me if I would remember her when she was no longer there. I recall that her question filled me with panic. How could she be out of my life? How could she no longer be there? She was an essential part of my small world. The idea was horrid, scary, and unthinkable. I had no idea how to respond. I didn't want to believe that she could die. But there was nothing I could say. But her question stayed with me. Thinking about it as I write, her question and the feelings it gave rise to are as fresh today as though it had happened yesterday. Like Siddhartha, I felt as though I had been thrown out of Paradise; it was as if I had lost my innocence. Of course, I had known about death, insofar as I had seen dead birds, insects, and animals lying at the side of the road. But

169

this was different. This was very personal. The notion of death would now be with me, a fear that would gnaw at my insides. Occasionally I would ask myself, how would I be able to live with it? When would the day of reckoning come?

A few years later—far too soon—my grandmother died of pneumonia. It was the first in a series of other death experiences. I remember very clearly how her body was laid to rest for all to see in the main room of my grandparents' farmhouse. Rows upon rows of visitors passed by to pay their last respects. I also remember the funeral procession in the village, with hundreds of people following the hearse.

I recall the grief of my mother, and my feelings of helplessness at how to deal with it. I felt somehow responsible. Had I been good enough? Was I to blame? But I was somewhat reassured that my mother was still there to take care of me. I stayed in the background of all the family activity, a small child overwhelmed by grief, trying to recapture all the good memories I had of being with my grandmother. It took me some time to accept that she would no longer be there, that she was gone, that things were irreversible. For some time, I even engaged in magical thinking that she would come back. I remembered a coin she had given me the last time I saw her, to buy some candy. Where was that coin, that memory of her? I kept on looking for it as if the possession of that coin would bring her back, in a magical way. I didn't want to accept that death was irreversible. But I had to learn to accept that death, the one certainty in all life, would be life's greatest uncertainty.

THE VICISSITUDES OF GRIEF

But the story is not finished. Fifty-five years later the thing happened that I had been dreading for many years: my mother died. Although her death, given her advanced age and state of health, didn't come as a surprise, the impact was far more devastating than I ever expected. Anticipatory grieving, which I had thought would mitigate the pain, turned out to be nothing compared to the feelings I experienced when her death really happened. I had been fooling myself into thinking that I was prepared for her death. It has been said, "The death of a mother is the first sorrow wept without her." I was surprised by the intensity of my emotional reactions. I also felt deeply—and I realize that I'm not alone in having these feelings—that I could have done so much more before she had died. I felt guilty. So many things were left unsaid; so many questions remained unanswered. I hadn't asked them before, and now I couldn't ask at all. It really brought home to me that there is a high price attached to our fear of death; it deprives us of the opportunity truly to say goodbye, leaving unfulfilled a basic human need for making meaning and achieving closure.

When I was informed of my mother's death, I experienced a kaleidoscope of reactions. I was overwhelmed with sorrow, depression, guilt, loneliness, and intense longing for my lost mother. Most strikingly, there was a sense of disbelief at the finality of her death; I found it difficult to accept that there was no way I could talk to her any longer. At the same time, I felt numb. It was as if I was going through the motions of life while actually feeling very little. I had a sense of depersonalization. Although I normally have a busy life, I felt a loss of interest in the outside world; there was an inhibition of all activity. I felt paralyzed. Only my interior world seemed to matter.

In hindsight, I realize that by shielding myself from all external stimuli, I was striving for some kind of psychological restoration through grieving. I was taking stock of what would never be the same again. Of course, my behavior could also be seen as a way of negating what had happened, of denying the reality of what had happened, of refusing to believe that my mother was dead. Confused thoughts kept popping up. I had a sense of disbelief that this had happened to me. I wondered if it was just a bad dream. I kept searching for my mother. I had continual flashbacks of her, and dreamed about her. I had seen her body laid out in the funeral parlor. Recalling the sight, my mind would be flooded once more with the feelings of dread, horror, and sadness I had felt at the uncanny—to use the German expression, "*unheimlich*"—combination of familiarity and the unknown, of being attracted to, yet repulsed by the dead object that was once my mother. I would hear her talk—and then realize it was only my imagination. Admonitions she had given me kept floating through my mind. Objects, incidents, encounters, everything that came my way, reminded me of her presence. And I remembered other deaths—in particular my grandmother, a close cousin, and two friends.

Ironically, dealing with the loss of my mother, being in the throes of the grieving process, meant that she was more than ever present in my inner world. The work of mourning can be defined as excessive attention paid to a person in order to come to terms with his or her definitive demise. It made me more than ever aware of the fact that while it's true that we require air, food, water, clothing, and shelter in order to survive, we must also add relationships to the equation. It's a rare person who is able to thrive in the absence of intimate relationships with other people, places, and things. Having taken my mother for granted, I now realized how much she had contributed to my mental equilibrium.

In my state of grief, I was on emotional roller coaster. Tears would flow easily. It was very difficult for me not to cry. Having so little control over my emotions wasn't easy. I found it difficult to accept being in a situation that I couldn't control. Anything that I associated with my mother would set this grieving process into motion. In hindsight I look at this period as part of a struggle to maintain the emotional bond with my mother, while simultaneously experiencing the reality of loss. I became aware that the goal of the grieving process was learning to live with her absence. I had to accept, not just rationally but also emotionally, that death is part of the cycle of life. It dawned on me that we do not forget the person who has died, nor stop loving that person. The memories remain. The challenge is to grow to accept the death and our feelings about it, and move on with our own life.

Interestingly enough, trying to deal with my own grief I was reminded of a painting by Edvard Munch, "The Dead Mother and Child." I have always found it a very striking but disturbing piece of work. Death was a recurring theme in Munch's life and illness a frequent visitor. As a child he had lost a young brother and sister to illness and one of his younger sisters was diagnosed with mental illness. Another brother died only a few months after he had married. Both of Munch's parents died early, his mother of tuberculosis when Edvard was only five years old. Munch himself was also often sick.

The painting is a striking portrait of a young girl with her back to her mother, who is lying on her deathbed. Nobody else is there to break her sense of isolation. The eyes of the girl are wide with disbelief, her face distorted in sorrow, her hands cover her ears as if to block out reality. It looks as if the girl is ready to scream—in that way, the painting is reminiscent of Munch's most famous work, "The Scream." "The Dead Mother and Child" very much portrayed the feelings I experienced on the death of my mother.

I was entering an unknown territory characterized by an overwhelming sense of pain and loss. I was totally preoccupied with thoughts about my mother. I felt her presence more than once. I was taken with feelings of anger, guilt, and regret. I was mad at myself for what I had or hadn't done while she was still alive. The words "I should have done more" haunted me. I could have done so many things differently "if only I had known." Although my rational self told me that "grief work" was a necessary process to enable me to resume daily life, it also involved separating from my mother, adjusting to a world without her, and forming new relationships. I wasn't yet ready to do so.

I realized that grief is the internal meaning given to the experience of bereavement. It is an integral part of most life changes and experiences. It stands for the emotional, cognitive, behavioral, and physical reactions that follow the death of a person close to us. In contrast, mourning is taking this internal experience of grief and expressing it outside oneself. It's the formalized process of responding to a death. It includes the funeral service, the wake, the dress code, and other formal conventions. In a way, we can look at mourning as "grief gone public." The funeral service is a ritualized way to comfort the living, a communal effort to share thoughts of the dead.

The death of my mother brought home to me the degree to which grief and mourning are part of the human condition. These painful processes are ways of acknowledging the significance of the person who has been lost, and to take stock of how one's life has been affected by that person both before and after the loss. It's a way to honor the strong feelings that are stirred by the sense of sadness and unfairness at having a loved one taken away.

Gradually, I began to realize that there is a tendency in our society to move away from their grief instead of toward it. This made grieving more difficult. I felt, from some of the reactions around me, that grieving is not encouraged in present-day society. People (particularly men) are supposed to keep a stiff upper lip. Crying was an embarrassment. After all, men are not supposed to cry. Many people view crying as a sign of weakness. In contrast, suffering in silence is considered admirable behavior. The all-too-frequent advice is to "carry on" with whatever you are supposed to be carrying on with, and "to keep busy." I was supposed to deal with my grief in isolation or find a way to run away from it, or repress it. Expressing my grief openly might be seen as "weak," "crazy," or "self-pitying." Grieving should be done efficiently. But I became aware that my attempts to mask or move away from the grief resulted in greater internal anxiety and confusion. Keeping a "stiff upper lip" is not only difficult, but it represses your feelings, often bottling them up only to have them erupt at a later time and in a way you do not expect. I had to give myself permission to express through crying the many thoughts, feelings, and memories going through my head.

Just as failing to take care of a physical injury is likely to result in further physical damage, failing to attend to an emotional hurt can lead to a similar outcome—from grief to depression. I realized that I had to face my pain and emotions. All losses need to be mourned in one way or another. I also came to be aware of the fact that families who can acknowledge their grief and learn healthy ways to express their pain can then free their emotional energies to focus on life and the challenges ahead. It was important for me to share my pain with family members and friends. It was important to talk about it.

In spite of my hesitancy to cry, I found crying a very good way of releasing internal tension in my body. It made me feel better. I looked at crying as a way of ridding my body of "toxic" thoughts of self-blame. Indirectly, I think that crying was a way of asking to be comforted. It helped me to start a discussion about my mother with others. Also, crying had a delusionary component. It felt as if I was trying to express my sense of abandonment through crying. It was a magical way of creating a reunion with my lost mother. I also think that being able to cry helped me in the work of grief and the mourning process. While I cried, I thought about past joys and sorrows, decided what to do next, faced the guilt that I felt, and acknowledged the hostility and resentment I felt toward the hospital that wasn't able to keep my mother alive.

As the days passed, I realized that things would never be the same. I came to understand that I needed to integrate the new reality of moving forward in life without the physical presence of my mother who had died. I needed to acknowledge the reality of her death and that pain and grief are inevitable parts of living. I needed to work intellectually and emotionally through a life without my mother. Although my sense of loss didn't disappear, it became somewhat less acute and the intense pangs of grief became less frequent. I knew that I couldn't call her back. But I also knew that my mother would live within me and never be forgotten. However, I also became more cognizant of the fact that I had to move forward in my own life and find the capacity to re-engage with the activities of living. I had to become reconciled to my loss.

I was greatly helped by going through albums of photographs of my mother. I seemed to develop an inner representation of her by recognizing her behavior in myself, seeing the degree to which I had internalized her attitudes, behavior, and values. When I looked in the mirror, I would recognize aspects of her face in my reflection. I became much more aware how much I resembled her and to what an extent I was my mother's living legacy. I realized how interdependent I had been with my mother. Many elements I disliked in my mother were really parts of myself. It seemed that I was making a heroic effort to find a place for her inside me.

Looking at those old photographs, I became aware of the continuity between past memories and present events, the extent to which memories constitute a meaningful life. Relationships with others, living or dead, seemed to frame my sense of self and the way I was living. Throughout this process of reconciliation, I talked to my mother, a process that had begun when I was alone with her at the mortuary; I talked to her in my dreams, and felt her presence at certain places. She was both always present and absent. Furthermore, I had to talk *about* her. Although I wanted to be left alone, I also needed the help of others to assist me through the grieving process. To quote a Turkish proverb, "He that conceals his grief finds no remedy for it." Grief has to be dealt with, otherwise it will come back with multiple strength. It needs time to be digested. It's an essential process of the human condition.

I realized that I was not going to find a simple formula for getting over the loss of my mother. It was going to be slow, hard work. In order to metabolize my loss, it was going to be essential to allow myself to feel all the emotions that would arise, painful as they might be, and to be patient. Some words from Shakespeare's *Richard II* resonated with me: "My grief lies all within, / And these external manners of lament / Are merely shadows to the unseen grief / That swells with silence in the tortured soul." Grief has no timetable: there would be no completion date for grieving. Most likely, the emotions would come and go for weeks, months, or even years. Time would be the only but the best medicine. From a conceptual point of view, I knew that I should not suppress these feelings, but emotionally I was not so consistent. I realized the importance of talking about my feelings but sometimes I was hesitant to do so. Unresolved grief tends to close our hearts down. At the same time, although other people made efforts to console me, I realized that no one can really feel another's grief.

THE STAGES OF GRIEF

Researchers have distinguished four stages in the grieving process:

1. *Shock and numbness*: This stage usually occurs immediately after a death. As my example illustrates, the grieving person will find it difficult to believe the death has occurred. He or she feels stunned and numb.
2. *Yearning and searching*: As the feelings of shock and numbness recede, there is a tendency to "forget" that the person has died. The person in mourning tries to maintain the illusion that it all has been a bad dream.
3. *Disorganization and despair*: The reality of the absence of the person who has died makes itself felt. This is the period of grief during which the person gradually comes to terms with the reality of the loss. The suffering process typically involves a wide range

of feelings, thoughts, and behaviors, as well as loss of a sense of meaning in life. As my own experience illustrates, it is common to feel depressed and have difficulty thinking about the future. It's a period in time when interest in the external world has diminished and planning for the future is put on hold.

4. *Reorganization*: Gradually, the reality of what has happened will filter through. The person realizes that life has dramatically changed because of the loss. But one has to move on and lead a more normal life. A sense of reorganization and renewal begins to evolve. The person who has died will be remembered but one begins to learn how to live with the loss.

The poet Henry Wadsworth Longfellow once wrote, "Well has it been said that there is no grief like the grief which does not speak." We cry most about the things we left unsaid and undone concerning the dead. All of us deal with grief differently. It's a process that we have to do alone, everyone in their own way. Tears can be compared to the blood of the soul; they are a way to heal the wound. But as Epicurus said, "It is possible to provide security against other ills, but as far as death is concerned, we men live in a city without walls." Grief never dies and it doesn't take much to reawaken it.

23

DEATH AND THE HUMAN LIFE CYCLE

While I thought that I was learning how to live, I have been learning how to die.

Leonardo da Vinci

Ivan Ilych's life had been most simple and most ordinary and therefore most terrible.

Leo Tolstoy

Since the day of my birth, my death began its walk. It is walking toward me, without hurrying.

Jean Cocteau

Death is psychologically as important as birth ... Shrinking away from it is something unhealthy and abnormal which robs the second half of life of its purpose.

Carl Gustav Jung

As my personal example has illustrated, death is perhaps the most difficult of life's events to cope with, yet one that we prepare for least. We've to come to grips with the fact that loss and grief are a natural part of life. Unfortunately, rationality and emotionality do not go hand in hand with death. Instead, the denial of death is a more common pattern of human behavior and remains a force throughout the human life cycle. Fortunately, the forces of suppression, repression, and other mind-numbing practices help to reduce our preoccupation with death and facilitate our ability to function. Whatever we do, however, a lingering feeling of sadness remains. This feeling has been described by the Japanese as the experience of *mono no aware*, the "pathos of things."

Human behavior reveals that the adult outlook toward death is not greatly different from that of children. What's remarkable is not that children arrive at adult views of death, but rather how tenuously adults hold on to childhood beliefs throughout life and how readily they revert to them. Children's views of dying and death are inseparable from the psychological defenses against the reality of

177

death that they acquire early in life. The study of child development reveals that death anxiety and the misery associated with separation from the original object of attention and preservation—the mother or other caretaker—have a lot in common.

From an ethological perspective, the source of these behavior patterns is basic attachment behavior with species survival as its original objective. As I have noted in Part One, on sexual desire, attachment behavior (like crying and searching) among young children can be viewed as an adaptive response to separation from a primary attachment figure, the person who provides support, protection, and care. Because human infants, like other mammalian infants, cannot feed or protect themselves, they are initially totally dependent on the care and protection of others. Over the course of evolutionary history, infants who were able to maintain proximity to an attachment figure were more likely to survive to reproductive age. Species survival means that attachment behavior is a basic characteristic of humankind and attachment behavior patterns dominate the human experience from the cradle to the grave. The more secure the mother-infant relationship has been, the fewer problems the adult will have with issues of separation and abandonment—and less death anxiety also. How an adult deals with separation in his or her adult relationships—and by extrapolation death anxiety—can be presumed to be a reflection of the quality of his or her attachment experiences in early childhood.

Our fear of death changes with age. As we age, getting closer to an appointment with death contributes to a change in attitude. Under the age of forty, we're immortal, measuring our lives as time-lived-so-far; over forty, and probably more aware of our physical frailties, our measure of life changes to time-left-to-live. To the young, death is merely a distant rumor: no young person truly believes he or she will ever die. But our awareness of death becomes clearer as age and infirmity bring it nearer.

Adolescents can simultaneously harbor a sense of immortality but experience feelings of vulnerability and incipient terror when they first begin to think about death. This is a point in life where they frequently transform suppressed death-related anxiety into death-defying, daredevil activities. Young adults are often concerned about dying before they have had the chance to do and experience all they hope for in life. Adult parents are more likely to worry about the effect of their possible death on other family members. Elderly people often express concern about "living too long" and becoming a burden on others and useless to themselves.

These perceptions of death at different points in the life cycle remind me of a story. One day a rich merchant asked a Zen master for a good saying that would help preserve the prosperity and happiness of his family. The master took brush and ink, and wrote: "Grandfather dies, father dies, son dies."

The merchant was very angry. "What kind of evil spell are you writing against my family?" he demanded. "It is no evil spell," said the master, "but a hope for your greatest good fortune. I wish that every man of your family shall live to be a grandfather. And I wish that no son may die before his father. What truer happiness than life and death in this order can any family desire?"

INTEGRITY VERSUS DESPAIR

An astute observer of human development, the psychoanalyst Erik Erikson, describes the last phase of life as a conflict between two opposing positions or attitudes (or dispositions or emotional forces) in the form of a polarity between integrity and despair. According to Erikson, integrity has to do with our capacity for creating order and meaning in life, a feeling of being at peace with oneself and the world, and having no regrets or recriminations. People with this disposition are more likely to look back positively on their lives and feel that they have left the world a better place than they found it. Despair represents the opposing disposition, a "sour grapes" attitude toward what life might have been, a feeling of wasted opportunities and regrets, the yearning to turn back the clock and have a second chance. People with this disposition are also characterized by a strong fear of loss of self-sufficiency and of their own death.

Erikson also points out how generations affect each other. A parent's or grandparent's behavior obviously affects a child's psychosocial development (which will include attitudes toward death and dying). In turn, the parent's or grandparent's psychosocial development is affected by their experiences of dealing with the child.

Leo Tolstoy's famous story *The Death of Ivan Ilych* is one of the single most moving and unforgettable works of fiction to explore the psychology of mortal illness, the act of dying, and spiritual resurrection.

The Death of Ivan Ilych

This novella, written in 1886, is an account of the writer's personal struggle for meaning in the face of the terrifying inevitability of death. Tolstoy's story is an exposition of everything contemporary culture tells us is important: wealth, stability, reputation, and family. It also presents a rich kaleidoscope of how others react to the process of dying. Tolstoy's story is a challenge to all who would like to die well, to make the most of the little time we've on earth, to create a life that has sense, and to build a life that is real.

Ivan Ilych is a conventional family man, and a judge, with a high social standing. He seems to have it all: a good career, a wife, children, friends, and hobbies. He is married to a handsome woman, although theirs is a marriage based more on external qualities than mutual attraction. He's a very successful judge, with the political savvy to advance his career.

Over time Ivan has developed an attitude of complete indifference toward his family. From his wife, he requires only general conveniences such as serving him dinner, being a housewife, or being a companion in bed. His relationships with his children aren't much better; his dealings with them are quite superficial. Moreover, his activities as a judge are perfunctory. The story leads us to understand that, like many people in contemporary society, money and work is the root of all happiness for Ivan. However, work and money also seem to be an escape from his artificial married life. His is an unexamined life, in which he is simply going through the motions. Ironically, although he's a judge dealing with death all the time, he never seems to have given much thought to his own life.

As the story continues, it plunges us into the confused mind of Ivan who wakes up one day with a pain that will not to go away. It becomes more and more excruciating, and Ivan is forced to visit physicians. None of them, however, can give him a solid diagnosis, although it soon becomes clear that his condition is terminal. Ivan is now brought face-to-face with his mortality, a baffling process, as until now the idea of death and dying has been a complete abstraction to him.

As Ivan's pain continues, it contributes to an increasing number of problems in his life. First it interferes with his ability to work, so he can no longer use work as an escape. Then, because of his illness, people begin to look down upon him. There's very little sympathy for his ordeal. His illness frightens them. They are very uncomfortable dealing with a dying man.

The people he once called his friends treat him the same way he treated them in the past: with total indifference. Even his wife considers his illness a nuisance. All he wants is pity, but nobody is prepared to give it to him. These disturbing experiences make Ivan increasingly aware that he has lived his life as an automaton, never allowing his emotions to affect the way of how he acted or performed his duties. He never has built up true, meaningful relationships. But now when he's dying, he permits himself to be more reflective.

On his deathbed, Ivan still hopes for a miraculous recovery. At the same time, he consoles himself with the thought that although his death will be an unfortunate event, his wife and children will be taken care of after he is gone. Then Ivan comes to the sudden realization that the accumulation of wealth, the big house, political power, and a beautiful wife, turn out to be meaningless, sterile things. Terrifyingly, he confronts the question, "What if my whole life has been wrong?" It's a frightening conclusion for a person to arrive at just before dying, and it causes Ivan more pain than his illness. It's the pain of knowing the truth that his life, which could have had meaning and substance, has been of no value. And now it is too late to do anything about it.

Many of us, like Ivan Ilych, lead shallow lives of quiet desperation. Many of us do not dare to probe into the feelings deep down inside us, fearful of what we may find. Many of us disregard the feelings and sufferings of others, fearful of stepping outside the lines of propriety. Many of us don't create meaningful relationships. Ivan Ilych's life demonstrates all of this.

Tolstoy's story shows us that what's really important in life is creating meaningful relationships, having people around who care. He also shows us that death is an inevitable part of life, and the active acceptance of this simple fact is a necessary precondition for leading a meaningful life. None of the characters surrounding Ivan (with the exception of his servant), seem to have yet understood these lessons, however. They all treat the dying Ivan as an unpleasant and foreign intrusion into their otherwise comfortable world. They hope that his bothersome presence will just go away.

Tolstoy describes how on his deathbed Ivan seems to oscillate between despair at the expectation of incomprehensible and terrible death and hope. At the end of the story, Ivan's pain becomes not only the central fact of his existence but also the means of his salvation. The pain saves him by sharpening and heightening all his senses. Ivan discovers that the pain that accompanies the process of his dying is a catalyst for self-knowledge and spiritual renewal. Ironically, in accepting the pain of death, Ivan symbolically rediscovers life.

This epiphany underlines the grave consequences of a life lived mechanically rather than holistically. But with this story, Tolstoy also shows us that a person can change, even at the eleventh hour. Even if it has to be through pain and suffering, every one of us is capable of redemption. Only in the face of death, however, is Ivan able to gain the requisite distance to behold the true meaning of his sense-less life. Once he sees this, he sees the trajectory of a life well lived. At the end, seconds before his death, Ivan sees what he describes as a light, and realizes that his past life was death itself and that the real life is only beginning.

Although *The Death of Ivan Ilych* is the story of a nineteenth-century man, it has all the characteristics of a modern, twenty-first-century individual: a person alienated from others, and one only compelled by his impending death to seek and find true meaning. Before death knocked on his door, Ivan happily believed that death was something that happens to other people, not to himself. The denial of death had been a major theme in his life. As we see in his situation, hope is independent of logic. Ivan's fate, however, which is everyone's fate, suggests that the inevitability of death ought to have consequences for how we live our lives. And here we have to thank Tolstoy for delivering this seemingly simple message in a story that transcends both time and culture.

Furthermore, as Tolstoy unravels Ivan's ongoing struggle to come to grips with his own mortality, we're faced with the challenge of looking at our own life and the manner in which we are living it.

24

TRANSCENDING THE ULTIMATE NARCISSISTIC INJURY

Trust yourself, then you will know how to live.

Johann Wolfgang Von Goethe

The most I ever did for you was to outlive you. But that is much.

Edna St. Vincent Millay

Pray that your loneliness may spur you into finding something to live for, great enough to die for.

Dag Hammarskjold

There is a Tibetan Buddhist saying that tells, "When you are born, you cry, and the world rejoices. When you die, you rejoice, and the world cries." Because our apprehension about death has its precursor in separation anxiety, complete severance from life can be viewed symbolically as the ultimate form of separation. Like Ivan Ilych, we use denial and ritual to cope with our lingering knowledge of death and keep our basic anxiety under control. We like to exert a modicum of control over the cycle of life. Rituals help us deal with the distress that accompanies death.

Symbolically, death is a long goodbye, the final separation, the ultimate rejection. Death is interpreted by loved ones as a form of total abandonment, creating a sense of complete loneliness. Our helplessness in the face of death contributes to deflation of the self; it is the ultimate narcissistic injury.

RITUALS OF DYING

It's not only the idea of death but encounters with death that trouble all of us. Coming face-to-face with death has an enormous effect on our thought processes and behavior. To deal with this dreaded encounter, we've devised numerous rituals to work through the horror that death represents to many of us.

With every death, the first question that people ask is: who's next? When will it be my turn? Human beings have always looked for ways to overcome this anxiety. This explains why every society has constructed rituals around death that do more than simply address the practical disposal of the corpse. The dead need to be mourned properly; they aren't surrendered that easily. To deal with our own fear of dying, we have developed a plethora of ways to mitigate our fear of annihilation, or total loss of the self.

Many societal beliefs and practices in many cultures appear to be in denial of death. Primitive societies rely heavily on ritual and ceremony to shield individuals and their community from evil and death. To placate the living, in many cultures the dead are surrounded by elaborate rites and ceremonials that provide some form of continuity. These rituals are connected to the cycle of life and attribute cosmic meaning to suffering and the ending of life. They are ways to ease the terror of death, to provide reassurance, enabling people to die with courage and dignity, and to help the living continue their journey, having mourned their loved ones. Cultural traditions vary, however. Some cultures view death as a transition to other forms of existence; others propose a continuous interface between the dead and the living; some cultures conceive a circular pattern of multiple deaths and rebirths; and yet others view death as the final end, with only nothingness following.

Whatever form these rituals take, these processes of mourning are very important to the living. The main purpose of all these rituals is to alleviate our anxiety about the inevitable encounter with death—to help us to go on with life. They help us to cope with our existential dilemma (fueled by death anxiety), making us feel that we're still alive. Without these rituals, the fear of death would not stay submerged but would be far more present and possibly deflect us from living. With the help of ritualistic cultural activities, however, we're more able to manage our fear of death and create meaning, organization, continuity, and instill hope in our lives. To create hope, these transition rituals provide a broad context of meanings and routines for securing the doubts and unknowns of individual experience. These rituals offer solace both to dying individuals and to their loved ones.

FEELING ALIVE

From the primary, self-contained narcissism of the infant, to the narcissism of the adult, a degree of narcissism—the possession of a solid dose of self-esteem—is necessary for human functioning and survival.

Feeling good about ourselves—having a narcissistic investment in the self—forms the foundation for self-assertion, creativity, and leadership. A solid dose of self-esteem reassures us that we count, and that we can make a difference, in spite of the knowledge of our inevitable, impending demise. Demonstrating our accomplishments to others is a way of asserting our existence. It's a way of reassuring ourselves that we aren't dead yet. Our capacity to believe in ourselves is vitally important.

The most important judgment we make in life is our judgment about ourselves. But to establish a positive sense of self-esteem, we must appreciate our successes and not just harp on the negatives in our lives. Having a morbid preoccupation with death is like driving through life with the handbrake on. Obsession with our future encounter with the Grim Reaper isn't a great way to build (and maintain) our sense of self-esteem. To retain a sense that we've a role to play in our world, we need to remain with the living. At the same time, we shouldn't be blind to the fact that our role is temporary.

Dealing with our fear of death while maintaining our sense of self-esteem isn't easy. Self-esteem doesn't exist in isolation. Societal validation will always be needed to establish and maintain a positive sense of self-esteem. The help of others is vital to our mental equilibrium. We judge and measure ourselves not against our own norms but against the norms of people who are important to us. We make a great effort to have our cultural worldviews validated by others, and compliance with cultural values will enhance our feeling of belonging and our sense of self-esteem. Being part of a greater scheme of things, from the nuclear family, through social groups, to society as a whole, makes us feel better. Feeling good about ourselves is an excellent antidote to death anxiety. Nothing builds self-esteem as much as others acclaiming our accomplishments.

Self-esteem should be seen as a cultural construct, starting with the kind of developmental experiences we've with our parents. In all cultures, the family imprints its members with selfhood. Our families introduce us to systems of meaning that are compatible with societal belief systems—including beliefs about the nature of death. We acquire a positive sense of self-esteem when we believe that we're living up to the values inherent in the cultural worldview of which we are a part. Failing to live up to these standards creates a sense of insecurity. For reasons of self-affirmation, we want others to subscribe to our way of looking at the world. If they do not, it may be interpreted as an assault on the self, a threat to our existence.

To reaffirm our self-esteem, to assert our existence and ward off the ultimate assault against the self—the inevitability of death—we go to great lengths to invent systems of "meaning" and "immortality." These "immortality" systems are ingenious ways of repressing and overcoming our inner fears about being insignificant within the greater scheme of things. To ward off the fear of death and nothingness, we're compelled to create mental constructs to create continuity. The creation of self-esteem enhancing systems seems to be the garment with which we protect our nakedness; the creation of systems of meaning helps us reaffirm that there is more to life than death. We hang on to the wish that life has meaning and that each of us has a special mission in life to negate the deterministic notion that we live to die.

To illustrate this point, I would like to refer once more to Ingmar Bergman's memorable film *Wild Strawberries*. In the opening scene of the film, Isak Borg is haunted by a nightmare that is full of death symbolism. The dream features a funeral procession, imagery of clocks and time running out, and Isak Borg finding himself in a coffin. Almost paralyzed with fear he wakes up and says aloud, "My name is Isak Borg. I am still alive. I am 76 years old. I really feel quite well." While he's awake, Isak tries to push away what his dreams are trying to tell him at night: he is very close to death. He reaffirms that he's still alive and who he is. Anxious not to fall back into his nightmare and have another encounter with death, Isak becomes restless. He wakes up the whole house and decides to drive from Stockholm to Lund where, at the university, a great affirmation of the self will take place, in the form of an honorary doctorate. He needs this flight into action to re-establish that he still exists, enhance his sense of self-esteem, and ward off his emerging death anxiety. His nightmare about his approaching death appears to have increased his need for self-affirmation. It also contributes to his need to repair conflict-ridden relationships before it is too late, especially rebuilding a relationship with his son.

This vignette within a film illustrates why we do what we do—how self-affirmation, self-esteem, and death anxiety are closely linked. However, we've to bear in mind—strange as it may sound— that our awareness of death remains quite symbolic. Most of our lives, we look at death as a merely abstract possibility. As Freud noted, we assume the role of spectators, even when contemplating our own death. Death only becomes a reality—as Ivan Ilych discovered—when we are actually dying, when we experience a serious decay of the body, or when we see someone or something die. But whether we're spectators or not, there will always be lingering feelings of anxiety about loneliness, and the ultimate separation. These thoughts touch the narcissistic core of our being. Loneliness is very frightening. It's a feeling that can break our spirit.

Self-esteem can only serve its anxiety-buffering function as long as faith is sustained in a specific cultural worldview about the continuity of the self in the greater scheme of things. Faith in a specific cultural worldview is maintained through secular and religious teachings, associated cultural rituals, and continual social validation in interpersonal and intergroup contexts.

Because faith in the cultural worldview depends on continuous consensual validation from others, those who question that worldview, or advocate a different one, threaten our equilibrium. Doubts are perceived as an attack on the self and create existential anxiety. If history is a teacher, it shows us that we're prepared to do anything to ward off these threats to our self-esteem. This explains our often violent reactions to people with different ideological or religious outlooks.

To maintain our sense of who we are, to create a strong foundation of the self, we try to adhere to the standards of appropriate conduct associated with the social roles that exist in the culture in which we live. Ideas right or wrong vary from culture to culture. Our need for affirmation of the self means that outsiders are frequently considered a threat. Being different is interpreted as a rejection of the belief systems we cherish—and those most susceptible to attack are those that concern our efforts to deny our mortality. Noncompliance with the prevalent systems of meaning will arouse an enormous amount of anxiety, all too frequently followed by aggression.

Unfortunately, human history is full of inhuman acts, acted out as a way to deny our mortality. Homo sapiens seems to be reluctant to follow the rule that when you can't have what you want, it's time you started wanting what you have. Instead we resort to violent action to demonstrate to others that what they believe is wrong. Anxiety about the inevitability of death is the greatest threat to our self-esteem, and explains the passions that become aroused when other people's systems of meaning don't conform to ours. Ironically, being a meaning-making species seems to be accompanied by intolerance for systems of meaning that differ from our own. As the Arab proverb says, "Make sure you have a different opinion and people will talk about you." In general, however, I have learned that arguments only confirm people in their own opinion, or, as Voltaire said, "Opinion has caused more trouble on this little earth than plagues or earthquakes."

25

IMMORTALITY SYSTEMS

Everything is the product of one universal creative effort. There is nothing dead in Nature.

Seneca

Do every act of your life as if it were your last.

Marcus Aurelius

What matters, therefore, is not the meaning of life in general, but rather the specific meaning of a person's life at a given moment.

Victor Frankl

Man is not just a blind glob of idling protoplasm, but a creature with a name who lives in a world of symbols and dreams and not merely matter. His sense of self-worth is constituted symbolically, his cherished narcissism feeds on symbols, on an abstract idea of his own worth, an idea composed of sounds, words, and images

Ernest Becker

A sense of meaning counters feelings of worthlessness and alienation. Creating meaning means creating hope. And hope is to the meaning of life what breathing is to the body. If we can find something to live for, if we can find some meaning to put at the center of our lives, even the worst kind of suffering becomes more bearable. In this context, the torturous lives of many saints can be read as examples of people who managed to transcend suffering. Meaning, self-affirmation, and self-esteem are closely intertwined. Finding meaning in whatever we do will bolster our sense of self-esteem as it affirms our existence.

WHERE ARE WE GOING?

As I have already suggested in my comments on Gauguin, we ask ourselves existential questions like "Who am I?"; "Where did I come from?"; "What should I do?"; "And what happens when I die?" to try and make sense out of things, to establish our place in the general scheme of things. Reflecting on these questions helps us to construct meaning, permanence, and stability. It fosters our sense of self-esteem and conveys hope of symbolic and even literal immortality.

Immortality through a religious belief system

Every culture, in upholding standards by which its people are supposed to abide, affords opportunities for us to find meaning and to live forever—symbolically, through the production of great works, creating institutions that extend beyond an individual's lifetime, through political ideologies, philosophical systems, scientific theories—and/or literally, through religious beliefs of an afterlife in heaven or by means of reincarnation. We base our self-esteem on something that offers permanent or enduring meaning: the nation, the tribe, the race, the new world vision, the timelessness of art, the truths of science, the rhythms of nature, or religious belief. Identifying with religious, political, or cultural immortality systems is a way of assuring ourselves of continuity and permanence.

Each of these belief systems promises to connect our lives with an enduring meaning that will not perish. These immortality systems help us believe that despite our personal insignificance, our weakness, and our inevitable death, our existence has meaning in some ultimate sense because it exists within an eternal and infinite scheme of things designed and brought about by some creative force.

All of us are aware of our need to combat our fear of insignificance. We want to be recognized; we want to be appreciated; we want to affirm our self. Our narcissistic disposition, our need to be recognized as important, our wish to be part of a greater scheme of things, is an essential part of the struggle to deal with our lingering fear of death. It appears to be the tragic destiny of our species that we feel this need to justify ourselves as an object of primary value in the universe; we want to stand out; we want to be heroes; we want to show the world that we matter. We want to be able to say, and have other people say when it's all over, that we made a difference. But the deeper we plunge into our narcissistic soup of self-admiration and idolization, the harder it becomes for us to come to terms with our inevitable fate—and the less able we are to face up to the fact of death in our daily activities. But as we have to accept that we all die—that we will not live forever—the challenge for many becomes to find something that does not die, something that will outlive us.

Religion has always been a great ally in alleviating feelings of annihilation, helplessness, separation, and abandonment, thoughts viewed as threats to the self, endangering self-esteem. The Bible tells us, "The last enemy that shall be destroyed is death," and offers eternity as the Promised Land. Religion, a complex belief system and set of rituals used to ward off feelings of fear and anxiety, is one of humankind's most ingenious solutions for dealing with our fear of death. By fostering a belief in a life hereafter, religion has assumed a consoling function and has played an integrative role in society. Moreover, with heaven as the ultimate destination, a religion like Christianity has provided an obvious incentive to living a true life, even if that means more melancholy and less fun. And religion presents a specific proposition: the reward we get in heaven will be proportionate to the amount of suffering we're prepared to endure on earth. If there is heaven, then of course we may be willing to accept the world's suffering for greater, later, longer lasting rewards. It has been suggested that true believers whose head is in heaven need not fear to put their feet in the grave.

Thus in our search for immortality systems we identify with religious or even political ideologies (Communism includes many aspects of an immortality system) and adopt a specific, culturally sanctioned viewpoint that we invest with ultimate meaning, and to which we ascribe absolute and permanent truth. But although religions emphasize leading a virtuous life on earth, all too often religious conviction has resulted in endless cycles of violence. Religions tend to single themselves out by a sense of invulnerable righteousness. Having selected one specific immortality system seems to necessitate protecting it against other "false" systems. The way we do this is to insist that all other absolute truths, all other systems of immortality, are incorrect. Time and again, we see religious leaders and followers incite aggression, fanaticism, hate, and xenophobia—inspiring and even legitimizing violent and bloody conflicts. At the core of these we frequently find a mindset that limits eligibility for immortality only to true believers. As the French mathematician-philosopher Blaise Pascal once said, "Men never do evil so completely and cheerfully as when they do it from religious conviction." So we attack and degrade—preferably kill—the disciples of different immortality systems. Christians kill Jews or Muslims, Protestants kill Catholics; Muslims vilify and kill Christians, Buddhists kill Hindus, and so the murderous clash of belief systems goes on. It seems as if we're asked to believe—madly—that a country or a specific group of people is ordained by heaven to commit unspeakable acts in the name of God.

Immortality through procreation

However we view the role of religion in society—as either a force for good or for evil—religion is the most prominent of our immortality systems. But there are many other ways of denying the reality of death and pursuing the concept of eternal life. We only have to remind ourselves of Freud's dictum that the "normal" personality should possess the ability "to love and to work." Deconstructing the first part of Freud's statement brings us to the act of procreation. One way of coping with the unacceptable notion of death is through the creation of children. As the philosopher John Whitehead said, "Children are the living messages we send to a time we will not see." Children are reflections of the self on which the adult can project his or her own aspirations and achievements. Children will perpetuate our beliefs and values. If we can't come to terms with the annihilation of our own aspirations and achievements, children may become our escape valve. Living through one's children—sending them on this "mission impossible"—is a way of overcoming death anxiety and arriving at a new psychological equilibrium that centers on life's meaning and continuity. Procreation is a natural immortality system. As Albert Einstein once said, "Our death is not an end if we can live on in our children and the younger generation. For they are us, our bodies are only wilted leaves on the tree of life." The creation of children as a way of indulging in the myth of immortality is a crucial variable in many societies. A Moroccan proverb explicitly states, "If a man leaves children behind him, it is as if he did not die." One hundred years from now it will not really matter what kind of car we drove, or what kind of house we lived in. It will not matter how much money we had, or what our clothes were like. What will matter are the memories about ourselves we give to our children.

Immortality through work

But there was a second part to Freud's equation. Work is another way of coping with the anxiety of death. Work can be an effective immortality system in many different ways. Some people—hyperactive individuals, workaholics who are totally preoccupied by work—overdo it. They only feel alive when they're working. They need to be engaged; and to accomplish things. This manic defense is their way of dealing with death anxiety.

Some may also suffer from the "edifice complex," the need to create a legacy in the form of a company, a building, or other tangible achievements. These are the people who like to see their name on the building. Creating a business entity that will be continued by other family members is their way of attaining some form of immortality. Many family business dynasties—especially those who are determined to keep the business in the family—have the search for immortality at its core.

For some people, work becomes a narcotic. They cannot relax. They are consistently preoccupied with performance, adding responsibility to responsibility, working incessantly to ward off the specter of the Grim Reaper. To them, life without the continuous pressure of work would be unimaginable. Only through work—reaching specific targets—can these people ward off depressive thoughts (which have death anxiety at their core) and share up a fragile sense of self-esteem. Their motto is, "I work, therefore I am." Work is their means of self-affirmation, their way to feel virtuous. These people need the structure of work to ward off the demons of loneliness, separation, and death anxiety. Unfortunately, their manic behavior to ward off these fears can be counterproductive. Increased anxiety leads to increased activity, which instead of having an anxiety-reducing effect, leads to even more activity, making the person a slave of specific metrics. The question is then, how long can they keep up the pace? How long can they drive away the depression that dogs our awareness of the end of life?

Several times, I saw an executive—I will call him Armand—who exemplified this flight into work. Armand was the CEO-owner of a construction firm. During my discussions with him, I saw him demonstrate increasingly manic-like behavior to fight his fear of getting older. He "worked hard but not smart," doing more and more work for work's sake. Sundays—days without a specific structure—were difficult for him. What he was failing to deal with was the big question: life after him. Although I tried to bring up this issue in our conversations, it was clear that Armand didn't like to think or talk about succession. Merely touching on the topic was anxiety provoking. From his reaction, he experienced it as a threat to his sense of immortality.

From what I could infer, Armand—who had evidently always been somewhat hyperactive—had been pushed into overdrive by a recent coronary bypass operation. His elevated mood state, expansive talking, and increased activity—although seductive—had begun to worry other executives in the corporation. They were concerned about his new, poorly thought-through efforts at diversification, especially recent investment in a film company, which they thought was too risky.

Not only did Armand invest in the film company, he also asked it to make a very expensive documentary of his organization. Its alleged purpose was to help them better articulate their brand identity. The documentary turned out to be a hagiography about the Armand's career. It was as if he had wanted to create a monument for posterity. This action (confirmed in further discussions with him) amounted to some kind of "anti-necrologic notice"—a major defense against emerging death anxiety. The work with the film crew, however, had given Armand an even greater taste for the film business, which increased the anxiety of other executives in the company. A small investment was one thing but taking the company into the film industry on a large scale was another matter altogether. It was not a domain where they had any expertise. What would be next? Would other film projects follow? Not only were his executives worried that Armand's frantic work pace would contribute to another coronary incident, but they also began to question his sense of judgment. They were fearful about the company's future viability. And there was still that unsolved problem of succession.

Armand's case is only one among many examples I have seen of people using work to ward off the fear of death. Besides engaging in frantic, even meaningless business activities—a process where means and ends may have lost their significance—at the other end of the spectrum there is the example of creative work. Creative work is not the monopoly of artists, writers, or scientists. Any work that is innovative, deviates from routine activities, or—more importantly—is valued by the creator, is creative. It is done in the hope and belief that the things that are created are of lasting worth and meaning, that will outlive or outshine death and decay. The art of creation, supposedly for posterity, is another immortality system that may provide historical continuity. It is an open question, however, how many of us are truly creative or even have the opportunity to be so. Maybe Woody Allen had a point when he said, "I don't want to achieve immortality through my work. I want to achieve it through not dying."

Immortality through nature

In the book of Genesis we are told, "Dust thou art, and unto dust thou shalt return." All that lives rises from the body of earth, and will go back into that body. Our ancestors never lost sight of this truth. In many primitive cultures, cycles of existence, life and death, body and soul, earth and underworld, were interwoven in the cycle of the seasons. Many of these cultures honored the Fruitful Provider, often imagined as Gaia, the Great Mother. Mother Earth may sustain the crops, but Mother Earth can also generate terrible forces—earthquakes, floods, and volcanic eruptions. Thus the Great Mother needs to be pacified. Grain from the first harvest of every season was offered to her, and nourishing gifts of milk, wine, or blood were poured directly into the ground as an expression of gratitude. Remnants of these traditions still survive, even in developed countries. In addition, earth is also home to the dead. Agricultural peoples all over the world would plant their dead into the ground like seeds, expecting them to be born again from the earth in one way or another—to spring up new from another woman's womb, or in the body of an animal.

Dante said, "Nature is the art of God," and Rembrandt, "Choose only one master—nature." A Greek proverb says: "A society grows great when old men plant trees whose shade they know they shall never sit in." These sayings suggest that nature can be viewed as another immortality system—and that we don't inherit the earth from our ancestors; we borrow it from our children.

I subscribe very much to this feeling of unity with nature—viewing the earth as a single integrate organism—having crossed many rivers, forests, steppes, and mountains. Climbing to the top of a mountain, and seeing the landscape—sky, snow, rivers, other mountains—these images always leave me with a feeling of being part of a larger whole.

Many other people seem to agree. For example, the French Renaissance scholar Michel de Montaigne once noted, "If you don't know how to die, don't worry; nature will tell you what to do on the spot, fully and adequately. She will do this job perfectly for you; don't bother your head about it." Or to quote Albert Einstein, "What I see in nature is a magnificent structure that we can comprehend only very imperfectly, and that must fill a thinking person with a feeling of humility. This is a genuinely religious feeling that has nothing to do with mysticism."

To some of us, nature is full of meaning while to others it means little. But symbolically, our perceptions of nature and our associations with immortality are closely connected. Whatever an individual's inner world, nature contains imagery that simultaneously frightens and attracts. There is respect and fear for the elements—storms, floods, thunder, and lightning. But besides the awe for nature, people also experience a feeling of warmth and continuity fostered by the existence of natural laws: the daily cycle of darkness and light, the passing of the seasons, the growing of plants, and the falling of leaves. Being surrounded by mountains, valleys, forests, streams, and oceans becomes a form of communion of life and death for many. Merging with nature in death is viewed as being part of an eternal cycle of life of the self with others, a place of resurrection. Every night that folds us up in darkness may have associations with death but with the first of dawn, life seems to be renewed. All forms of decay are just masks for regeneration and life.

People with this particular outlook toward nature don't view death as an end, but as a transition. They may even experience a sense of *unica mystica*, or oceanic feeling, a state of boundlessness whereby the individual seems to merge with the universe. To quote the aviator Charles Lindbergh, "In wilderness I sense the miracle of life, and behind it our scientific accomplishments fade to trivia." This is one thing that makes the threat of global warming and the destruction of nature such a frightening possibility.

But do these various immortality systems still fulfill their purpose? Do these edifices of self-affirmation still function effectively in post-industrial society? These are not easy questions to answer. Obviously, many people still resort to them. They need these systems to overcome existential anxiety. Doing without them would be catastrophic. Others, however, have a more pragmatic outlook, acknowledging the finality of their stay on earth. For them, it is only a brief visit. For them, to pick up a phrase I used earlier in this book, "The journey is all, the end nothing." They take to heart the text written on a Roman tombstone:

> Do not pass by my epitaph, traveler. But having stopped,
> listen and learn, then go your way.
> There is no boat in Hades, no ferryman Charon,
> No caretaker Aiakos, no dog Cerberus.
> All we who are dead below
> Have become bones and ashes, but nothing else.
> I have spoken to you honestly, go on, traveler,
> Lest even while dead I seem loquacious to you.

When we finally are able to face the fact that we will die, as will everybody else, we will come to the realization of the fragility of life and the preciousness of every moment. And hopefully, from this realization of the tragic transience of things will grow a deep compassion toward humankind.

This sense of pragmatism doesn't mean, however, that we should adopt a mechanical outlook on death. We need to respect the mourning process. Whatever society we live in, we need rituals, specific rites of passage, to help the living deal with the dying. Rituals are very important in the transition process; they create peace of mind and reassurance.

26

DEATH IN OUR POST-INDUSTRIAL AGE

Old friends pass away, new friends appear. It is just like the days. An old day passes, a new day arrives. The important thing is to make it meaningful: a meaningful friend— or a meaningful day.

Dalai Lama

I often say a great doctor kills more people than a great general.

Gottfried Leibniz

To die proudly when it is no longer possible to live proudly. Death of one's own free choice, death at the proper time, with a clear head and with joyfulness, consummated in the midst of children and witnesses: so that an actual leave-taking is possible while he who is leaving is still there.

Friedrich Nietzsche

We all die. The goal isn't to live forever, the goal is to create something that will.

Chuck Palahniuk

But how effective are these rituals in our post-industrial society? Haven't they become rather hollow and stale?

In his age of narcissism, preoccupied as we're with our personal well-being, hedonism reigns. Sleeping pills, anti-depressants, and Prozac have become popular crutches. What our reliance on these kinds of drugs tells us about the society we live in? Why are people drugging themselves out of awareness?

Emptiness, anomie, and alienation have become the great afflictions of modern life. The sense of community so common in pre-industrial society has largely been lost. Many of the meaningful rituals that once bound members of society together have vanished. In our narcissistic age, self-seeking materialism and the promised salvation by science and technology have become the prominent forces that shape our daily lives.

In this environment, the notions of suffering, dying, and death have been pushed to the periphery of cultural experience. In the process, however, we are violating something that is most sacred to us. Fueled by man's denial of death, popular culture—more than in the past—has found it expedient to expel any thoughts of dying and death from our daily existence. However, things that are pushed out of conscious awareness will re-emerge from a more subterranean terrain through our dreams, daydreams, and fantasy life. Creating a culture of denial will not create a stable mindset and drugging ourselves into denial will bring only temporary respite.

Medical technology, in particular, has been instrumental in pushing death anxiety underground and has contributed to the depersonalization of the death experience. While death is already frightening enough in itself for many people, our ways of dying in contemporary society have become an additional terror. Dying has become extremely undignified, depersonalized, and dehumanized. As the Swiss playwright and novelist Max Frisch stated, "Technology is a way of organizing the universe so that man doesn't have to experience it." Medical technology has steamrolled us. For some of us, it's not the ending of life that precipitates the most fear but the thought of how life ends. As the American architect Buckminster Fuller once said, "Humanity is acquiring all the right technology for all the wrong reasons."

Technology is replacing meaningful ritual with the mechanization of death. Dying people are defiled, stigmatized, and relegated to the role of second-class citizens. They aren't listened to or taken seriously; things are done to them. This situation is aggravated by the view that dying people can have a contaminating effect on others: we try to contain and sanitize their experiences so that they can't push our noses in the kind of reality that we'd rather not see. Technological advances aid and abet this process by fostering a culture of detachment, disengagement, and depersonalization.

The tendency to hide and exclude death from everyday life has been helped by the transfer of the place of death from the home to the hospital. The social innovator Florence Nightingale was already worried about this trend, and its implications for the dying, when she said, "It may seem a strange principle to enunciate as the very first requirement in a hospital that it should do the sick no harm." In pre-industrial society the care of the dying took place at home, in plain sight, as it did for my grandmother. It was part of the cycle of life. But in post-industrial society the burden of care has been delegated to medical professionals. The dying process has been confined to hospitals and long-term care facilities. Nowadays, family members and friends who used to accompany the dying on their last journey are largely removed from the equation. To quote the movie tycoon

Samuel Goldwyn, "A hospital is no place to be sick." He had a point. For most of us, dying in a hospital is a highly unattractive prospect.

Delegating the dying process to the medical profession, with its "professional" resources and sophisticated medical equipment, is now de rigueur. Hospitals, it's argued, can take better care of the dying. But underneath the rational explanations of this systematic delegation lurks another: the unpleasant and disturbing sights of the dying process are removed from our day-to-day experience. And this delegation—where death is hidden away and institutionally confined—is quite an attractive option. It's a very effective way of neutralizing our anxiety about death and dying. It's the story of Siddhartha revisited.

MANAGING DEATH

In the hospital, dying is redefined as a technical process that's professionally and bureaucratically managed. The horribleness and enormous suffering of dying is banished from public visibility as it's isolated within the professional, technical confines of the health care facility. But although the dying process is removed from public sight, it's very much present for the professional caretakers. Hospital personnel have to cope with their own death anxiety, reactivated when dealing with the dying. They have to manage these fears one way or another.

The psychoanalyst Isabel Menzies, in a study of nurses who dealt with the seriously ill or dying, noted that their work was organized to maximize containment and modification of emerging anxiety. There was a prevailing perception within the medical establishment that if the relationship between nurse and patient was too close, the nurse would experience too much distress when the patient died. Consequently, nurses were required to perform a few specialized tasks with a large number of patients, restricting contact with any single one of them. This approach helped foster a culture of distance, detachment, and depersonalization. According to Menzies' observations, no direct attempts were made to address the issue of the fear of death and develop the nurses' capacity to respond to anxiety in a more psychologically healthy way. Menzies' example is revealing of how the medical establishment tries to shore up dysfunctional methods of death denial. And her disturbing observations are still valid. One of the most difficult things to contend with in a hospital is the assumption by the staff that if you're old and sick, you have also lost your mind.

The problem is aggravated by the tendency of many health professionals to view death as a defeat and a failure on both personal and professional fronts. Death is seen as a sign of incompetence. They are trained to prolong life: dealing with the dying isn't really part of their education.

So it shouldn't really surprise us that not only nurses but also most doctors have very poor training in talking to patients, especially about death. Because of their discomfort, these final guardians of life assume a professional shell of detachment, denial, and depersonalization. It's interesting here to turn to an insightful and touching book, *Final Exam*, by Pauline Chen, a surgeon specializing in liver transplants, who wrote: "During almost fifteen years of school and training, I faced death over and over again. And I learned from many of my teachers and colleagues to suspend or suppress any shared human feelings for my dying patients, as if doing so would make me a better doctor." She describes how, in a patient's final hour, the doctor would close the curtain around the hospital bed, and disappear quickly, leaving family members alone with their dying relative.

The training these doctors receive may supply a high level of professional competence but fall desperately short in helping them to express empathy or confront their own fears of death. Death presents medical personnel with a double whammy: a reminder of their personal vulnerability and a signifier of professional failure. It's no wonder that the profession seems to have instituted a strong aversion to anything to do with death. Ironically, in the dying process, many things happen to the dying person, but he or she has very little say in what goes on. In modern medicine, death is everywhere and nowhere at the same time.

Death denial by health professionals and the people close to the dying hampers our ability to understand that some very elderly people, with no hope for recovery, may have reached the point when they want to die naturally. Instead, hospital personnel, often encouraged by distraught family members, may resort to overly complex technological solutions to prolong life, regardless of the patient's wishes, in an effort to master their own anxiety. They are in denial of what they're really doing, and how the patient experiences it. People in the helping profession may act in this way as a reaction to their own fear. These practices, however, degrade the dying process. It's a very troublesome development that contributes nothing to dying with dignity.

In modern society, forces in the cultural and medical establishment converge in a conspiracy of silence surrounding suffering, dying, and death. Many of the norms and rituals that once helped to sustain, guide, and comfort people in the dying process have vanished or have been downgraded. Death has been managed out of common awareness and incorporated within a technological, medical model. Death and dying now lie at the periphery of human existence.

Reflecting on this, I realize that I've never been taught many of the important things in life. Death wasn't discussed when I was at school. In retrospect, now I have reached a different stage in life, these unsaid things may be the most important things that are to be learned. But as these things were never taught to me, like many people, I had to learn about them on my own. Why are these important issues not taught? It almost makes me wonder why we have schools. Schools don't teach us how to love; they don't teach us how to deal with money; they don't teach us how to be somebody; they don't teach us how to divorce; they don't teach us how to grieve; and, to top it all, they don't teach us how to die.

But perhaps I'm getting things out of perspective. No form of teaching will be enough to create a greater understanding of what dying is about. Certain things can't be taught; they have to be experienced. As Jim Morrison, the American poet and singer once said, "I wouldn't mind dying in a plane crash. It'd be a good way to go. I don't want to die in my sleep, or of old age, or OD ... I want to feel what it's like. I want to taste it, hear it, smell it. Death is only going to happen to you once; I don't want to miss it." Perhaps the important thing—when we're at death's door—is to have no regrets. We should do the things we want to do, and do them now. The elderly rarely express regrets for the things they did, but rather for the things they didn't do. Perhaps the only people who fear death are those with regrets.

There is a Zen story about a monk who asked his master, "What is the way?" The master responded, "An open-eyed man falling into a well." Our challenge is to keep our eyes wide open as we look death in the face.

27

GOING INTO THAT GOOD NIGHT

The art of living well and the art of dying well are one.

Epicurus

Only cowards insult dying majesty.

Aesop

There's nothing glorious in dying. Anyone can do it.

Johnnie Rotten

Dying is a very dull, dreary affair. And my advice to you is to have nothing whatever to do with it.

William Somerset Maugham

I recently (and belatedly) saw the movie *Sophie Scholl*. This is the true story of a twenty-one-year-old university student in Nazi Germany who had the courage to stand up to the Nazi regime and state that what they were doing was wrong. It tells the story of the White Rose resistance movement. The film portrays Sophie Scholl's last days before she was executed by the Nazis in the afternoon of February 22, 1943. Although originally both Sophie and her brother Hans believed that Hitler would lead Germany to greatness—and had even been members of the Hitler Youth—they had become increasingly disillusioned. In their outlook, they were influenced by their father, the mayor of Forchtenberg, who felt that Hitler was leading Germany down the road to destruction.

Throughout her childhood, Sophie's parents emphasized the importance of following the dictates of the heart, to do what was right. They encouraged her in whatever she wanted to do, including her choices in education. After a stint as a kindergarten teacher, in May 1942, Sophie entered the University of Munich to become a student of biology and philosophy, a period when she became increasingly disenchanted with Hitler's regime.

201

Although the members of the White Rose knew that open dissent was impossible, they felt that it was the duty of citizens to take a stand against the Nazi regime. They distributed a series of leaflets that stated that the Nazi system had slowly imprisoned the German people and was now destroying all of them. The regime had turned evil; it had become like the mythological figure Cronos, who ate his young. It was time, one essay said, for Germans to rise up and resist the tyranny of their own government.

These leaflets had a dramatic effect on the student community. It was the first case of internal dissent against the Nazi regime in Germany. The Scholls and their friends had to be cautious, however, as they knew what would happen if they were caught by the Gestapo. As well from distributing flyers, the members of the White Rose engaged in other, highly visible actions, like producing graffiti in numerous locations, saying "Down with Hitler," "Hitler the Mass Murderer," and "Freedom." The Gestapo was in a frenzy to identify the members of the group.

On February 18, Sophie, Hans, and Christoph Probst were caught leaving pamphlets at the University of Munich and arrested. After their arrest, the true test of Sophie's character began. But the Gestapo official who interrogated her realized that he would not convince her of being wrong, even under threat of death. Sophie had the moral high ground, and he knew it. He tried to get her to sign a statement that would have led to lesser charges. She refused his offer.

Four days after their arrest, the three members of the White Rose were tried by the presiding judge, the chief justice of the People's Court of the Greater German Reich, who came especially from Berlin. The judge played the role of Grand Inquisitor in a farcical trial in which it was almost impossible for the accused to defend themselves. He acted as both judge and jury and the lawyers for the defense did nothing to defend them.

The judge ranted at Sophie, saying that he couldn't understand what had twisted the students' minds. Sophie was on record as saying "Somebody, after all, had to make a start. What we wrote and said is also believed by many others. They just don't dare express themselves as we did." She continued: "You know the war is lost. Why don't you have the courage to face it?" In the context, her bravery and refusal to cower before Nazi authority appears remarkable. When Hans and Sophie's parents tried to get into the courtroom, they were refused entry. The entire courtroom could hear their father shout: "One day there will be another kind of justice! One day they will go down in history!"

Predictably, the judge sentenced all three to death. Hans and Sophie's defiance, however, in the face of terrifying consequences, gained them enormous admiration. Sophie remained forthright, steadfast, and hopeful in the face of the Gestapo and the Nazi kangaroo court which condemned her. It was clear that even the spectators in the court room were extremely uncomfortable about the way the proceedings had been going, not knowing where to look. Deep down, they admired Sophie's courage.

In prison, Hans and Sophie were permitted one last visit from their parents. Although profoundly distressed by the immediate fate of their two children, they were very proud of them—proud that they would rise to such acts of courage and conviction—that they stood up for the oppressed, that they would not merely swallow what their government told them, but followed their curiosity to the truth. Before leaving her parents with a smile, perfectly composed, Sophie was reminded by her mother to think of Jesus. On entering her cell, she immediately broke down. She had held out before her parents, not wanting to distress them further. The Gestapo official who had arrested her saw her crying and Sophie apologized. She had not cried once during his interrogation.

The prison guards allowed Hans, Sophie, and Christoph to have one short, last visit together. Soon after, Sophie was then led to the guillotine by two men in top hats—the usual funeral attire. One observer described her walking to her death "without turning a hair, without flinching."

When she was laid on the block, her last words were *"Die Sonne scheint noch,"* meaning "The sun still shines." Christoph Probst was next. Hans Scholl was last; just before he was beheaded, he cried out: "Long live freedom!" Afterwards, more members of the group were executed or sent to concentration camps. Following Sophie's death, a sixth leaflet was smuggled out of Germany and dropped by the millions by Allied Forces over Germany under a new title: "The Manifesto of the Students of Munich."

What made Sophie so courageous? How did she manage to keep her cool throughout the interrogations? It is clear that Sophie Scholl's Christian faith gave her a strong sense of the right thing to do and helped her transcend death. Of course, her way of looking at the world didn't emerge out of a vacuum. Her parents had played an important role in instilling values—her father's stand vis-à-vis Hitler was very telling.

Today, every German knows the story of the White Rose movement. A square at the University of Munich is named after Hans and Sophie Scholl. And there are streets, squares, and more than a hundred schools all over Germany named after the members of the White Rose. Even today people leave white roses in a square near the university where their deeds are commemorated. In 2005, a ZDF Television audience survey voted Hans and Sophie the fourth greatest Germans of all time. Sophie Scholl's sister Inge wrote: "Perhaps genuine heroism lies in deciding to stubbornly defend the everyday things, the mundane and the immediate."

The question that this remarkable story raises, what went through Sophie's mind just before she laid her head on the block of the guillotine? How did she manage to face her death so courageously? What did her last words—"The sun still shines"—mean? Furthermore, how did the people who condemned her to death feel—the Gestapo officer and the judge? Did they feel a sense of righteousness or did they have second thoughts? What would be foremost in *their* minds when their time was up? Sophie's last moments raise important questions for all of us. How would we have acted in this situation?

LAST WORDS

There are many examples, real or apocryphal, of famous last words. Voltaire is supposed to have said on his deathbed—in response to a priest who asked him to renounce Satan— "Now, now my good man, this is no time to be making enemies." "Why are you weeping? Did you imagine that I was immortal?" were the last words of the French King, Louis XIV, to his servants. The poet Heinrich Heine said, "God will pardon me. It is his trade." For Goethe it was, "More light!" "My wallpaper and I are fighting a duel to the death. One of us must go," were the last, probably apocryphal, words of Oscar Wilde. One of the early leaders of the French revolution, Georges Danton, instructed his executioner, "Show my head to the people, it is worth seeing." Cecil Rhodes bemoaned, "so little done, so much to do," while Winston Churchill declared, "I'm bored with it all." "Don't worry! It's not loaded," were the last words of rock musician Terry Kath, who was playing Russian roulette. And George Eastman, the founder of Eastman Kodak, announced "My work here is done, why wait?" before he killed himself.

And of course there are many, many more on record. Reading people's last words from this side of the grave, I can't help speculating how true a window they offer into the soul. What do they say about the people who uttered them? What insights do they give to each individual's personal demons? Quite a lot, I suspect.

Last words hold a fascination for us because they respond to our need for closure, desire for immortality, and attraction to the mystique of death scenes. Last words, handed down from generation to generation, bestow some kind of immortality on their maker, surviving in our collective memory. The content epitomizes a life, or conveys a sense of irony: it might even represent the last performance before an audience.

"Die Sonne scheint noch—the sun still shines." What did these words, uttered between this world and death, mean to Sophie Scholl? That she still believed in the goodness of humankind, in spite of all the signs she had seen to the contrary? That there was eternal hope? That she trusted that the actions of the White Rose wouldn't be forgotten— that what they did would stand out as an example for future generations? We will never know. But this young woman's simple statement remained with the people present at her death. It became part of Germany's collective unconscious, creating a form of immortality.

The remarkable story of Sophie Scholl tells us that it's one thing to deal with death in the abstract, but a very a different thing to face it directly. Facing the condemned or the terminally ill is not easy, because we can project on to what they are enduring, what we will eventually face ourselves. Nevertheless, we have always been morbidly attracted to death scenes. Our fascination seems to be based on a tension between our inability to accept the reality of our own death and the reality of seeing it happen to someone else.

Most people—even those who, in a professional capacity, are used to seeing it at close quarters—are so steeped in death denial that they are caught by surprise when death appears at their door. Overwhelmed and confused, they miss out on the extraordinary opportunity for peace and resolution that is inherent in the dying process. Instead of learning from it, they engage in technological flight behavior.

STAGES OF TRANSITION

The challenge for all of us is to move beyond denial and to view death as part of a natural process. The death of a person shouldn't only be seen as a normal stage in nature's biological rhythm—in the words of the British philosopher Jonathan Miller, "a natural appointment that must be kept"—but also as part of the immense, physical universe. Death, like birth, should be seen as an essential element of life, a transition or another form of separation. And like any form of separation it follows certain patterns.

The theme of separation brings us once more to the work of John Bowlby, whose seminal theory of mother-child separation identified his famous thesis of the triad of reactions to separation: protest, despair, and detachment. In the first phase of protest, the young

205

child appears acutely distressed at having lost its mother and seeks to recapture her by the full exercise of its limited resources. After the initial protest, this phase is followed by despair. The child seems to lose all hope of reunion, although its preoccupation with the missing mother is still evident. But the child's behavior suggests increasing hopelessness. It becomes withdrawn and inactive, making no demands on its caretakers. The child is in a state of deep mourning. In the final phase, detachment, the child seems to overcome its loss and become responsive, sociable, and even cheerful. As the child shows greater interest in its surroundings, this phase is often welcomed as a sign of recovery. But viewing it this way is overly simplistic. The child's sociability is superficial. In effect, the child has adopted an "I don't care" attitude. A child that can speak may even go so far as to say, "I don't want mommy." In fact, the detachment response is a shutdown of loving feelings, a strategy that helps the child deal with loss in a number of different ways: it punishes the person who has gone. Detachment is a disguised expression of rage: intense and violent hatred is a common response to abandonment. It may also be a defense against the agony of loving, and possibly losing, again. Contrary to the old cliché, absence makes the heart grow colder, not fonder. At this point the child no longer seeks out the mother and may even ignore her if or when she returns.

Bowlby's theory has universal implications for the way we deal with any form of loss or transition in life, including the process we go through when we enter the final stage of our life. But if Bowlby dealt with attachment and separation in a generic way, the psychologist Elisabeth Kübler-Ross has done more than anyone to bring the final stage of life out into the mainstream of cultural discussion. She became a spokesperson for the needs of the dying, and a pioneering advocate for death with dignity.

Unlike many health care professionals, Kübler-Ross made it a point to spend time with terminal patients. She was appalled by the standard treatment they received. She felt that their needs were ignored, that they were abused, and that nobody was being honest with them. She criticized the effects of the increasingly technological management of modern death—loneliness, mechanization, dehumanization, and depersonalization. She portrayed the terror of dying, and how the medical treatment the dying received came at the cost of compassion and sensitivity. While the dying looked for peace and recognition of their suffering, and hoped for dignity, they found themselves instead on the receiving end of invasive procedures like infusions, transfusions, and other technologically driven plans of action.

Kübler-Ross also introduced a stage model of grief, identifying five stages most people tend to go through when faced with the realization of their own impending death: denial and isolation, anger, bargaining, depression, and acceptance. These five stages have since been applied to the grieving process the bereaved go through as well.

The first stage, denial and isolation, is usually a temporary shock response to the bad news. Isolation arises when other people, including family members, start to avoid the dying individual, because of their own uncomfortable feelings. This stage is followed by anger, which can be expressed in various ways. There may be a "Why me?" reaction, a feeling that others deserve to die rather than oneself. This reaction may be accompanied by envy and a sense of unfairness: other people don't seem to care; they are still enjoying life. The subsequent stage is bargaining, a brief stage that is hard to observe because it's often a process between the patient and God, or fate. The next stage is depression, mourning what will be lost. The final stage is acceptance, a stage reached only after working through some resistance. It takes a while to reach this stage, which fundamentally involves giving up, recognizing the inevitability of death.

Some critics point to dangers involved in using this sort of stage theory, concerned that it might turn into a deeply embedded ideology about dying, something that doesn't simply describe the dying process that people go through but ends shaping or prescribing the dying process. A person may be considered to fall short if he or she does not systematically plod through each of these stages. It may be more appropriate to regard these five stages as steps that we use to help us work through catastrophic news and cope with trauma.

Kübler-Ross also argued that dying doesn't need to be terrible and tragic, but could be a springboard for courage, growth, and enrichment, much as is suggested in the last part of Ivan Ilych's story. In that respect her outlook has been refreshing. It's fair to say that Kübler-Ross's idea of dying with dignity has been welcomed in a society that was becoming increasingly fearful of the indignities of technologically managed death. Her work was not only welcomed by the general public but has also been influential in the medical community, which has taken many of her observations to heart.

THE HOSPICE CARE SYSTEM

Kübler-Ross's contributions have been responsible for the development of a movement that has sought to eliminate our long-standing cultural taboos about suffering, dying, and death. Her theory offered alternative ways of dealing with death, in the transformation of dying into an opportunity for growth and dignity.

Kübler-Ross has also been a powerful influence on the hospice care system, a program of humane and supportive care for the emotional, social, and spiritual needs of dying people and their families. Hospice work is founded on a philosophy of care, recognizing death as the final stage of life and providing the dying with palliative care so that their last days have dignity and quality, and the opportunity to spend this time with their loved ones. Hospice care is an alternative to hospitalization. The dying are supported at home for as long as possible, and given relief from pain. The hospice itself provides an attractive environment for respite care and when the patient eventually can no longer be cared for at home. Hospice staff also provides personal and family counseling.

Guided by this philosophy, an increasing number of health care professionals make great efforts to reduce the anxiety of the terminally ill by providing accurate and reassuring information, using relaxation techniques, anxiolytics, or antidepressants. Of course, we need to consider whether the hospice philosophy, with its focus on dignity and its preparedness to welcome death as a vital part of the human experience, really marks a sea change in attitude, or is merely a reconfiguration and continuation of a culture of denial in a new form.

We can also ask whether the final acceptance stage of life can best be compared to early infancy, a stage of narcissistic bliss, when nothing was asked of us and we were given all we wanted. Maybe at the end of our days, when we've worked and given, enjoyed ourselves and suffered, we go back to where we started. We do sleep a lot, retreating to a postfetal state.

During the last two years of my mother's life, her interest in the external world started to diminish. She withdrew increasingly into her inner world. She felt that her body had worn out and that her time was up. But, as she said herself, her mind was definitely present. Like a baby, she began to spend more and more time in her inner world. Her dream life took over from her waking life. She slept a great deal, and when she woke recounted to me in great detail the vivid dreams she had had while asleep. These dreams were full of imagery of important figures from her past; her parents, old, long-deceased friends, memories of the war. Her increased dreaming was a sign to me of her impending end. The twilight zone between waking, sleeping, dreaming, and dying in which she lived made every time of waking a surprise—until the final moment came.

Arriving at this stage of acceptance brings life full circle. It's accompanied by a sense of resignation. However, even the most accepting, most realistic patients always leave the possibility open for some cure, for the discovery of a new miracle drug. Our denial of death informs an extremely strong life force. To quote Samuel Johnson, "The natural flights of the human mind aren't from pleasure to pleasure but from hope to hope."

28

THE DYING OF THE LIGHT

The dream crossed twilight between birth and dying.

T. S. Eliot

A man's dying is more the survivors' affair than his own.

Thomas Mann

To live in the hearts we leave behind is not to die.

Thomas Campbell

Life is no brief candle to me. It is a sort of splendid torch which I have got a hold of for the moment, and I want to make it burn as brightly as possible before handing it on to future generations.

George Bernard Shaw

The Buddhist parable of the mustard seed tells the story of a woman grieving uncontrollably over the death of her son. She doesn't understand the terminal nature of death and, searching for a cure for her son's "illness," asks the Buddha to heal him. The Buddha tells her to find a few grains of mustard seed from any house in the city. These mustard seeds will serve as an antidote for the "illness." But there's one condition; she can accept the mustard seed only from a house in which no one has ever died. After an exhaustive and fruitless search she finally realizes the truth—death is everyone's inevitable destiny. The tranquility this realization brings her enables her to submit her son's body to the funeral pyre.

As the story reiterates, death comes to all of us. We can take any number of escape routes—getting high, getting drunk, engaging in one kind of death-defying adventure or another—in order to forget our mortality. Or we can join a religious movement, associate ourselves with an ideology, build charitable institutions and put our name on them, build a business, fill a house with children, or produce an enduring work—but all our attempts to ensure our immortality are futile. Death does not forget us, nor does it let us ignore reality for very long.

We all have to accept the mystery and responsibility that come with a life structured by death. Flight into denial is not a satisfactory solution. Death and dying can't be pushed out of our conscious awareness; we can't avoid dealing with this critical fact of life. We need to change our attitude to death and dying, and move from denial to acceptance, without losing our vitality and our will to live.

WHAT ABOUT YOU?

By virtue of being human we all know that we're alive, and are more or less aware of ourselves as separate entities and beings. We also know that a point will come when we will cease to have life and no longer function. But beyond these conscious thoughts, we are not really sure what death entails or means. It's the greatest of mysteries.

Living also means incorporating death. But as I discussed here, dealing with the reality of our own death is still highly uncomfortable. We avoid talking about it. But we must have the courage to look our fear of death in the face. We have to learn how to prepare for it, and live courageously despite our awareness of it.

A modest, uncomfortable assignment

The following assignment can help us confront how we deal with this disquieting truth, and on the way learn more about ourselves.

Do you think about death often or rarely? Are there special circumstances that make you think about death? Are you afraid of death? Do you know why? What do you imagine death to be like? Do you discuss these questions with others?

Have you ever lost someone close to you? If so, how did you experience this? What went through your mind as you watched, waited, and anticipated the pain of this person's absence from your physical world? How did you prepare for this person's disappearance? What did you do at the time to help them? Did you say anything to them before they died? Did you find it a difficult process to go through?

Take some time out to write down what you would do if you had only five years to live; then repeat the exercise for only one year, six months, one month, then one day. Try to be as precise as possible. This assignment will help you to identify some of the most important issues in your life. It will set into motion the process of becoming aware of things you would like to accomplish before you die. It may help you to find peace and fulfillment in your life.

Are there friends and family you would like to say goodbye to before you die? Are there relationships you would like to repair before it is too late? Imagine, for example, that you are going to die soon and can only talk to one person: who would you talk to and what would you say? Why aren't you talking to this person right now? What's holding you back?

Reflect on your answers to these questions. Think about how you've appreciated your life up to this very moment, its joys and pleasures. Have you stopped to smell the roses and be nice to yourself? Are you being "selfish" enough—allowing yourself to do the things you like to do? Or are you like Sisyphus, always pushing some rock up some hill? What will you miss most from your life? And what keeps you from living your life more fully *now*?

How would you like to die? What would you consider a "perfect" death? Would you like it to be quick and easy? Or would you like it to happen very differently? Would you like to die in your sleep? In a car? While making love? Do you want to die in a specific place? And who would you like to be with you in your final moments on earth? How would you like to script your death? What do you want to do with your remains? Is there a special place where you would like your remains to be interred or disposed off?

What kind of immortality system is important to you? Do you believe your soul lives on in an afterlife or do you believe that once you are dead there is nothing more? Have you spent time reflecting on this? Have you talked to others about it?

The next step is to write your own eulogy. What would you like people to say about you at your funeral or memorial service? What would you like to be written on your gravestone? How would you like your children to remember you after your death? How will others remember you? These questions may help you to articulate better your "mission" in life. What do you have to do to attain maximum self-realization, love, and enlightenment? What are your unique potentials? How can you fulfill them? Is there someone you can talk to, to find answers to these basic questions?

Finally, write your will. This is something we all tend to put off until too late. But writing a will is a valuable exercise: you will generate greater awareness of the inevitability of death but also have the opportunity to evaluate the things that are important in your life and decide how you would like your personal possessions to be divided, and to whom to give them.

Most people who work through this assignment emerge more fully aware of life's possibilities, prepared to reconsider how they can live their lives more fully. These questions may also shed more light on the changes you may need to make in the way you live from this moment on. It's important to live your life: as the old Scottish saying goes, you're a long time dead.

If you're open and honest with yourself about these issues, you will be able to come to a deeper understanding and acceptance of death. Furthermore, when you share this kind of information with your family, friends, or other people you care about—however uncomfortable it may be at first—even more meaningful relationships can be developed. Openness will enable you to embrace death through living life more fully and learning from those approaching the end of their lives. When you share with others the things that are really meaningful to you, others are encouraged to open up themselves, forging closer connections.

Facing death in a way that affirms life results in reverence for human life. Denial of our mortality is often a root cause of our devaluation of human life. To identify with our humanity is to face our animal physicality—the fact that we're housed in bodies that decay and will one day die. While we are in that body, there is much to revere about the human journey. We must learn to conquer our fears, seize the day, and make the most of the moments we're living. There is much to be said for exploring life, beauty, and human achievement, and it is important to live our lives without regrets.

THE NEXT GREAT ADVENTURE?

But even if you take this assignment seriously, it will still be hard for many to conquer our deepest weakness: our psychological reluctance to accept the inescapable truth of our personal disintegration and decay. Socrates' insight remains deeply challenging: "For fear of death, gentlemen, is nothing other than to think oneself wise when one is not; for it is to think one knows what one doesn't know. No man knows whether death may not turn out to be the greatest of blessings for a human being."

It would be interesting to imagine a world without death, wouldn't it? How attractive would it be? What's the downside? If we think about this even half seriously, we realize that death is an essential condition of life, and not necessarily an evil. Mark Twain once said, "Whoever has lived long enough to find out what life is, knows how deep a debt of gratitude we owe to Adam, the first great benefactor of our race. He brought death into the world."

There is an old Arab tale called *Appointment in Samarra* in which Death tells the following story. There was a merchant in Baghdad who sent his servant to buy provisions from the market. After a little while the servant came back, white and trembling, and said, "Master, just now in the market-place I was jostled by a woman in the crowd and when I turned I saw that it was Death who jostled me."

"She looked at me and made a threatening gesture. Now, master, do lend me your horse, and I will ride away from this city to avoid my fate. I will go to Samarra where Death will not find me."

The merchant lent him his horse. The servant mounted it, dug his spurs in its flanks and galloped away as fast as the horse could go. Then the merchant came down to the marketplace and saw me standing in the crowd. He came up to me and said, "Why did you make a threatening gesture to my servant when you saw him this morning?"

"That was not a threatening gesture," I said, "I was startled by surprise. I was astonished to see him in Baghdad, for I have an appointment with him tonight in Samarra."

As this story makes clear, we can't control our destiny; there is only now, and there is only here. We often meet our destiny on the road we take to avoid it. There is a Yiddish proverb that says, "If a man is destined to drown, he will drown even in a spoonful of water." What's meant to be, will find its way. The boundaries between life and death are at best shadowy and vague. Perhaps the fear of death will prove to be worse than death itself. The nineteenth-century American novelist Nathaniel Hawthorne wrote, "We sometimes congratulate ourselves at the moment of waking from a troubled dream—it may be so the moment after death." What is certain in death is somewhat softened by uncertainty. For all we know, death will be the next great adventure.

AFTERWORDS: THE QUEST FOR AUTHENTICITY

The happiness of your life depends on the quality of your thoughts.

Marcus Aurelius

Land of Heart's desire,
Where beauty has no ebb, decay no flood,
But joy is wisdom, Time an endless song.

William Yeats (*"The Land of Heart's Desire"*)

The art of being wise is the art of knowing what to overlook.

William James

When you cease to make a contribution you begin to die.

Eleanor Roosevelt

This above all: to thine own self be true,
And it must follow, as the night the day,
Thou canst not then be false to any man.

Shakespeare, (Hamlet, act 1, scene 3)

Writing these essays was the result of learning from experience—and the ability to make sense of these experiences. Without practical exposure—without the contributions of my students and clients—it would have been impossible to write them. "Praxis" is a Greek word meaning action with reflection, or learning from what we do. Educators use the word praxis to describe a cyclical process of experiential learning, whereby a theory, lesson, or skill is enacted or practiced. Praxis implies the acquisition of tacit knowledge, the sort that is embedded in personal experiences and can't be effectively transferred without personal interaction.

215

Praxis is important to me, in that I learn by reflecting on my own experiences. In my efforts to turn executives into reflective practitioners, questions are more important than answers. When I interact with executives I learn by having to deal with a question, a problem, a dilemma, or a challenge. As a teacher, however, I am often expected to make bold assertions and confident statements because they convey a sense of mastery and control (and certainty) about the world around us. Unfortunately, heroic as this may sound, it's not the way to further learning by my students or for myself. I learn most from dealing with knotty questions, issues for which I don't readily have answers. Questions force deep thinking and reflection. They are an invitation to a conversation. Questions are the royal road to insight and further learning. In contrast, dealing only with answers is a prelude to shutting down the learning process.

BEING AUTHENTIC

Having written these chapters, I realize the importance of authenticity in my own life and the life of others. I have seen how easy it is for someone to follow a route to self-deception and illusion. Fooling ourselves—as many of us learn the hard way—isn't sustainable in the long run. We lie the loudest when we lie to ourselves. But if we don't tell the truth about ourselves, how can we be genuine with other people? How can we deal with the important existential questions discussed in these chapters?

To quote Nathaniel Hawthorn once more: "No one man can, for any considerable time, wear one face to himself, and another to the multitude, without finally getting bewildered as to which is the true one." Assuming a mask, not being true to ourselves, comes with a heavy price. The problem with being inauthentic is that whatever we say or do will come back to haunt us. Inauthenticity will stab us in the back. As the American novelist Mark Twain said, "If you tell the truth you don't have to remember anything." If we're not honest with ourselves, how can we possibly be honest with other people?

To me, being authentic implies being honest, truthful with myself and others, living in an integrated fashion with my own values and principles, and experiencing a sense of meaning in what I am doing. Authenticity implies a willingness to accept what I am and not attempt to pass for something or someone else. Authenticity means not only trusting my strengths but also facing my weaknesses and being patient with my imperfections. It has to do with having the courage to say how things are, to say no, to face the truth, and to do

216

the right thing because it is right. Being authentic also means being able to set boundaries. Doing everything either to please others or to keep others from getting upset with me is not authentic. Authenticity also entails seeing others not as extensions of myself but as individuals in their own right, deserving respect. Authenticity also means letting go of the false things in my life, the things that don't mean anything. It has about being genuine, not being an actor, not wearing a mask.

It is this authenticity that makes the story of Sophie Scholl and the White Rose movement so memorable. Many people in Germany recognized what the Nazi regime really stood for; they knew that the war was lost and that Hitler was deluding himself about winning it; but they kept silent. Sophie and her collaborators didn't. They had the courage to act while fully aware of the terrible price they might have to pay for doing so. They recognized that there was a time for silence, and a time for action. They knew that words without actions are mere hallucinations.

While authenticity is grounded within us, it will affect all our inter-actions, like a diamond that scratches other stones. If we're authentic, we inspire confidence in others. We raise the spirits of those around us. We're empathic friends and good listeners. By showing genuine concern to others, we provide "containment" and create a "hold-ing environment," that safe place that helps other people to cope with conflict and anxiety. We're kind to others, nurturing the spirit of generosity, while humble about our efforts. If we're not at peace with ourselves, how can we find or share peace elsewhere? If we lack confidence in ourselves, how can we inspire others?

Sincerity lies at the heart of authenticity. If we're authentic, we're credible and trustworthy and abhor hypocrisy in ourselves and others. Authenticity makes trust possible: the trust we put in our-selves permits us to trust others and to establish meaningful relation-ships. Trust also gives us the courage of our convictions in difficult situations, helping us to remain faithful to our values and beliefs. If we're authentic, we're the embodiment of endurance and perse-verance; we're not flags in the wind, changing with every influence that comes along. Anyone can steer a boat when the sea is calm. It's in rough seas that the real helmsman—the authentic individual—emerges. Because adversity is a great teacher, peril is the scaffold on which self-reliance is built.

As we search for authenticity within ourselves, it's important to realize that if we're on a clear path, with no obstacles, it's probably a dead end. The best lessons are learned not through success but through failure. Surmounting difficulties hardens us for future strug-gles. Authenticity contributes to the courage to be different. And the real test of courage comes when we find ourselves in the minority. Because we're social animals, we often have difficulty standing alone in our opinions. As the playwright Henrik Ibsen said, "The strongest man in the world is he who stands most alone." Although we might not all be capable of rising to the courage of Sophie Scholl, we're all called to stand alone at times. When we follow the dictates of our heart and mind and do what we believe is right, we sometimes displease those we'd prefer to accommodate. And when what we believe so strongly turns out to be wrong, we have to summon up the courage to acknowledge our error.

Authenticity implies doing things that have meaning for us and that make us feel useful. Unfortunately, too many people go through life without identifying any meaning or sense of usefulness. They are like sleepwalkers, even when they're busy doing the things they think are important. It's because what we're pursuing is meaningless. We only truly live when we have a cause. As Carl Jung once said, "The least of things with a meaning is worth more in life than the greatest of things without it." As I suggested in my discussion of immortality systems, we need something to believe in, something for which we can have wholehearted enthusiasm. We need to feel that we're needed in this world, that we count for something.

SEARCHING FOR MEANING

Living without meaning results in an empty existence. We need to transcend feelings of boredom, disconnection, and alienation—familiars in this age of plenty and convenience. We accomplish that transcendence by forming an attachment to something larger than ourselves.

The novelist and political activist Elie Wiesel said, "Our obligation is to give meaning to life and in doing so to overcome the passive, indifferent life." The Spanish poet Pedro Calderon de la Barca concurred: "Even in dreams doing good is not wasted." The pursuit of goodness, the search for meaning, leaves a pleasant aftertaste when we wake in the morning, motivating us to continue. In my experience, the happiest people are those who make a conscious effort to live meaningful lives. These aren't the people whose life is a movable feast, who try to drown their underlying depression in continual meaningless activity and partying. This kind of behavior has a pseudoquality. True happiness is based on the sense of inner peace that comes from believing that our lives have meaning because we are doing good for others. We are at our very best, and we are happiest, when we are fully engaged in work that we enjoy, working toward a goal that we've established for ourselves.

Meaning is not something that suddenly happens to us. It needs to be built into our lives. Grounded in our developmental history, meaning derives from significant experiences we've had in our lives; it's part of the network of relationships we build over time; it depends on our talents and skills; it's constructed on the things that make us feel alive. It's up to us, however, to create from these ingredients a creative cocktail that makes sense to us. After all, all meanings depend on interpretation.

In searching for the meaning of life, we're really aiming to feel alive. We want our experiences, the external reality, to resonate with our internal reality. Only when our personal activities are consistent with our values, commitments, and other important elements of our concept of ourselves will meaning be attained. As Michel de Montaigne, the Renaissance scholar, wrote, "The great and glorious masterpiece of humanity is to know how to live with a purpose."

Thomas à Kempis, the Renaissance Roman Catholic monk, told the story of a disciple who complained to his master, "You tell us stories, but you never reveal their meaning." The master replied, "How would you like it if someone offered you fruit and then chewed it before giving it to you?" Like this disciple, our challenge is to extract meaning from everyday experience. We have to do this ourselves. We don't start with meaning; we end with it. The true meaning of life may be to plant trees under which we know we will never sit.

Authenticity and our search for meaning are twins. As the saying goes, "Say what you mean, mean what you say." Nothing has meaning unless we give it meaning. And happiness is only found in the company of meaning. In the chapters on happiness, I mentioned the Greek self-realization theory—*eudaimonism*. Although the noun is usually translated as happiness, it might more properly, if less efficiently, be translated as "the feelings accompanying behavior consistent with one's true potential." The *daimon* in *eudaimonia*—"spirit"—signifies that which strives to create direction and meaning in our lives.

The educator Helen Keller once said, "Many persons have a wrong idea of what constitutes true happiness. It is not attained through self-gratification but through fidelity to a worthy purpose." She knew this better than most, growing up blind and deaf following a severe illness during infancy. Through her own heroic efforts, and those of her teacher Anne Sullivan, who had herself been cured of partial blindness, Keller learned to read and write in Braille. As an adult she devoted her life to helping the deaf and the blind. Her many books became the basis for a play by William Gibson, *The Miracle*

Worker, which won a Pulitzer Prize and was later made into a motion picture. Helen Keller toured the world promoting the cause of people similarly afflicted. Her spirituality, selflessness, courage, and perseverance inspired many, as did her civility, compassion, and caring. Those traits served her well, too, contributing to her self-worth and emotional health.

Most of us would like to be remembered for doing our best to help others. In my own personal journey, through my work with organizational leaders, I seek meaning in helping others develop their full potential, acting as a guide in their inner journey, and encouraging them to actualize their strengths and face their limitations. I like to guide them in their transitions. I want people to be aware that mental health is the result of choice. It's not a given. I want people to own their own lives, not to be manipulated by others. I want to help people find a meaningful balance in their lives. My hope is that when people in leadership positions are committed to these goals, they'll positively affect the organizations they run. In a small way, I'm trying to contribute to the creation of organizations in which people find purpose, feel a sense of wholeness, perceive themselves as complete and alive, have the opportunity to learn and grow, and believe that they can make a difference. Sometimes I dare to hope that in a small way (who knows?) the creation of such organizations—places that are fair to everyone and abhor injustice—will contribute to a better society.

I encourage executives to create what I call "authentizotic" organizations, a description I have drawn from two Greek words, *authenteekos* (authenticity) and *zoteekos* (vital to life). Authenticity implies that an organization offers its members a compelling connective quality through its vision, mission, culture, and structure. In other words, it creates meaning for the people who work there. In the organizational context, *zoteekos* describes the way in which people are invigorated by their work. It applies to organizations that allow self-assertion in the workplace and produce a sense of effectiveness and competency, autonomy, initiative, creativity, entrepreneurship, and industry—organizations in which people generally feel happy. Companies with a higher purpose than just making money are intrinsically more credible and worthwhile of support. And ironic as it may sound, companies that create meaning may also be more profitable, as their employees will be more committed. It's impossible to have a great life unless it's a meaningful life. And it's very difficult to have a meaningful life without meaningful work.

One of the people who have explored humankind's search for meaning most extensively is the father of logotherapy Victor Frankl. He used his experiences in a Nazi death camp to demonstrate that by focusing on the reasons behind a situation, rather than on the results that would follow, a person was more likely to survive even the most appalling circumstances. While Frankl was incarcerated in some of these camps, he noted that those who survived were able to transcend their suffering by finding meaning in life, despite the miserable circumstances in which they found themselves. Apathy and the death rate were lower among inmates who retained a purpose in living and dying. Frankl's observations of the behavior of people in extreme circumstances have helped us understand better how meaning enforces our sense of self-esteem and supports self-affirmation. Frankl also argued that every individual has an innate propensity to search for the meaning of his or her existence.

Frankl made it his life's work to advocate that humankind's primary motivational force is the search for meaning and purpose. He suggested that people aren't really in pursuit of happiness; rather, they're looking for reasons to be happy. If they attempt to make the best of a given situation, to find meaning in even the grimmest circumstances, they will achieve satisfaction. According to Frankl, when a person is prevented from connecting with this desire for meaning, it results in extreme frustration and can eventually lead to mental breakdown.

Frankl also promoted a sense of "tragic optimism," the ability to turn suffering into achievement, to strive for improvement no matter how bad things look, to be motivated (despite the transitional nature of life) toward responsible action. In his words, "A man who becomes conscious of the responsibility he bears toward a human being who affectionately waits for him, or to an unfinished work, will never be able to throw away his life. He knows the 'why' for his existence, and will be able to bear almost any 'how.'" According to Frankl, without meaning, we end up in an existential vacuum; we suffer from "abyss experiences" and simply give up. To be mentally healthy, we need the feeling that there's a purpose to life and that what we're doing is consistent with our values, commitments, and other important aspects of self-identity. Thus a sense of directedness and intentionality, whatever form it takes, helps our mental equilibrium. It is—as I said in my chapters on death—one way of creating immortality.

Meaning can be found all around us. It can be discovered in relationships, work, a good cause, even in religious beliefs. What all of these sources of meaning have in common is a motivation to go beyond narrow self-interest, to engage in something on a more substantial scale. While selfish people look out for number one, selfless people attempt to bring happiness to others—and lay their own happiness in that. Since people engaged in altruistic behavior feel better about themselves and the world, altruistic behavior can be reframed—here's a paradox—as acting in one's own self-interest.

THE ALTRUISTIC MOTIVE

What is altruism? It is derived from the Latin word "alter" (the other), literally translated as "other-ism." According to the French philosopher Auguste Comte, who coined the term about 150 years ago, altruism is devotion to the welfare of others, based on complete selflessness. Altruism can be viewed as a motivational state with the ultimate goal of improving another person's welfare. Altruists are happy when others thrive, sad when they suffer. A truly altruistic act must be free of self-interest, a sort of transcendent self-sacrifice.

Why do we engage in altruistic behavior? Why do we help others? There's a very utilitarian answer to this question, which is that we help others because we have no choice, because it's expected of us, because it is in our own best interest. Perhaps we do someone a favor because we want to ensure that the relationship continues or because we expect to see the favor reciprocated. The bond of reciprocity is a universal human pattern that plays an important role in all forms of human society.

An interesting question arises when we speculate about whether our helping is always and exclusively motivated by the prospect of some benefit for ourselves, however subtly this plays out. For example, kinship is probably the most basic and widespread bond that exists between human beings. Most of us show kindness to our parents, spouse, children, and friends. In general, we tend to be most kind, most altruistic, to the people closest to us. A bias toward the interests of our own family, rather than those of the community in general, is a persistent tendency in human behavior, for good evolutionary and biological reasons.

But can people transcend the bounds of kinship and self-interest and help out of genuine concern for the welfare of others, no strings attached? Can altruistic behavior be part of the human condition? Is it possible to engage in altruistic acts that we genuinely hope will go unnoticed? Or do we always do whatever we do for selfish, egotistical reasons?

The question whether true altruism exists has been heavily debated. The majority view among biologists and psychologists is that we are, at heart, purely egotistical, that we care for others only to the extent that their welfare affects our own. Everything we do, no matter how noble and beneficial to others, is really directed toward the ultimate goal of self-benefit. As a person's actions can only be called altruistic if all selfish motives are entirely absent, as soon as people start to consider their own benefits, they are no longer acting altruistically. And since we'll always have—in whatever we do—somewhat egotistical motives, true altruism doesn't exist.

Of course, some forms of egotism are obvious, as when we receive money or recognition for something we have done. Even if the rewards aren't so obvious, we may still gain some benefits. For example, seeing a person in trouble may distress us. In spite of what seems to be a purely altruistic act, helping that person also can be seen as an instrumental way to relieve our own unhappiness. In addition—as an extra "selfish" motivator—it may even make us feel good and virtuous, as we compare ourselves to those who do nothing. From this strict interpretation of what constitutes an altruistic act, even the Mother Teresas of this world may have a selfish component woven into their behavior.

This kind of nit-picking about what is selfish and what is selfless may be an admirable exercise for social scientists, but do we really care? For most of us our motivations are not so clearly defined. Much of what we do may have an underlying component of self-interest, but it doesn't mean that doing something with the ultimate goal of benefiting someone else is not within the repertoire of the human animal. Most of us show a mixture of selfish and selfless motives in our behavior.

Resorting once more to a personal example, during World War II my grandparents and my mother took care of many "*onderduikers*," (people who went into hiding for long periods of time to avoid being sent to concentration camps by the Nazis). When they took these people in, were my relatives thinking, "If I help these people now, they may do something for us later, when the war is over"? Were they showing off their bravery to other people in the village? Did the thought cross their mind that—because of their deeds—there was the possibility that they would later be honored by the state of Israel? I cannot ask them now what went through their minds when they decided to take a stand—but to the best of my knowledge, given the stories they told me when I was a child, I doubt that they were motivated by any of those thoughts. From what they told me, they saved these people because they felt *it was the right thing to do*. They were compassionate enough to give them shelter and to find them food, even at the risk to their own lives. They did what they did because helping others, under the circumstances, was important to them. In fact, the members of my family were eventually honored as "Righteous Gentiles" by the state of Israel, but by that time my mother was the only one still alive.

Obviously, human beings sometimes help others because they get something in return; whether it's positive self-esteem, recognition from their peers, relief from the stress of seeing others in pain, or even avoidance of the guilt that they would experience later if they didn't help. But the truth still remains that sometimes human beings help other people at the expense of their own well-being. Sometimes they help when there is no possible apparent reward for their behavior. Sometimes they help because it makes them feel better. Sometimes they help because it makes them happy to see other people happy. Sometimes they help because it gives meaning to their lives.

The financier George Soros is a good example of an individual who has gone a long way toward finding meaning through altruistic behavior. Soros was born in Budapest to a prosperous Jewish family, but his childhood was disrupted by the Nazis' invasion of Hungary. The family fled the country to escape the concentration camps. The uprooting of his family marked Soros for the rest of his life. They moved to London, where Soros chose to study philosophy. For practical reasons, he abandoned his plans to become a philosopher and joined a merchant bank. Over time, he established his own investment fund, which became extremely successful and remained so for many years. Instead of retaining all his earnings for himself, Soros used a generous share of his profits to create a network of philanthropic organizations. Much of the work of the Soros Foundations has been directed at Eastern Europe—starting with Hungary—where he has awarded scholarships, provided technical assistance, and helped modernize schools and businesses. His way of finding meaning in life has been through building stable democracies in these countries.

I believe very strongly that our feeling of well-being increases when we give happiness away through active altruism. All the people I interviewed who were involved in volunteer activities reported an increased feeling of well-being when undertaking their particular volunteer project; they felt energized and alive. They reported that their activities filled a sense of inner emptiness—the price many pay for rampant individualism. We are happiest when we reach out and help others, moving from individualistic behavior to good citizenship.

The Stoic philosopher Epictetus said, "All human beings seek the happy life, but many confuse the means—for example, wealth and status—with that life itself. This misguided focus on the means to a good life makes people get further from the happy life. The really worthwhile things are the virtuous activities that make up the happy life, not the external means that may seem to produce it."

Finding meaning through altruistic actions that go beyond rampant individualism brings people together, helping them to feel part of the human community and allowing them to feel good about themselves. Leo Tolstoy maintained that "The sole meaning of life is to serve humanity." The people who work for the Red Cross, the World Economic Forum, or *Médecins sans frontières* have a commitment to their work that's hard to match. They radiate a sense of responsibility, nurturance, and civility, believing that their contribution makes for a better world. Their work gives them a deep sense of satisfaction and happiness. It is not what we get but who we become and what we contribute that gives real meaning to our lives.

We must not forget that egotism is the anesthetic that dulls the pain of stupidity. It may be an effective tranquilizer, but it doesn't diminish the foolishness of hanging on to such a life strategy. Narcissists and egotists end up lonely and unhappy. The self-focused, those who have difficulty reaching out to others, are among the unhappiest people in the world.

HAVING WISDOM

Authenticity and wisdom are the result of learning from many hardships. As the saying goes, "No mistakes, no experience; no experience, no wisdom." Wisdom is usually found only in people who've gone through difficult life experiences and have surmounted the setbacks they encountered. As the French novelist Marcel Proust noted, "We don't receive wisdom; we must discover it for ourselves after a journey that no one can take for us or spare us." Failure and anguish pave the way to insight, and mistakes are the bridge between inexperience and wisdom. Defeat is thus the cornerstone of wisdom and a complement to authenticity. And the memories that defeat bequeaths us are great catalysts for self-reflection.

There's a story about a famous Zen master who was approached by a young monk who wanted to become his disciple. The master invited the young man to have tea with him. When the tea was prepared, the master began pouring the tea in the novice's cup. But when the cup was full, the master didn't stop. He kept on pouring, letting the tea spill out. The novice asked him why he was he doing such a thing. The master replied, "Your mind is like the cup. It is bursting full. There is no place for anything new. I can't teach you anything. Go away, and come back when you have made some room." Narcissism and self-knowledge rarely go together. To acquire self-knowledge and wisdom, we need an open mind; we need to be prepared to experience new things. As the book of Proverbs says, "Experience is the mother of wisdom."

Being authentic and possessing wisdom are closely related human dynamics that reinforce and build on each other. They focus on our life's existential journey. And if we want to understand what our life is all about, we have to face the facts about ourselves, unpleasant as these sometimes are. Being prepared to look into ourselves is a necessary condition for acquiring wisdom. As the Greek dramatist Aeschylus puts it, "Wisdom comes through suffering." Only by understanding the unpleasant parts of ourselves can we deflect and overcome our darker side. Wisdom comes not only come from experience but also from meditating on experience. On the gate of the temple of Apollo in Delphi were written the words "Know thyself"— words that still reverberate today.

Wisdom implies a high degree of personal and interpersonal functioning. The psychoanalyst Erik Erikson tied wisdom to integrity and generativity (the desire to care for others). He clarified the different challenges we face at each stage of the life cycle to reach an increasingly higher level of functioning as life unfolds, identifying a host of traits essential to wisdom. In Erikson's schema, wisdom implies a concern for the well-being of others, affirmation of differences, tolerance for ambiguity, and acceptance of the uncertainties that our world brings. I believe that it also implies the capacity for empathy and mood regulation, the ability to listen and understand, and the capacity for judgment and advice. Finally, wisdom involves mastery of the strategies that concern the conduct and meaning of life, a knowledge of life's obligations and goals, and a degree of understanding of the human condition. But in the end, as Epictetus reminds us, wisdom is revealed through action, not talk.

Acceptance of one's self and one's past life isn't always easy. All of us have a great capacity to delude ourselves, a unique defensive structure composed of many resistances that need to be overcome as we go through the process of personal discovery. Until we break down those resistances and understand ourselves, we're not really free or really alive. Understanding our inner world is the key to conquering our outer world—and to arriving at a state of wisdom. To be a good judge of people, we need to know what we're all about ourselves.

So how do we gain self-knowledge? In more religious periods, people spent much of their time in church. Prayer gave them an opportunity to reflect on life and take stock. Nowadays, however, structured religious activities are less common, though quiet moments to ourselves are just important today as they were in the past. We all need time for self-renewal and self-reflection. For reasons

226

of personal development, we need time alone to examine what we're doing and think about what's right and good for us. We need time to contemplate our strengths and weaknesses, to give play to our imagination, and to dream.

Arriving at self-reflection alone isn't always possible. Paradoxically, in the search for meaningful moments for self-reflection, we may need professional help. We may need to consult someone who will listen to our ideas and fantasies, help us make sense of our dreams and daydreams, get us unstuck when we're caught in a vicious circle, help us see crucial links between past and present, and guide us into a better future. Dialogue of this sort isn't typically comfortable. Because it requires opening up to another person to an extent that we don't often experience, it demands tremendous trust. But finding a companion for our journey of self-discovery can pay great dividends in terms of personal growth, awareness of alternatives, and preventing errors that would haunt us later in life.

Many people who lack the courage to engage on such a personal journey instead adopt what I described earlier as "the manic defense." They run away from self-discovery—and can't stop running. They delude themselves into thinking that activity equals happiness. They're afraid that if they stop running, they'll see the emptiness of their lives. Though time is short, these people waste what years they have in pointless activity. What are they running for? What are they running to? As Mahatma Gandhi once said, "There is more to life than increasing its speed." For people who rely on the manic defense, most of life is spent before they know what it is and what it means.

Unless we're willing to forego happiness, we need to strive for wisdom and refuse to become victims of hurry sickness. We don't want to become one of those unfortunates who discover that, in John Lennon's words, "Life is what happens when you're busy making other plans." We need to reflect on what's important to us and make an effort to set our priorities accordingly. If we choose to do what we really enjoy and live life to the full, we've got a serious shot at attaining happiness.

SMELLING THE FLOWERS

Finding happiness isn't like arriving at a station. We don't get to a certain place one day and feel flooded with happiness. No miracles happen when we arrive at a final destination because there *is* no final destination. There will always be a next stop. Happiness is in the way in which we travel.

There's another Zen story about a woman who had been told about an enchanted valley in a faraway place, full of the most beautiful flowers. She decided to search for this place and see it for herself. Though she set off eagerly, she was daunted at the length of the journey. Days turned into weeks, weeks into months, and months into years. Finally, totally exhausted, she arrived at the edge of a forest where she found an old man leaning against a tree. She said, "Old man, I have been traveling now for longer than I care to remember. I have been looking for an enchanted valley with beautiful flowers. Please, could you tell me how far I still have to go?" The old man replied, "The valley is right behind you. Didn't you notice? You passed it on the way."

As this parable illustrates, it's important for us to focus on our route, the scenery, and our fellow travelers than on our destination. We need to enjoy the journey rather than impatiently counting the kilometers we clock up. Too many people spend their lives climbing ladders only to find out that they had placed them against the wrong wall. We need to enjoy the little things, since they often turn out to be the big things in the end.

Socrates once said that an unexamined life isn't worth living. Equally, we could say that an unlived life isn't worth examining. If we're serious about the pursuit of happiness, meaning, wisdom, and leading an authentic life, we have to make the journey worthwhile, cherishing each moment. To quote Marcus Aurelius, the philosopher-emperor, "It is not death that a man should fear, but he should fear never beginning to live." It's already later than we think.

The Roman poet Horace wrote a dedicatory poem (Odes 1–XI):

> Ask not—we cannot know—what end the gods have set for you, for me ... How much better to endure whatever comes, whether Jupiter grants us additional winters or whether this is our last, which now wears out the Tuscan Sea upon the barrier of the cliffs! Be wise, strain the wine; and since life is brief, prune back far-reaching hopes! Even while we speak, envious time has passed: seize the day, putting as little trust as possible in tomorrow!

Carpe diem—seize the day— may be a cliché but it's no less true now than it was when Horace first wrote it. And at the same time, take the road you want to travel. I often remind myself of the story of the businessman who kept promising his children that he would take them fishing. He was always too busy, however, to do so. One day a procession carrying a corpse passed their house. "Where do you think he's going?" the executive asked his children. "Fishing," they replied.

ABOUT THE AUTHOR

Manfred F. R. Kets de Vries applies a unique perspective to the much-studied subjects of leadership and the dynamics of individual and organizational change. Bringing to bear his knowledge and experience of economics (Econ. Drs., University of Amsterdam), management (ITP, MBA, and DBA, Harvard Business School), and psychoanalysis (member of the Canadian Psychoanalytic Society and the International Psychoanalytic Association), Kets de Vries scrutinizes the interface between international management, psychoanalysis, psychotherapy, and dynamic psychiatry. His particular areas of interest are leadership development and coaching, career dynamics, executive stress, entrepreneurship, family business, succession planning, cross-cultural management, creating high performance teams, and the dynamics of corporate and individual transformation and change.

A clinical professor of leadership development, Kets de Vries holds the Raoul de Vitry d'Avaucourt Chair of Leadership Development at INSEAD (France, Singapore, and Abu Dhabi). He is also the Director of INSEAD's Global Leadership Centre. In addition, he is program director of INSEAD's top management seminar, "The Challenge of Leadership: Creating Reflective Leaders," and the executive program "Coaching and Consulting for Change" (he has received INSEAD's distinguished teacher award five times). He has held professorships at McGill University; the Ecole des Hautes Etudes Commerciales, Montreal; and the Harvard Business School, and lectured at management institutions around the world. He is also the distinguished professor of leadership development and research at the European School of Management and Technology in Berlin. He is a founding member of the International Society for the Psychoanalytic Study of Organizations. The *Financial Times, Le Capital, Wirtschaftswoche,* and The *Economist* have rated Manfred Kets de Vries among the world's top fifty thinkers on management and among the world's most influential people in human resource management.

Kets de Vries is the author, co-author, or editor of more than thirty books, including *Power and the Corporate Mind, The Irrational*

229

Executive, The Neurotic Organization, Leaders, Fools and Impostors, Handbook of Character Studies, Life and Death in the Executive Fast Lane, The Leadership Mystique, The Happiness Equation, Struggling with the Demon, Organizations on the Couch, The New Russian Business Elite, Leadership Lessons of Alexander the Great, Leadership by Terror, The Global Executive Leadership Inventory, The Leader on the Couch, Coach and Couch, The Family Business on the Couch and *Reflections on Character and Leadership.* Four new books are in preparation.

In addition, Kets de Vries has published over 300 scientific papers as chapters in books and as articles. He has also written approximately a hundred case studies, including, to date, eight that received the Best Case of the Year award from the ECCH. His work has been featured in such publications as The *New York Times*, The *Wall Street Journal*, The *Los Angeles Times, Fortune, Business Week*, The *Economist*, The *Financial Times*, and The *International Herald Tribune*. He writes regularly for a number of magazines. His books and articles have been translated into more than thirty languages. He is a member of seventeen editorial boards and is one of the few Europeans elected as a Fellow of the Academy of Management. He was also the first non-American recipient of the International Leadership Award for "his contributions to the classroom and the board room."

Kets de Vries is a consultant on organizational design/transformation and strategic human resource management to leading U.S., Canadian, European, African, Australian, and Asian companies. As a global consultant in executive leadership development his clients have included ABB, ABN-AMRO, Accenture, Aegon, Air Liquide, Alcan, Alcatel, Bain Consulting, Bang & Olufsen, Bonnier, BP, Deutsche Bank, Ericsson, GE Capital, Goldman Sachs, Heineken, HypoVereinsbank, Investec, KPMG, Lego, Liberty Life, Lufthansa, Lundbeck, McKinsey, National Australian Bank, Nokia, Novartis, NovoNordisk, Russian Standard, SABMiller, Shell, SHV, SpencerStuart, Standard Bank of South Africa, Unilever, and Volvo Car Corporation. He has worked in more than forty countries as an educator and consultant.

In November 2008, Manfred Kets de Vries was one of six recipients of the International Leadership Lifetime Achievement Award at the International Leadership Association's 10th conference in Los Angeles, for his founding work in the development of leadership as a field and as a discipline. The Dutch government has made Kets de Vries an Officer in the Order of Oranje Nassau. He was the first fly fisherman in Outer Mongolia and is a member of New York's Explorers Club. In his spare time he can be found in the rainforests or savannas of Central Africa, the Siberian taiga, Arnhemland, the Pamir Mountains, the high Altai, or within the Arctic circle.

SUGGESTED BIBLIOGRAPHY

While I've avoided using references in the text, below are a number of books and articles that were influential in my writing of this book.

Argyle, M. (1987). *The Psychology of Happiness*. London: Methuen.

Argyle, M. (1997). "Is Happiness a Cause of Health?" *Psychology and Health*, **12**, 769–81.

Batson, C. D. (1991). *The Altruism Question: Toward a Social-psychological Answer*. Hillsdale, NJ: Erlbaum

Becker, E. (1973). *The Denial of Death*. New York: The Free Press.

Boothby, R. (2005). *Sex on the Couch*. New York: Routledge.

Bowlby, J. (1969). *Attachment* [vol. 1 of *Attachment and Loss*]. New York: Basic Books.

Bowlby, J. (1973). *Separation: Anxiety & Anger* [vol. 2 of *Attachment and Loss*]. New York: Basic Books.

Bowlby, J. (1980). *Loss: Sadness & Depression* [vol. 3 of *Attachment and Loss*]. New York: Basic Books.

Buss, D. M. (1994). *The Evolution of Desire*. (Revised edition). New York: Basic Books.

Chen, P. W. (2007). *Final Exam: A Surgeon's Reflections on Mortality*. New York: Albert A. Knopf.

Cousins, N. (1991). *Anatomy of an Illness*. New York: W. W. Norton.

Csikszentmihalyi, M. (1990). *Flow: The Psychology of Optimal Experience*. New York: Harper & Row.

Dawkins, R. (1976). *The Selfish Gene*. New York: Oxford University Press.

Dalai Lama (1998). *The Art of Happiness*. New York: Penguin Putnam.

De Unamuno, M. (1954). *The Tragic Sense of Life*. New York: Dover.

De Waal, F. (2006). *Our Inner Ape: A Leading Primatologist Explains Why We Are Who We Are*. New York: Riverhead Books.

Diamond, D., Blatt, S. J., and Lichtenberg, J. D. (2007). *Attachment and Sexuality*. New York: Routledge.

Ellis, A. (1954). *The American Sexual Tragedy*. New York: Twayne.

Erikson, E. H. (1963). *Childhood and Society*. New York: W. W. Norton & Society.

Fenchel, G. H. (2006). *Psychoanalytic Reflections on Love and Sexuality*. New York: University Press of America.

Fisher, H. (1992). *Anatomy of Love*. New York: Random House.

Frankl, V. (1962). *Man's Search for Meaning: An Introduction to Logotherapy.* Boston: Beacon Press.

Freud, S. (1911). Formulations on the Two Principles of Mental Functioning. In J. Strachey (Ed.), *Standard Edition of the Complete Psychological Works of Sigmund Freud* (vol. 12). London: Hogarth Press and the Institute of Psychoanalysis.

Freud, S. (1915). Thoughts for the Times on War and Death. In J. Strachey (Ed.), *Standard Edition of the Complete Psychological Works of Sigmund Freud* (vol. 14). London: Hogarth Press and the Institute of Psychoanalysis.

Freud, S. (1929). Civilization and its Discontents. In J. Strachey (Ed.), *Standard Edition of the Complete Psychological Works of Sigmund Freud* (vol. 21). London: Hogarth Press and the Institute of Psychoanalysis.

Friedman, M., & Ulmer, D. (1984). *Treating Type A Behavior-and Your Heart.* New York: Knopf.

Fromm, E. (1956). *The Art of Loving.* New York: Harper & Row.

Kahneman, D., Diener, E., and Schwarz, N. (Eds.). (1999). *Well-Being: The Foundations of Hedonistic Psychology.* New York: Russell Sage Foundation.

Kaplan, H. S. (1979). *Disorders of Sexual Desire and other New Concepts and Techniques in Sex Therapy.* New York: Simon & Schuster.

Kapleau, P. (1971). *The Wheel of Death.* New York: Harper Colophon Books.

Kets de Vries, M. F. R. (1995). *Life and Death in the Executive Fast Lane: Essays on Irrational Organizations and their Leaders.* San Francisco: Jossey-Bass.

Kets de Vries, M. F. R. (2001a). *Struggling with the Demon: Perspectives in Individual and Organizational Irrationality.* Madison, Conn.: Psychosocial Press.

Kets de Vries, M. F. R. (2001b). *The Leadership Mystique.* London: Financial Times/Prentice Hall.

Kets de Vries, M. F. R. (2006). *The Leader on the Couch.* New York: Wiley.

Kets de Vries, Carlock, R, with Florent-Treacy, E. (2007). *The Family Business on the Couch.* London: Wiley.

Kets de Vries, Korotov, K., and Florent-Treacy, E. (2007). *Coach and Couch.* Basingstoke: Palgrave Macmillan.

Kinsey, A. C., Pomeroy, W. B., and Martin, C. E. (1948). *Sexual Behavior in the Human Male.* Philadelphia: W. B. Saunders.

Kinsey, A. C., Pomeroy, W. B., Martin, C. E., and Gebhard, P. H. (1953). *Sexual Behavior in the Human Female.* Philadelphia: W. B. Saunders.

Klein, M. (1948). *Contributions to Psychoanalysis.* London: The Hogarth press.

Kuebler-Ross, E. (1969). *On Death and Dying.* London, Macmillan.

Kubler-Ross, E. (1997). *Living with Death and Dying.* New York: Scribner.

Lichtenberg, J. (1989). *Psychoanalysis and Motivation.* Hillsdale, NJ: Analytic Press.

Lorenz, K (2002). *On Aggression.* London: Routledge Classics.

Masters, W. H. and Johnson, V. E. (1966). *Human Sexual Response.* Boston: Little Brown.

Masters, W. H., Johnson, V. E., and Kolodny, R. C. (1982). *Human Sexuality.* Boston: Little Brown and Co.

McDougall, J. (1995). *The Many Faces of Eros.* London: Free Associations Books.

Menzies, I. E. (1960). "A Case Study of the Functioning of Social Systems as a Defense against Anxiety: A Report on a Study of the Nursing System in a General Hospital." *Human Relations*, **13**: 95–121.

Michael, R. T., Gagnon, J. H., Laumann, E. O., and Kolata, G. (1995). *Sex in America: A Definite Survey.* New York: Warner Books.

Miller, W. R. and Rollnick, S. (2002). *Motivational Interviewing.* New York: The Guilford Press.

Nietzsche, F. (2000). *Basic Writings of Nietzsche.* New York: Modern Library.

Parson, T. (1967). *Essays in Sociological Theory.* New York: The Free Press.

Regan, C. P. (1999). *Lust.* Thousand Oaks: Sage.

Reik, T. (1945). *Psychology of Sex Relations.* New York: Grove Press.

Russell, B. (1930). *The Conquest of Happiness.* London: George Allen & Unwin.

Seligman, M. E. P. (1990). *Learned Optimism.* New York: Simon & Schuster.

Seligman, M. E. P. (2002). *Authentic Happiness.* New York: Free Press.

Seligman, M. E. P. and Csikszentmihalyi, M. (2000). "Positive Psychology: An Introduction." *American Psychologist*, **55** (1), 5–14.

Shorter, E. (2006). *Written in the Flesh.* Toronto, University of Toronto Press.

Sternberg, R. J. and Barnes, M. L. (1988). *The Psychology of Love.* New Haven: Yale University Press.

Tatelbaum, J. (1980). *The Courage to Grieve: Creative Living, Recovery and Growth through Grief.* New York: Harper Books.

White, R. (1966). *Lives in Progress.* New York: Holt, Rinehart and Winston.

Wolfelt, A. (1997). *The Journey through Grief.* Ft. Collins, CO: Companion Press.

INDEX